DANCING
with the
DEVIL

DANCING
with the
DEVIL

THE WINDSORS AND JIMMY DONAHUE

CHRISTOPHER WILSON

St. Martin's Griffin
New York

Grateful acknowledgement is made to Macmillan Books for use of material from *Change Lobsters and Dance* by Lilli Palmer.

Lines from Irving Berlin's 'This Army, Mr. Jones' quoted courtesy of Warner/Chappell Music Ltd © 1942 Irving Berlin Music Corp, USA. Used by permission of International Music Promotions Ltd.

www.stmartins.com

ISBN 0-312-27204-9 (hc)
ISBN 0-312-28896-4 (pbk)

First published in Great Britain by HarperCollins*Publishers*

First St. Martin's Griffin Edition: February 2002

10 9 8 7 6 5 4 3 2 1

Contents

To
The Boys in the Band

The author and publisher are grateful to the following for permission to use copyright photographic material: 1 © Michael Bloch; 2, 13, 21, 22, 28, 29, 30, 32, 33 © The Board of Trustees of the Victoria and Albert Museum; 3, 4, 5, 6, 8, 10, 19, 36, 38 courtesy of Mrs Woolworth Donahue; 7 courtesy of the Historical Society of Palm Beach; 9, 11, 20, 34 © *New York Journal-American* archive/University of Texas at Austin; 12 © The Illustrated London News; 14, 16, 17, 18, 25, 27 © UPI/Corbis; 15 courtesy Lilian K. Gardiner; 23 © E. Haring Chandor; 24 © Sotheby's Picture Library; 26 © *Daily Mirror*; 31 © Associated Press; 35 © John H. Deming Jr; 37 © Gerry Atkins; 39 © David Heymann

Illustrations

Author's Note

This story starts in the Jazz Age and finishes at the onset of flower power; but though fashions changed and governments changed, the one immutable commodity throughout those decades is money. But the value of the dollar in 1920, when Jimmy was five years old, is the equivalent of $8.31 today. By 1930 it was $9.95, by 1940 $11.87, by 1950 it was back to $6.90. So unpredictable are these fluctuations that I make no apology, when referring to cash sums, for bracketing afterwards the present-day equivalent.

Foreword

From those who still live and took part however vestigially in this story, I received a curious reaction when I approached them to talk about Jimmy Donahue. Many spat out his name as if wormwood. Others agreed to talk, but not to be quoted. A few were prepared to be quoted, but were cautious in what they said. Others hinted that what they knew about him was too terrible to repeat, even though he has been dead for over thirty years.

Close friends of the Windsors, like Lady Mosley, cannot bring themselves to speak of Jimmy in the same breath as the Duchess. Given her unflinching support of her friend over two-thirds of a century, that is entirely understandable.

Others felt angry that a skeleton, successfully buried for nearly fifty years, was about to be disinterred. Many blame Jimmy for triggering the love affair which nearly ended the Windsors' marriage, because it seemed like just another Jimmyesque prank. The Duchess was bored, vulnerable, of a certain age. Jimmy was young, naughty, sexually promiscuous, unfrightened. He had nothing to lose. She did.

Nobody who subscribes to the myth of the Duke and Duchess of Windsor as the twentieth-century's greatest love affair wants to think about Jimmy Donahue. It is too unsettling, it destroys the symmetry of the Windsor story. In the eyes of these adherents, Jimmy put Wallis in a position to fatally compromise the man who had given up his throne, his crown and his empire for the woman he loved. For four years and three months, the Duke of Windsor was cuckolded by, and remained in danger of being rejected for, a homosexual.

The Duchess was infatuated with Jimmy, but in the end the affair ran its course. It was not his charm alone which seduced her – if anything, she seduced him – it was Woolworth money. Jimmy Donahue's mother put at the Windsors' disposal her share of the multi-million fortune created by her father F. W. Woolworth, founder of the five-and-dime store chain, and both the Duke and Duchess helped themselves liberally.

It was not a unique situation – others had assisted the Windsors financially, and to a certain group of people it was a positive pleasure to shower upon this historic couple gifts they felt were suitable to their status as the grandest royal exiles ever to have existed in modern history. Indeed, if one looks at the sale of Windsor jewels executed by Sotheby's in Geneva in 1987 it becomes clear quite how much the Windsors were on the receiving end of people's generosity. No man with the Duke's resources could have collected such a treasure-trove for his wife without considerable outside assistance.

It was money, then, that first attracted the Windsors to the Donahues, mother and son. What they lacked in ancestry they made up for with style; their mansion in Palm Beach, Cielito Lindo, was truly a magnificent creation, quite worthy to receive kings and queens. But it was Jimmy – the camp, beautiful, funny, talented, devilish Jimmy – who stunned Wallis Windsor the most, and rattled the iron self-discipline which, for fifty-four years, had propelled her ever upwards.

Jimmy Donahue was lawless, and above the law. Yet he never once saw the inside of a jail cell. The millions and millions made by his grandfather Woolworth helped Jimmy keep a healthy distance from the law but then, apart from his unfailing good manners, he never saw a reason to accept society's conventions. His life was a ceaseless round of laughter, practical jokes, bibulous merriment and zestful energy. He filled his life with music and personalities, surrounding himself with beauty and describing the set among whom he moved as 'all the beautiful people', pre-dating that phrase's overuse in the 1960s by a decade or more.

A child of exceptional beauty, bright, loving, intelligent and swift to learn, he turned into an isolated adolescent, marginalised by his contemporaries, in large part by the suicide of his father and the negligence of his mother. His education was a shambles, with his parents – while his father lived – mostly absent on world tours at crucial turning-points in his development. He was taught to understand that he would never have to work in his life, nor should he contemplate such an eventuality, and so he devised a career for himself – one of mischief, some said evil.

Of F. W. Woolworth's six grandchildren, the most prominent was Barbara Hutton, who inherited one-third of his estate – worth $238 million in today's money – on her twenty-first birthday. Barbara and Jimmy understood each other and, at an early age, became as brother and sister, a relationship that was as strong at the end as it was in childhood. Barbara, the legendary poor little rich girl, with seven husbands and a burning desire to be a princess, played a major role in Jimmy's life, acting as confessor and banker, and she plays a significant part in this story. Indeed, in pure publicity terms Jimmy lived in her shadow all his life; and while there are several books which have documented Barbara Hutton's riches-to-rags story Jimmy Donahue's own life, by far the more amazing, has been ignored.

In large part this has to do with the fact that previous generations remained unsure of what to make of Jimmy Donahue's relationship with the Duchess of Windsor. That the couple became infatuated with each other was beyond question, but the ignorance and prejudice of a less emancipated age allowed a certain conviction that it was not possible for a man who was so palpably gay to have a sexual affair with a woman, and a woman old enough to be his mother at that. Furthermore, the cataclysmic effect on the world of King Edward VIII's abdication for 'the woman I love' was seen to be a landmark of twentieth-century history, something not to be sullied by gossip. 'Jimmy and the Duchess' was a conundrum historians found easier to ignore.

I came across the existence of Jimmy Donahue when reading Caroline Blackwood's sulphurous, cranky, memoir *The Last Days of the Duchess*. The people she interviewed about the Duchess gave Jimmy such a universally bad press I had to discover more; it was not possible that one person could be so absolutely awful. Yet, nearly a quarter of a century after his death, of the survivors from that time who remember Jimmy, there are two equally strongly-held views. The first is that Jimmy was mad, bad and dangerous to know, a user and a profligate, an untrained mind and an unstemmable sexual glutton; the other that Jimmy was a divine amusement, someone who gave generously to his friends and to charity and the Church, someone who never bore a grudge and only existed to amuse.

Lady Mosley wrote to me quoting Count Jean de Baglion. 'He used to say, *Je deteste la bassesse*, and I think he found a good deal of *bassesse* in Donahue.' Billy Livingston, who had known Jimmy from Palm Beach childhood days, told me that whatever the enormity of his actions, however badly he behaved, Jimmy was the one person who could be forgiven.

Because of his life of excess, because of his vulgar display of homosexuality in polite society, when people observed Jimmy they often did not bother to look too deep. But beneath it all, he had the capacity to be tender and loving. It may have seemed the most wonderful prank to indulge in oral sex with a member – however marginalised – of the British royal family, but a prank does not last for four years and more. The Duchess had come through the menopause when they first made love; soon she was to undergo a hysterectomy as a result of the discovery of fibroid tumours. Some men, many perhaps, might take this as a signal or encouragement to abandon sexual activity but Jimmy, with a degree of sensitivity, encouraged his lover back into bed and their resumed love-life took the Duchess through an emotionally bleak patch. He made her feel wanted, he convinced her of her own sexual allure, and the strength which she derived from that directly benefited her hopeless and childlike husband.

Some may consider it prurient to delve into the mysteries of the bedroom, but in the case of Jimmy and the Duchess there is a vital need, for this story to make sense, to explore how they surmounted an apparent incompatibility of age and sexual orientation to find such profound delight in each other. The Duchess's biographer and, some might say, chief apologist Michael Bloch raised in 1996 the question of her gender. In an article, he quoted Dr John Randall, consultant psychiatrist at the Charing Cross Hospital in London and an expert in the differences between men and women, in a conversation which took place in 1980. Randall told him: 'I want to tell you something extraordinary about her, to keep at the back of your mind. The Duchess was a man. There's no doubt of it, for I've heard the details from a colleague who examined her. She was a man.'

Michael Bloch was unable to pursue the conversation and two years later, Randall died. However a colleague of Randall's sought to shed light on this awesome statement by suggesting that what Randall had been referring to was a rare condition known as Androgen Insensitivity Syndrome. In the case of AIS, a child is born genetically male with the male XY chromosome, but owing to the fact that the body does not respond to the male sex hormone it develops as a female. When they reach maturity such women exude certain male characteristics and can have unusually strident personalities. Such people cannot bear children and unless aided by surgery often cannot experience sexual intercourse.

There is of course no direct evidence of this syndrome in the Duchess, beyond the hearsay account of an eminent doctor. All it can do is point towards a possible answer as to why the Duchess endured with such equanimity a lengthy marriage without, for her, the least sexual gratification. The Duke's own proclivities, as revealed by his former mistress Freda Dudley Ward, were masochistic and, argues Bloch, it is highly possible that penetrative sex never took place between the couple during their marriage. Given these circumstances, finding a lover who could accommodate her own needs and difficulties would have been well-nigh impossible – until Wallis met Jimmy.

From Jimmy's perspective, though he was a practising and promiscuous homosexual, he had always been attracted to older women. In the following chapters a member of his family makes it clear that Jessie Donahue was a cold, hands-off mother who was constantly absent abroad during his formative years. He yearned for a mother's love, but the only way that Jessie cared to demonstrate it was through the opening and shutting of her cheque-book. Other women became mother-substitutes, before and after his affair with the Duchess: Lupe Velez, Libby Holman, Martha Raye, Ethel Merman. In the case of Jimmy and the Duchess, the magnet which drew them together was non-penetrative oral sex. Later, when the affair was over, Jimmy was able to make wry jokes about the nature of their intimacy, but for the time it held them together, its effect on both parties was electric.

C.W.
Swallowcliffe,
Wiltshire
April 2000

CHAPTER 1

PARIS, 1951

Paris in the 1950s was the epicentre of civilisation. The world's poets, painters, writers and film-makers raced, as if to a child who has tripped and fallen, to help revive the City of Light after the cruel dark days of war and privation. Socialites and aristocrats, newly-minted millionaires and ordinary tourists crowded its wide boulevards, injecting life and hope and, just as important, much-needed foreign currency.

This second Occupation was led by America and Britain, two great allies who, having given France its liberty, now sought their own spoils of war – food, wine, culture, music, frivolity. Paris had them all, and much more besides. The Ritz Hotel in the Place Vendôme was permanently fully booked, the great restaurants such as Maxim's and the Tour d'Argent were full. Theatres, music halls and nightclubs echoed to the sound of joyous alien tongues celebrating the city's release from subjugation.

Paris, in the spring, was the place to be in love. Two figures, clenched tightly on the dancefloor of Jimmy's nightclub in Montmartre, moving in harmony, challenging the dawn to come, exemplified the spirit of the age, this essence of post-war liberation. The man was tall, slim, still carrying some of youth's bloom, dressed languidly in dinner-jacket, black tie, and with a gardenia in his buttonhole. The woman was older, darker, more intense; sheathed beautifully in a Jacques Fath velvet dress, a diamond brooch at the shoulder, a fantastic sapphire ring flashing on her right hand.

A black dance band played and Henri Salvador sang, champagne flowed and assignations were kept. In the crowd of no more than a hundred which surrounded the dancefloor sat the Portuguese Duke de Cadaval, next to him Comtesse Cléclé de Maille. Though Jimmy's was no more than a humble couple of rooms in the rue Huygens, its clientele was far from lowly. One person who was there that night, E. Haring Chandor, describes the scene: 'It was late. I suppose the crowd was beginning to thin out, but they stayed on the dancefloor. And then, suddenly, they kissed . . . it went on and on. People were looking, but it made no difference. They didn't care. It was the kiss of two lovers.'

A black Cadillac awaited them in the street. They were driven up the Champs Elysées, across L'Etoile and over the Pont de l'Alma to the Quai Branly in the seventh arrondissement. They stopped outside a building which contained the apartment of Count Jean de Baglion, a well-known and much-loved French aristocrat. It was to be their haven for the night, for the woman's husband was in England.

The date was Tuesday 5 June 1951. The Duke of Windsor, a figure unique in world history for having abandoned power, status, riches, and a throne all for the love of a woman, had left Paris two days earlier to visit his ailing mother, Queen Mary, in London. His wife – who was, it might be argued, the most admired woman in the world at the time – followed the young man into the apartment and together they walked to the window. In the dawn light the grey River Seine beneath them was touched with the first rays of summer sun. It was possible to glimpse over the rooftops the Arc de Triomphe and its great tricolour flapping gently in the warm morning breeze. As Paris began to waken, the couple took off their evening clothes and went to bed.

In the history of love, it was possibly the greatest betrayal of all time.

The Duke knew, and looked the other way. He may not have known everything, but into every single day, ever since the previous summer, there had danced the elegant figure of Jimmy Donahue: at luncheon, at cocktails, at dinner, and in the nightclubs after dinner. Once, there had been two Windsors; now, it seemed, there were always three. Jimmy was with the Duke and Duchess in New York, in Palm Beach, in Paris – laughing, camping, effervescing. Jimmy with his jokes, Jimmy with his money, Jimmy with his stories and rudery – Jimmy, Jimmy, Jimmy . . .

'The Duchess was infatuated by him,' recalls David Metcalfe, the Duke's godson. 'He had control of her. She couldn't do without him.'

For though he was homosexual, Jimmy had discovered the key to unlock the pent-up desires and frustrations of a woman who had spent the previous fifteen years, since the Abdication, in a virtually sexless marriage. She was both suffocated by her husband's love, and unfulfilled; for though Wallis may have found the secrets to the Duke's innermost desires, love her though he might, sexual gratification was not something the Duke was able to reciprocate.

Jimmy was, for Wallis Windsor, a last throw of the dice. There had been other men before the Duke and Mr Simpson,

3

some of whom found the trigger to her ambiguous sexuality. But the Duchess was moving towards old age, her husband leading the way with his fussy, obsessive habits, and she wanted one last reminder that she was still desirable as a sexual being, not simply an icon, a footnote in history.

That week in June 1951, Jimmy and the Duchess went everywhere together. They lunched, as they had done so often over the past year, at their favourite rendezvous, the Méditerranée; at the time the smartest fish restaurant in Paris, it was said that the chef committed suicide because he lost a Michelin star. At night they would dine at the Relais des Porquerolles, then visit the clubs less associated with the Windsors' habitual trawl of the city's night-spots: the Pam Pam, the Val d'Isère, l'Ascot on the Champs Elysées; and the Vieux Colombier where they bumped into Prince Aly Khan – the man who with his sexual prowess brought an end to Thelma Furness's affair with the then Prince of Wales, thus opening the door for Wallis.

Jimmy took his lover to see how the other side lived: to Le Boeuf Sur Le Toit and Le Carrousel and La Vie en Rose, known as 'la salle viande', the meat market, where an orchestra played and men danced cheek-to-cheek. Lady Diana Cooper, wife of Britain's ambassador to France, recalled: 'A *patron*, with a face painted an inch thick, hangs about waiting for the moment when his shirt and trousers are exchanged for a sequinned Edwardian gown and hat, à la Boldini. Then, at a beat from the band, out troops a *corps de ballet* of oldish gentlemen *en décolletage and maquillage* – delight as best they can, while between numbers the male couples go prancing round with here and there a couple of tweedy women.'

Each night they made their way back to the Quai Branly before Jimmy's chauffeured black Cadillac, by now bearing a single passenger, finally nosed its way back to her home on the Rue de la Faisanderie.

Yet apart from that one night in Montmartre, Jimmy and the Duchess were not observed kissing. Indeed they usually travelled with a chaperone in an attempt to deflect the already burgeoning gossip about their closeness. The Countess of Romanones, who sometimes sat as Jimmy and Wallis's chaperone till five in the morning, says, with decorum, that she never knew for certain the exact nature of their relationship. But the evidence was there. Count Jean de Baglion – gay, plump, wickedly funny and exceptionally clever – had provided the perfect backdrop for the affair with his exquisite apartment in the Quai Branly, with its panoramic views of the Seine and its black satin-lined bedroom. What occurred behind those doors remained secret – until Jimmy, after the affair was over, started to tell tales.

Jimmy's cousin Barbara Hutton housed the couple at her suite at the Paris Ritz. There, they sometimes spent afternoons together, but the lovers were more vulnerable to discovery. 'I knew it was physical, I knew from the maid there was sexual activity,' says Mona Eldridge, then Hutton's secretary. She continued: 'She was in love with him, she was besotted by him, she chased him. She really fell for him.'

Apart from a sexual re-awakening the affair's allure, for the Duchess, was its clandestine nature. She became skittish at the prospect of secret nocturnal forays and Billy Livingston, Jimmy's childhood friend, recalled: 'Jimmy once picked me up in his limousine and I found the Duchess crouched on the floor – she didn't want to be seen. She enjoyed all this wildness and the crazy things they did.'

She enjoyed, too, the fruits of being wooed by a Woolworth heir. The huge sapphire ring she wore that night at Jimmy's was a Christmas present from her lover, made by Van Cleef and Arpels in New York. Its provenance emerged thirty-six years later when the Duchess's jewels were auctioned by

5

Sotheby's and their history researched. The auction house was able to identify several lots which came ostensibly from Jimmy's mother, Jessie. Though the accounts at Van Cleef and at Cartier were in Jessie's name, Jimmy often shopped and ordered for the Duchess through them.

Many more jewels were bought in the name of love. 'Barbara Hutton paid for maybe $500,000 ($3.45 million) of presents Jimmy gave to the Duchess,' recalls her former boyfriend and biographer, Philip van Rensselaer. Charles Amory, a member of one of Palm Beach's oldest families, observed: 'Jessie paid for the affair because it was a feather in her cap.'

Indeed, she paid handsomely, effectively purchasing the Windsors' time for the duration of the affair. Her first present was offered soon after the Duke and Duchess, encouraged by a mutual friend, paid a visit to her Palm Beach mansion during the Second World War. To mark the occasion she commissioned a spectacular gold mesh, ruby, turquoise and diamond evening purse from Van Cleef. There followed many more such items which the Windsors were not too abashed to accept. The Duke, too, became ensnared by the Donahue largesse. Perfectly aware of the closeness between his wife and the man twenty-two years his junior, he nonetheless accepted from Jimmy jewelled cufflinks, tiepins and other male accoutrements. In 1950 Jimmy commissioned through his mother's Van Cleef and Arpels account a gold travelling watch with a slide-action basketweave case which the Duke was more than happy to receive.

For a time it seemed as though the Woolworth women, Jessie Donahue and Barbara Hutton, were pushing Jimmy from behind to take this love-match to the limit. Jessie hired yachts upon which the menage-à-trois holidayed, while Barbara, in recognition of Count Jean de Baglion's unselfishness in allowing his Quai Branly apartment to be used as a love-nest, bought him another in the Rue Washington. When Jimmy, spendthrift from beginning to end, ran short of cash, Billy Livingston recalls, 'She gave him a million dollars ($6.9 million) the next day.'

Such sums need to be seen in context. The one successful enterprise the Duke of Windsor ever undertook – the writing of his memoirs *A King's Story*, a project which took several years – earned him newspaper headlines around the world when it was revealed he had made $1 million from them. By comparison, all Jimmy had to do to raise the same amount of cash was ask his cousin; so it is unsurprising that the Windsors capitulated in the face of such uncountable wealth. Once they became a threesome, Jimmy paid for everything – dinners, cars, presents, holidays, even the redecoration of the Windsors' house in the Rue de la Faisanderie.

Jimmy's apparent homosexuality shielded the couple from any revelations in the press. The homosexual act was still illegal and references to it, in polite society, were usually circumspect. That is, apart from Jimmy: 'He didn't mind at all that people knew he was gay – he used to make all kinds of jokes about it,' recalls the Countess de Romanones. 'In those days, people were very different and Jimmy was very courageous.' It was the perfect camouflage, and though the rumour-mill in 1950s Paris worked overtime, seasoned correspondents including Sam White from London and Cy Sulzberger and Art Buchwald from New York were unable to grasp what was going on. Furthermore the Duchess sought ways of rationalising it to her friends: 'She told me she could relate very easily to Jimmy because they were both Southerners, even though there was a generation gap,' recalls Mrs Carroll Petrie, the former Marquesa de Portago. 'Certainly you could see the attraction – the Duchess with her colossal energy, Jimmy so young and vital. Jimmy had that energy and directed it at her – he must have made her energy even stronger than it already was.' Mona Eldridge adds: 'He played the piano, he could tell jokes, he was so witty. He was very intelligent, very clever, tall, goodlooking, wicked – very charismatic.'

Compare that with two views of the Duke of Windsor at the time: 'His face was wizened, his teeth were yellow and crooked, and his golden hair was parched,' wrote Harold Nicolson. And Cecil Beaton, who went to Paris to photograph him, wrote, 'His face now begins to show the emptiness of life. It is too impertinent to be tragic ... He looks like a mad terrier, haunted one moment, then with a flick of the hand he is laughing fecklessly.' Given these harsh portraits of a man in decline, there is little wonder the Duchess chased after Jimmy so hard.

Her energy and resilience in both matters of the heart and in everyday life remain astounding, even at half a century's distance. In February 1951, the Duchess had been hospitalised in New York and had undergone a hysterectomy, at the age of 54. She remained in hospital for three more weeks and did not resume her social round until the beginning of April, but by then she was determined that her life would return to normal – and that included Jimmy. When she and the Duke set sail on the *Queen Mary* for France on 24 May, Jimmy went too – just as he had the year before, when the couple consummated their love for the first time.

Within four days, the Duke had left for London. Up until then it had been difficult for Jimmy and the Duchess to resume their previous relations but now, after her operation, the affair increased its physical intensity; she became almost mad with the pleasure Jimmy gave her.

On a later occasion there was an incident in Paris which, as much as that passionate kiss on the dance floor at Jimmy's, was to give the game away. Lady Diana Cooper recalled the night the Duchess, wearing blue wig and red dress, attended a fancy dress party in a private house with Jimmy and the Duke. The band from the Duke's favourite nightclub, the Monseigneur, had been engaged and played tirelessly all night, but by four in the morning the Duchess wanted a change of scene and, not entirely sober, suggested a move to the Monseigneur. Someone gently pointed that there would be no band there, since it was here, in the house. Arrangements were made and the party, plus musicians, made their way to the Monseigneur as the Duchess required.

'In those days,' Lady Diana told Caroline Blackwood, 'they sold flowers and bottles of scent outside nightclubs. Once we got to the club, Jimmy Donahue really showed off and he went to town. He bought all the ladies flowers and expensive bottles of scent. But we all got very tiny bottles and rather measly little bunches of roses. But I can't tell you the size of the bunch of roses that Donahue bought for the Duchess. She also got a huge flagon, a sort of jeroboam of scent.'

Lady Diana continued that the Duchess instructed the band to play her favourite tunes, 'C'est Si Bon' and 'La Vie en Rose', and danced endlessly with Jimmy while the Duke looked on, becoming increasingly distraught. Finally she returned to her husband's table and, summoning a waiter, asked for a vase. Then, taking her trademark fan of ostrich-feathers fashioned in a Prince of Wales plume and Jimmy's roses together, she plunged them into the water. 'Look everybody!' she cried. 'The Prince of Wales's feathers and Jimmy Donahue's roses!'

The Duke burst into tears.

'It was ghastly,' Lady Diana said. 'The whole evening was ghastly. And once it was over, I ended up alone with Donahue. I had to drop him home in a car. I couldn't bear him, he was so pleased with himself.'

It was easier all round to blame Jimmy. The Duke's official

biographer Philip Ziegler described him as an 'epicene gigolo', but whatever Jimmy's sexuality, the transactions in the relationship were the other way round – Jimmy gave, Wallis took.

The apportionment of blame over the Jimmy-Wallis affair came later, however. For now, in the precious week they had together, they dined at the Ritz and went to see Josephine Baker sing, they danced at Scheherazade and watched the dawn come up over Les Halles, sharing a bowl of onion soup. Each night they made their way back to the Quai Branly before Jimmy's chauffeured black Cadillac, by now bearing a single passenger, finally nosed its way back to the Rue de la Faisanderie.

The Duke, having visited his mother, returned to Paris on 9 June. Jimmy and Wallis had had six nights together. There were to be longer periods in each other's exclusive company, but the week they had together in June 1951 marked the deepest, most intense time of the four years and three months in which they were lovers.

As the Duke reappeared, so Jimmy slipped away from Paris, travelling south to Cannes, to a part of his life which he kept unusually private; one which would have surprised and confounded the likes of Lady Diana Cooper and her contemptuous friends.

Despite breaking each one of life's tenets, and as often as he could, Jimmy struggled all his adult life to be a good Catholic. Since 1949 he had been on the advisory board of New York's Foundling Hospital, a Roman Catholic institution, and in the year his affair with Wallis Windsor began, he became its chairman. Now he travelled to visit the Benedictine monastery of Our Lady of Lerins on the recommendation of the Archbishop of New York, Cardinal Francis Spellman. Jimmy stayed for a few days and as he left, he handed the Abbé a cheque for a substantial amount of money; so big that later Spellman wrote to him saying 'I think that through your generosity you are

entitled to be known as the Second Father of this foundation.'
No greater compliment could be made by the representative
on earth of the First Father.

When Jimmy returned to Paris its allure was severely reduced
without the full-time companionship of the Duchess, for
Jimmy's Francophilia was only skin-deep, encouraged in its
shallowness by Wallis, who had her own ambivalent feelings
about the country which had welcomed her so generously. The
Duchess's friend Princess Ghislaine de Polignac recalls: 'He
never made any true friends in Paris, he never tried. Apart from
the Duchess he never made any social effort at all. People were
nice to him because he was a friend of the Windsors, but that
was it.' The suspicion was mutual, for Jimmy believed that the
French aristocrats who made up the bulk of the Windsors'
native acquaintance could be bought, just like anyone else.
Their insularity and snobbery left him unmoved.

Nonetheless Paris in these post-war years was a moment of
re-birth for Jimmy. He had had a poor war, being accused of
dodging his duty while contemporaries from school were giving
their lives or at the very least serving in uniform. His own
military record was brief, utterly undistinguished, and lowly;
but here in Europe these things were forgotten in the hedonistic
rush to return to pre-war style and pleasure. The Duke, with
a much-criticised role as Governor of the Bahamas and a flawed
military record in the months before his enforced exile there,
was equally happy to draw a veil over the years of conflict,
but it amused the Duchess no end to reflect on the fact that
she shared her bed with both a much-saluted former Field
Marshal and a reluctant army conscript.

Towards the end of 1951, when the Windsors arrived back in
New York, the Duke received a letter. It was from the American
Association of Marriage Brokers. They had written to inform
His Royal Highness that the Windsors had been chosen as 'one

of the happiest married couples in the land' and that it would be an honour to present them with a loving cup at their forthcoming convention.

The Duke, who so recently shed tears in a nightclub as he was forced to witness the antics of his wife and her lover, graciously declined the offer.

CHAPTER 2

A PIECE OF HEAVEN

Palm Beach, in the azure years between the wars, was a paradisiacal Mediterranean fantasy on the Atlantic shore. Colonised by the Astors, the Vanderbilts, the J. P. Morgans and the Wanamakers at the turn of the century, the finger-thin island off the Florida coast by now contained, in due season, the greatest concentration of personal wealth in the world. Here the super-rich could mix exclusively among their peers, uninhibited by the gaze of lesser mortals. The Breakers Hotel, the Everglades Club, the Royal Poinciana Hotel and Colonel Bradley's Casino were the island's four cornerstones, the land itself criss-crossed by dappled paths under a profusion of pines and coconuts.

Rich, but understated, was Palm Beach's keynote. When a wealthy New Yorker came down to join a friendly poker game he put down $10,000 on the table. In return he received a single chip. A woman, unexpectedly widowed, was amazed to discover that her husband had left her $62 million and could

13

not resist remarking upon her good fortune. She was silenced by Colonel Bradley's *sotto voce* advice: 'Don't mention it. They might not think that very much down here.'

Indeed they might not. The *Palm Beach Daily News* or 'Shiny Sheet' chronicled the arrivals, the important doings and the departures of Palm Beach illuminati with names like Guggenheim, Rockefeller, Whitney, Du Pont, Dodge and Mellon. Joe Kennedy, freebooting father of the future president, was considered a very low figure. By comparison Palm Beach adored Mrs E. T. Stotesbury, Queen Eva as she was known, after she decided she would like a modest beach-house on the island and Addison Mizner was commissioned to build it. With only thirty-seven rooms before she started adding on, it nevertheless had some thoughtful touches – a private zoo, housing for fifty servants, an underground garage for forty cars and a reception lounge for visitors' chauffeurs.

The automobile had only gradually supplanted the principal form of transport, the bath chair. With capacious wicker-seats to carry singles or couples, these vehicles were steered by capped and uniformed rickshaw-boys as the occupants were propelled under the trees to the Coconut Grove, a fashionable gathering place at tea-time. Later, after dinner, the bath chairs would make their way in procession, their lights winking, to Colonel Bradley's on the beach. Nevin O. Winter, a travel writer of the period, described the scene: 'People will part with fabulous sums of money with a mere shrug of the shoulder. The aggregate wealth of the crowd here on a typical February night is almost unbelievable – it would purchase a kingdom. The visitor almost stumbles over millionaires. One will see here those whose names are familiar the world over, because of their wealth and social prominence . . . Marvellous gowns sweep the soft carpets of the casino, and priceless diamonds glitter there in profusion.'

Away from Bradley's and other places of entertainment, these grandees were most likely to encounter each other on Worth Avenue, a long, straight boulevard of shops whose counterparts were to be found in Bond Street, Fifth Avenue and the Rue Faubourg St Honoré. There were, and still are, no funeral parlours or hospitals on the island, nor resident plumbers; neither could any line of laundry be hung in a place where the rich might chance to glimpse it.

Jessie Donahue, spectacularly rich from the efforts of her father Frank Woolworth, was attracted to Palm Beach not only because that is where, between January and April, *le gratin* were to be found, but because an advance guard in the shape of Jessie's sister-in-law Marjorie Merriweather Post had already arrived and found it indeed a pleasant place, so much so she encamped there and started to create a home-from-home. The resulting edifice, Mar-A-Lago, had 115 rooms, with grounds which spread from one side of the island to the other, from Lake Worth in the west to the Atlantic in the east. Guests dined off gold plate on a thirty-foot Florentine marble table, warmed on chillier evenings by six-foot logs in the fireplace.

The island was only a matter of hours from New York by train, but to ease the journey Jessie commissioned the building of the *Japauldon*, a sumptuous railway carriage which could be hooked to the back of a regular train and which she named with touching lack of modesty after her husband. It cost $145,000 ($1.29m), and boasted gold plumbing fixtures and a salon panelled in rarest *boiseries* with a ceiling of quartered oak beams.

This acquisition was not unique, indeed in her immediate family both Jessie's sister and niece used Woolworth money in this way to lighten the burden of travelling, and in the sidings next to the Royal Poinciana Hotel might be spotted a dozen or more such flamboyant vehicles. Once they had arrived, the owners and their friends would decamp to hotel or mansion, but rail-cars were useful for giving cocktail parties and the kind of attenuated poker games which might be frowned upon at Bradley's. The motorcar manufacturer John Studebaker turned up at one such railcar and asked to be excused as he had no ready cash in his pockets. He had just lost $200,000 to Colonel Bradley in a roulette game and was temporarily out of funds.

However common a sight these railway carriages were in Palm Beach, they were still deemed too expensive a luxury by most of America's grander dynasties. A typical excursion, recorded by the *New York Daily News*, sums up its use:

> 'All the horsy folk went down to Miami today to attend the running of the Florida Derby. Lots of Palm Beachers went in a train marked "Strictly Private". It was composed of three private Pullmans, the *Japauldon* owned by Jessie Woolworth Donahue, the *Curley Hut* owned by Barbara Hutton, and *Vietwood*, the property of Dr and Mrs John Vietor.
>
> 'The train was about twenty minutes late in getting started this noontime because when Mrs Donahue arrived at the private train, her Pullman held the rear, or caboose, position. And Mrs Donahue doesn't like to ride last. Car sways too much, she feels. So there was much switching until the Vietwood, in the first position, could be switched to the rear. Eventually everybody on board and everybody happy, the train rattled off down the tracks for Miami.'

Jessie May Woolworth met James Paul Donahue at an ice-skating rink on 1 February 1912. Of Irish stock, his family's rise in prominence was due to a fortune accrued from a fat-rendering business on the Upper West Side. On their wedding day Frank Woolworth wept.

The doughty founder of a mighty empire had failed to convince his daughter of the deep unsuitability of her intended, and he spent the morning on his office couch, crying uncontrollably. The cause of his despair was too well-dressed, too glibly-spoken, too evidently bisexual to pass muster with the old man, but Jessie was besotted, for her husband had a glamour and a mystery so lacking in the dullards her sisters had married. None the less her choice was a curious one, since the barriers of class, already erected in New York society, put Jessie in the category – extravagantly rich – which was just one notch behind the 400 families who appeared in the Social Register. Jim, by comparison, was a nobody. His father Patrick had worked for forty years at the helm of the Retail Butchers' Fat Rendering Company in a factory at the foot of West 39th Street. Finally enriched, the Donahues with their eight children moved uptown to 132 East 71st Street, a smartish address but one which, in those days, was still not a street in which millionaires lived.

But Jim, with his black hair and bright blue eyes, reflected none of his noisome upbringing. He emerged from boyhood as a gentleman, beautifully turned-out, and with a ready wit and ease of manner his children would inherit. That this exotic figure should find Jessie attractive when she herself was unable to do so was, to her, a miracle.

On her wedding day, dressed in a white satin gown with a train trimmed with point-de-Venise lace, she carried a shower bouquet of lilies of the valley and wore with pride her fiancé's wedding present, a diamond and sapphire brooch. On such a joyous day, who cared that it had been bought with her money?

The marriage ceremony, conducted in Frank Woolworth's New York town house at 990 Fifth Avenue, was the hardest work Jim Donahue would ever have to do. The bridegroom displayed all the hallmarks of a heavy stag-night spent at

Delmonico's as Frank Woolworth – his wife Jennie absent because of advancing senility – gave his daughter away. A reception was held for the small group of family and friends, then Jim and Jessie took their leave for a two-month honeymoon starting in Canada and wending its way through the United States. Jessie gave Jim a wedding present of $5 million so that no one could say he was living off her money. Not for a while, at least.

On their return from honeymoon the young couple were soon installed in a house on East 80th Street, created by the demolition of four older houses so that Frank's three daughters and their husbands – Edna and Franklyn Hutton, Helena and Charles McCann, and Jessie and Jim Donahue, could live cheek by jowl in a Woolworth enclave while the paterfamilias lorded it over them all, just round the corner.

There was very little expectation that Jessie's husband would make a career for himself, but some attempts were made for him in that direction, not least because Frank Woolworth himself, by now seventy-one, had spent every day of his working life creating the massive fortune which now cushioned his daughter and son-in-law. FW's mission to build New York's tallest skyscraper, the Woolworth building on Park Place and Broadway in Lower Manhattan, was nearing completion and though not yet part of the J. P. Morgan set, he was a commercial colossus. The family would have considered it unsporting for Jim to give up on his own career quite so easily. So the Irishman was sent to work first for his father-in-law, then his brother-in-law Franklyn Hutton. Both experiments were dismal failures. Jim was discovered to be idle, inadequate and unsure in his dealings as a broker, and eventually he left to create his own brokerage firm of which Jessie was virtually the only customer.

To compensate for this lack of assiduity, the Donahues made it their life's purpose to travel, and during the first ten years of their marriage, Jessie and Jim voyaged constantly to Europe, to Mexico and to South America. Paris, Monte Carlo and Biarritz were favourite watering holes, coincidentally where some of the better casinos were to be found, for Jim and Jessie loved to gamble, and gamble hard. Jessie was particularly addicted to the potent, tensely dramatic whirr of the roulette wheel, and with impassive face would lose $500 a turn.

The couple's first child, Woolworth, was born two years after the marriage on 9 January 1913. James Paul Donahue Jr arrived two-and-a-half years later on 11 June 1915. The opulence in which Jessie and Jim lived often proves too rich a diet for young children, but Jessie Donahue maintained a blithe and *dégagé* air when it came to the upbringing of her two sons. Too concerned with appearances to permit herself to be seen on the beach with bucket and spade, she encouraged her boys to develop tastes beyond their years in an unconscious attempt to grow them, thereby eradicating the tiresome business of parenting. The constant social round enjoyed by Jessie and Jim, from Long Island to New York to Palm Beach, and the constant foreign travel meant that both boys relied for friendship, support and comfort on the attentions of their respective nannies, Woolworth's who was French, and Jimmy's who was German.

Jessie saw her children as decorative adjuncts to a fragrant existence. Of the two she preferred Jimmy, mothering him in an unusually stifling way and, according to a family member, not allowing his hair to be cut until he was eight: 'She preferred him to look girlish, and he didn't seem to mind.' A friend who knew Jimmy all his life recalled: 'His mother favoured him over Wooly, no doubt about it, and took advantage of it – he was just plain mischievous. I remember playing with him at their mansion in Palm Beach when he was about five or six, and he turned the hosepipe on the cook and the butler through the open window. No-one would think of scolding him.'

Jessie and Jim and the boys enjoyed all that Palm Beach could offer – its platinum-blonde coastline and rocky pools, its exotic birdlife and gentle zephyrs – but it was Jessie's burning desire to give Palm Beach something back, or at least give it something to talk about in those long, long hours of indolence. She had arrived, in every sense of the word bar a mention in the Social Register, but now had to put down her marker. She conceived an extravagant summer palace, to be called Cielito Lindo, a little bit of heaven, which if not the first house on the island would run a close second to Mar-A-Lago.

Guided by the architect Marion Sims Wyeth, Jessie devised her new residence in the Mediterranean style surrounded by a vast estate which, like Mar-A-Lago, would stretch from Lake Worth in the west to the Atlantic in the east. Orange groves, tennis courts, a tea pavilion, a lily pool, boat houses and a finely planted formal garden surrounded the cloistered building supported by Moorish pillars. Inside, a drawing room, complete with Renaissance fireplace removed from Europe where it had given service for the past 400 years, stood next to a library decked with ornate pine panelling and hung with rare Gothic tapestries, and an Italianate dining room. It was massive.

Jimmy and Wooly had occasionally been allowed to trail round with their mother as she made bi-annual trips to Europe in search of artefacts with which to dress the house. By January 1927 the land had been identified – an impenetrable jungle facing the ocean front, separated from the sea only by the great Ocean Boulevard. 'The jungle was wild and beautiful, with yellow banana trees and coconut palms and banyan trees, blooming hibiscus in marvellous and startling colours, and tropical birds, the alemanda vine with its bright lemon-yellow blossoms, rubber trees, and orange trees in full blossom' went a contemporary account. Much of these natural assets were harnessed by Wyeth and incorporated into the finished estate, giving a timeless quality to his building.

Through 1927 workmen struggled to meet their deadline, and by December Cielito Lindo was complete, a fitting backdrop for this eminent sprig of Woolworth money. A stately residence had arisen, with walls of old ivory and roofs of rose-coloured Tuscan tiles, set in vast gardens of blue and emerald, the colours of the tropical sea twilight. Jessie and Jim, back from yet another European sortie, dined on the terrace on their first day home, 22 December. Paradise had taken less than a year to build.

It should have been enough for Jim. Palm Beach was his kind of place. There he was treated as though wealth had been in his family for generations. 'He swished', wrote the society author Philip van Rensselaer, 'around the dance floors of Southampton and Palm Beach.' Back in New York, though his new marbled residence on East 80th was a lengthy step away from West 39th, there were always those who could with a flip remark recall the fat-rendering factory whence his family arose.

Here, in the dappled glades on the Atlantic shore, and in Colonel Bradley's, he was accepted as an integral part of this recherché community. He was much liked, though not by all. The author Dean Jennings recalled: 'In addition to his contempt for money, Donahue was also noted for his malapropisms, which while they did not have the immortal quality of Goldwynisms, were at least considered collectors' items in the Palm Beach/Newport/Riviera set. He once asked a neighbour to inspect his dining room, saying "Come and see it. All the silver's gold." Another time, when the famous Webb Quartet

21

came to play at Cielito Lindo, Donahue rushed to welcome them. "What!" he yelled at the nonplussed musicians. "There are only *four* of you?'" Van Rensselaer called him an 'effeminate dandy' and Cholly Knickerbocker, the Hearst society columnist, wrote that the Donahues were 'rowdy and raucous'. If they were, they certainly didn't know it.

Indeed, the seasons of 1928 and 1929 saw a furious and successful round of lavish parties at Cielito Lindo, whether tennis tournaments for a hundred guests or a musical soirée – at which Florenz Ziegfeld, the famous Follies producer was usually an honoured guest – and rather more serious musical events to which principals of the Metropolitan Opera were invited to sing. Noted one diarist: 'A profusion of spring flowers and rare orchids were used in decorating the salons, the loggia, and the great patio, forming the most beautiful sight imaginable. The artists sang at one end of the patio and seats were arranged around the loggia facing the musicians. The program included many arias from the operas and was most artistic.'

In this the Donahues were following the example of their kinswoman Marjorie Merriweather Post, whose soirées were legendary. At Mar-A-Lago, with an indoor staff of eighty to support her, Mrs Post welcomed the rich and the noble. At Cielito Lindo mostly what they got was rich. Jimmy had the opportunity to sample a rarer atmosphere when he accompanied Barbara Hutton to Mar-A-Lago. 'I am having a little party for Grand Duke Alexander of Russia,' breathed Marjorie sweetly. 'Sixty will join us for dinner and eighty are coming in for dancing after.' These were still frontier days for Palm Beach, it was still finding its feet; and discovering people with titles, genuine titles, carried a great deal of kudos. Mrs Post's party also contained Prince Cyril of Bulgaria, Lady Wavertree, and Baron and Baroness von Einem.

It was heavenly. But in the Florida sunshine Jim Donahue

experienced a perpetual unease, for Palm Beach was too safe, and his native New York was not. While in Florida, or when *en route* for some new shore, he was Jessie's. She possessed him utterly. But in New York he would melt into the night, to resorts where homosexuals gathered such as the Paresis Hall on the Bowery and Billy's Place on Third Avenue, Bryant Park under the shadow of the Public Library and the wryly-named Vaseline Alley in Central Park, down by Columbus Circle. During the 1920s a vengeful police department turned its full might on what was seen to be the unacceptable growing tide of homosexuality, but the raids which were carried out all over the city merely served to heighten the delicious frisson of danger for the pampered and under-occupied Jim.

New York City was just beginning to create for itself a homosexual underworld, one which would be fully-formed by the time Jim's son entered it in the 1930s. But in the years after his marriage Jim found it difficult to find full expression or release in his own homosexuality. There had begun, however, a migration to New York from provincial cities of thousands of gay men whose own communities would not tolerate the unorthodox. These adventurers were not difficult to find, nor to attract, given Jim's customary largesse with Jessie's money.

Until now Jimmy's schooling had been a now and then thing, with nurses and governesses leading him with some success through the three Rs. Bright, quick to remember, and with a wealth of knowledge from his travelling, he showed early promise and displayed a lively intellect. These, coupled with his angelic looks, good manners and assured self-confidence, gave every reason to suppose that in Jimmy Donahue there was and would be a young man of substance.

23

An attempt to place Jimmy's education on a more formal footing was made after his tenth birthday, when he was sent off to the Harvey school at Katonah in upstate New York. Still in its infancy, Harvey – 'a school for boys in the English manner' – had small classes and Jimmy benefited from the close attention he received, first under headmaster John Miner, then Herbert Carter Jr, son of Harvey's founder. To begin with, Jessie played the doting mother, having a chauffeur-driven Rolls Royce swish her through the school entrance to deposit her, exquisitely clad in Russian sables and jewels, on the doorstep.

To Jimmy, there was nothing unusual in seeing his mother so magnificently turned out. To other boys, with parents from older families whose dress and manners were more low-key, a visit from Jessie was like the landing of an exotic parakeet in their playground. In time, Jimmy came to understand that his mother was not, perhaps, as other mothers, and maybe he was helped towards this realisation by the ribald comments of his classmates. Her showiness cannot have helped a boy who had been kept too long from the company of his peers and was finding it difficult to make friends. Nor, despite the high-profile visits, sometimes with her sister Helena McCann, did Jessie Donahue show much interest in her son's scholarly progress. Everyone was having too much fun for that.

Jimmy remained at Harvey for two years, but from the outset a pattern was established which would continue for the rest of his schooling. A childhood friend recalls: 'Jessie missed him dreadfully, and she would keep him at home. At Easter or Christmas if he said he didn't feel very well she would keep him from going back to school.'

He discovered that any onset of a minor 'illness' could save him from the scrutiny of masters who might otherwise suspect he had not done his homework. These illnesses, sometimes real, often imagined, developed into a routine where he would leave

school and return home, not to reappear for days and sometimes weeks. He cared not for schools, nor despite their best
efforts could he feel that they cared for him. He was too rich,
too quick, too beautiful, too uncommitted.

He left Harvey around the time of his twelfth birthday in
June 1927. There is no further record of Jimmy attending a
school until he arrived, several weeks late for the start of the fall
term, at The Hun school at Princeton, New Jersey, in 1928. He
had taken a whole year off, and had reverted to being educated
by a governess, Mrs Olivier. Notwithstanding this his scores at
The Hun were, to start with, creditable enough: 70% for maths,
80% for Latin. He went home for Christmas but did not return
when other boys did. His subsequent attendance at The Hun
remained patchy due to Jessie's indifference to school discipline.
She treated with blithe disregard the regular attendance which
was necessary in order to give the learning process a chance.

There was, admittedly, cause for distraction. Having made
such a success of Cielito Lindo, Jessie and Jim decided to buy,
rename and refurbish a vast 1905 mansion set in sixteen acres
next to the Beach Club in Southampton, Long Island. The
Tudor-style house, swiftly renamed Wooldon Manor, boasted
a fully-panelled drawing room measuring a hundred feet by
fifty feet, and fifty feet high. Other rooms were in proportion.
With twenty-six rooms, sixteen acres, six flower gardens, four
cottages, an eight-car garage, and a private 650-foot beach, it
was one of the most elaborate spreads on Long Island, and the
apple of Jim Donahue's eye. He particularly adored the beach
house he commissioned with its lounges, bar, dressing rooms
and indoor swimming pool for those who could not face the
force of the Atlantic waves. Extensive staff accomodation for
eleven gardeners and twelve indoor staff occupied part of the
estate, and soon expanding to fifty rooms, the edifice was the
showpiece of Southampton. The house cost Jessie $1m ($10m).

Jessie took Jimmy to witness the house's transformation into another summer palace but, by the time the work was complete, she had lost interest, and the house was never home to the family in the same way as Cielito Lindo.

During his first year at The Hun, Jimmy was doing work that was the equivalent of eighth grade studies, and which should have been completed at his previous school. But as the school record notes, due to 'poor health' he was absent a great deal during the course of the year and when he returned for a second year in 1929, he was forced to repeat the same sub-standard routine he had attempted the previous year. Though a bright, intelligent, worldly boy, this academic backsliding very soon set him apart in the competitive atmosphere of a school where, on arrival, boys of twelve nominated the university of their choice on the assumption that with hard work and no luck (beyond the fortune they were born with), they would get there. Jimmy's university of choice was Princeton, but from the outset it was clear he would never get there.

By the time he was fourteen the rot had set in. He hated the sporty atmosphere of The Hun and had, by his repeated absences, removed himself from the society of his peers. If he found any pleasure it was outside the school, and a long and pleasurable memory for him was being allowed a small walk-on part, dressed in top hat and Eton jacket, in a play called *Young Woodley* that was staged by a semi-professional cast at South-ampton, Long Island. So when he returned for his second year and was made to go round again, he stuck it out for a term but on returning for the Easter term in 1930, an illness was contrived and after a couple of weeks he was taken away again. He did not return to formal schooling for seven months. The overall picture was of a bright boy who could not – or was not allowed to – stick at anything.

Jimmy pleaded with his mother to be taken away from The

Hun to avoid further humiliation. A new start, somewhere more amenable, was the only thing – if he had to go to school at all. James Wendell, headmaster of the Hill School in Pottstown, Pennsylvania, was approached and expressed interest in taking the boy, but the plan fizzled out. Pottstown was too far from New York and Palm Beach, and in any event the Hill School had quite demanding entrance exams. As Jimmy's headmaster at The Hun, James Hubball, wrote dryly to Jessie's secretary Leonard Haynes: 'I am afraid Jimmy will not be very successful in the Hill School examinations . . . (there has been very little preparation for them and) even at this late date Jimmy has again been out of school. In May, he was said by Mrs Donahue to be suffering from an attack of bronchitis. He has not returned since last Friday when I was forced to allow him to go home at the request of Mrs Donahue.'

The same lackadaisical attitude which characterised Jessie and Jim's approach to their son's schooling could also be found in their disciplining him. A friend from that time recalls: 'Aged five or six you didn't notice it, but by thirteen or fourteen the result of his privileged lifestyle was more apparent. I'm sure that's why Jimmy went wild, went off and did some of the crazy things he did. He was spoilt and protected and had absolutely no idea of the true value of money, but, more than that, he craved attention. All the reckless things he did then, and later, were a huge cry for attention.'

There was a brief, singular, and highly questionable attempt by Jimmy's father to take an interest in his boy's schooling. There exists but a single letter in the school records where Jim, in responding to a complaint that his boy was not working, mused that he thought of taking a tutor, 'preferably a young boy from Princeton around nineteen or twenty who can live with me during the vacation . . . if you happen to know of a nice young fellow I would be very glad if you would let me know. I should want him to go horse-back riding, and play tennis golf, bathing and so on.' Hubball's tight-lipped response was to recommend that Jimmy instead join a group of boys on an educational trip to England.

⁂

Jim Donahue's grasp on what was morally acceptable and what was not was indeed slight. Never was it more palpably demonstrated than over the theft, in September 1925, of $683,000 ($6.07 million) worth of Jessie's jewellery at New York's Plaza Hotel. The couple had just returned from a four-month tour of Europe and were staying there while renovations were made to their house at 6 East 80th Street.

Described by the *New York Times* as 'the greatest jewellery robbery in the history of the city' – and by extension the world – the booty contained two pearl necklaces, a diamond ring, purse, and sundry other items. The theft took place at around 5 p.m. on a Wednesday afternoon, while Jessie lay in the bath in her six-room suite. 'When she found them missing she thought her husband had taken them, just to frighten her, because of her custom of leaving them carelessly around the apartment,' said a source.

The *New York Journal-American* revealed that Jim had made every effort to avoid publicity following the robbery because he feared that criminals might attempt to kidnap their two children for ransom. 'With quivering voice,' reported the newspaper, 'he exclaimed: "Night and day we've watched over Woolworth, who's twelve, and James, who is ten. When the robbery was discovered I thought immediately of the children. In withholding direct reports to the police I was moved only by the fear that the jewel thieves would follow this crime with an attempt to kidnap the boys".'

28

There was no evidence to support this fear, but Donahue already had in mind the sort of person who would steal his wife's jewellery: 'the thief must have been alone and well dressed, or he would have courted attention in the elevator and hall.'

The police commissioner, Enright, immediately expressed his confidence that the gems would be recovered; in the event it was not the work of his detectives but the telephone call of a mysterious intermediary which brought about their return. A private detective, Noel C. Scaffa, hired by the Donahues, recovered the jewels on 7 October, a fortnight after their disappearance, saying he received them from a man named Layton. Scaffa paid out $65,000 to Layton and asked no questions. But though Scaffa then claimed they lay in the safe of the Federal Insurance Company until he handed them over to the police a week later, Jessie was seen dining at the Old Colony on 8 October wearing a string of pearls 'so strikingly like the stolen ones' that it caused considerable comment by a fellow-diner who happened to be an expert in precious stones.

Charged with masterminding the thwarted police investigation, Assistant District Attorney Ferdinand Pecora was asked whether he felt the Donahues had been open with him and had told him everything they knew about the case. Swallowing hard, Pecora said he thought they had. But such was the feverish press coverage of the theft, and the anger among the New York Police Department at being kept completely in the dark about developments, that less than a month later it was announced there would be an investigation by a New York County grand jury and that 'several persons will be prosecuted for compounding crime'. Jim Donahue was repeatedly interviewed by police, his attorney John Nash by his side, but little was learned from his stonewall responses.

The case became even more bizarre. 'English Harry' Wallon,

29

the head of a bunch of desperadoes whose forte was robbing nightclubs, trucks, card games and safes, was arrested on suspicion of his part in the heist as he and several colleagues made a hasty exit from a card game. Sensing a police presence, they had run out into the street and, finding themselves outnumbered, threw away their handguns before engaging in a furious bout of fisticuffs. 'Dutch Adolph' Chrisano and William 'Cockeye' Baker were also arrested, but soon the police lost interest in this bunch of low-lifes since clearly their intelligence did not rise to the level required to pull off a sophisticated jewel heist.

Infuriated by the failure of the police to find a credible suspect, and of the grand jury to come up with a result on their investigation of the one man who knew the whole story, the authorities arraigned Scaffa, deciding it was better to string up the messenger than have no hanging-party at all. In an instant Scaffa invoked the help of a professional safe blower, Frank Adams, also known as Dillon, who had met an English criminal while they both served jail terms in Sing Sing prison. The Englishman, it was said, had returned from Europe on the same ship as the Donahues. He had heard of the pearls and had determined to steal them. This sparked an investigation by Scotland Yard and by mid-November their detectives revealed they were searching for a man among whose aliases was the name Edward Charles Stanley, and that although he had been apprehended at Croydon airport in connection with the death of a young women back in the States, he was also wanted for the jewellery robbery. Anyone on the run, it seemed, fitted the bill of jewel thief. Anyone, that is, apart from James P. Donahue Sr.

The investigation had become a joke in society and in the public prints. In the end, delaying tactics were employed to stop Scaffa's trial, not least by Jessie Donahue who, first, apparently felt the need to complete the 1926 Palm Beach season before playing her part in seeing justice done. Then, with days to go before Scaffa faced charges of compounding a felony, Jessie claimed illness had overtaken her and she sailed for Europe for a lengthy journey. The trial was unable to go ahead without her, and frustrated officials realised that, whatever the truth – and by now, with the absence of any other likely suspect, the finger pointed fairly convincingly to Jim Donahue – it was unlikely they would ever breach the wall of silence which now surrounded the event. For two years the matter hung fire. One trial fell through, but eventually Scaffa took the rap and was sentenced to six months, not for stealing the jewels, compounding a felony or perverting the course of justice, but for perjury.

Infuriatingly for Jim and Jessie, public interest kept the Donahue Jewel Heist affair alive. For several years after, whenever reference was made to Jessie or Jim in the newspaper columns, a rehash of the curious events of the afternoon of 25 September 1925 was served up; something which continued to depress Jim.

Long after, Wooly Donahue told a girlfriend what every tabloid reader had surmised at the time, that it was his father who had stolen the jewels, without the faintest idea of the commotion that would be raised. Jim Donahue had been having an affair with a black dancer, and was now the victim of a heavy blackmail campaign. It took a great deal of Jessie's money to quieten those who continued to probe the true story behind the heist of the century.

Of Jim's twin addictions, gambling brought him lowest. By the late 1920s his raids on the cash-safe at 83 East 80th Street had finally drained his own personal well dry. Down in Palm Beach his marker was no longer acceptable at Colonel Bradley's and, if Jim wanted to play, a discreet telephone call was made to

Jessie to see whether she would wear his losses. As his gambling increased he started to welch on his debts, but Jessie invariably squared things. Eventually it was agreed that he should have a ceiling of losses of $50,000 ($440,000) a night. Jim agreed to that figure, but as one newspaper later reported: 'Since any large-hearted gambling operator will let a man go a little over his limit – especially when backed by an heiress (like Jessie) – Donahue nearly always went $10,000 or $15,000 over his limit before he quit the tables.'

Friends who watched him night after night in the big *chemin de fer* game which ran in the upstairs room at Bradley's say they never saw Jim win. 'That big game in the quiet, simply furnished upstairs room is famous all over the world,' recorded one diarist. 'Only one table was working there, and only the richest of the rich dared to sit in. Night after night during the Palm Beach season you might see gathered there Florenz Ziegfeld, risking wealth garnered in showbusiness; Mrs Vanderbilt, hazarding some small part of the New York Central railway millions; Fifi Widener Holden, her arms blazing with diamond bracelets from wrist to elbow; and Jim Donahue, the latter risking – and generally losing – the millions of the Woolworth fortune. Speculators who watched mutely outside the silken rope often gasped as the banker's little wooden paddle disposed of tens of thousands in cash and chips within a ten-minute period.'

By 1931 it was estimated that Jim Donahue was losing at the rate of $1.5 million a year and had spiralled out of control. While Jessie merely frowned at his losses and sought to minimise them by tighter control of the purse-strings, the anxiety caused by his plight caused Jim to take comfort in greater extremes of behaviour. His visits to gay bars and nightclubs became more frequent, his drinking more excessive, his dependence on the fleeting relief that young men could provide more urgent.

By the end of the 1931 Palm Beach season he had lost
$900,000 ($8.95 million) in the space of a couple of months.
While much of this was covered by Jessie, other sums went
unrecorded, such as an excess of $150,000 over and above
Jessie's guarantees at Colonel Bradley's. Bradley, a gentleman
in an ungentlemanly profession, left it to Jim to approach his
wife but this Jim felt he could no longer do. But even now,
when her husband's human frailty was finally laid bare, Jessie
never lost her affection and admiration for him.

As New York society trooped back to the city after its Palm
Beach break, Jim became increasingly depressed. His depen-
dencies – on gambling, on alcohol, on his wife's purse, on the
young men who increasingly found it difficult to make him
smile – weighed him down, and the cruel attentions of one
particular suitor drove him to distraction. His hopelessness as
a broker was his final undoing. A month or two before, when
'bargain' stocks were being offered, he tried to recoup his massive losses experienced during the Wall Street Crash two years
before by buying up in bulk stocks which turned out to be
worthless.

How much of this he shared with Jessie, and how much she
uncovered for herself, family history does not relate. All that
is known is that during 13 April 1931 Jessie Donahue was
admitted to the Harbor sanatorium on Madison Avenue suffering from a nervous breakdown. During that week Jim visited
his lawyers and drew up a new will. Nonetheless, plans were
still going ahead for yet another European voyage, and on
Saturday 18 April the Donahue trunks were dispatched to the
pier in preparation for embarkation on the Monday.

On Sunday Jim invited two friends, a broker named Milton
Doyle and another, Gordon Sarre, to the house at 6 East 80th
Street. Also present were Woolworth, now sixteen and Jimmy,
thirteen. During luncheon Jim remained silent. He remained in

low spirits as the table was cleared and a card game was started. Finally he excused himself to go to the bathroom, followed by Woolworth.

'I'll be all right,' he told his son before closing and locking the door. Five minutes later he staggered out, violently ill.

'What have you taken?' Sarre demanded.

'You'll find the bottle in there,' Jim said, gesturing towards the medicine cabinet.

Sarre ran in to find a blue bottle labelled Poison on the wash-stand. In it had been nineteen blue hexagonal bichloride of mercury pills: Jim had swallowed seven of them.

This drama was enacted in front of both children, already battered by the removal of their mother to hospital in an advanced emotional state. Woolworth and Jimmy were dispatched to find milk and eggs, the antidote printed on the bottle label, and watched as Jim's friends administered the liquid. Their father was removed to the Harbor hospital where doctors ordered, without much hope, a series of blood transfusions. It was generally agreed among the attendant specialists that death was inevitable through the poison's paralysis of the kidneys.

'I can't tell you why I did it,' Jim kept repeating as he grew weaker. 'I'm a chump for doing such a thing. Please don't tell Jessie – I love her very much.' But as death approached Jessie was wheeled in from another ward to face the spectacle of her dying husband – the second suicide in her immediate family in sixteen years,[1] but not the last.

---

1 On 2 May 1917 Jessie's sister Edna Hutton, mother of Barbara, was found dead in her bedroom at New York's Plaza Hotel. She had died after swallowing strychnine crystals, spurred on by her husband Franklyn Hutton's promiscuity which culminated in a very public affair with a Swedish actress, Monica von Fursten. Her daughter, just four, was the one to find the body.

Nor was it to be the last cover-up presided over by Jessie. Spurred on by the memory of her sister's death, and the public announcement that it had been due to 'a chronic ear disease', she ordered that the word suicide should not appear on her husband's death certificate. A battle developed between the family and Dr Thomas Gonzales, the city's assistant medical examiner: 'It is an outrage that Mr Donahue's death should be listed as a suicide,' an incensed family member told the *New York Daily News*. 'Of course there were bichloride tablets, and the circumstances of his sudden illness after taking them. But Dr Gonzales does not know what Mr Donahue's condition was when he went into the bathroom where the tablets were.'

Perhaps bearing in mind the suborning with Woolworth money of his predecessor David Feinberg in the Edna Hutton case, Dr Gonzales was unmoved: 'If they want an investigation they can conduct one. In my opinion it was suicide.'

Woolworth Donahue, witness both to the suicide attempt and the subsequent death, later told a friend that his father's death was a combination of intense anxiety over his financial plight, and a broken love affair. He had fallen for a young sailor who, once having accepted his gifts, rebuffed him.

Mauve orchids, tied with a lavender satin ribbon, adorned the door at 6 East 80th Street and the Donahues' two boys, marooned in the house without their mother, but with their father in a casket and the press baying at the door outside, retreated to an upstairs room to look down on the scene. 'All day long socially prominent people called, their chauffeurs trailing after them with costly floral pieces' recorded one writer. 'Police were finally summoned to regulate the traffic in the precincts of the home.'

Despite self-inflicted death being against the tenets of the Roman Catholic Church, a requiem mass was hastily arranged by Monsignor Stephen Donahue, secretary to Cardinal Hayes and a second cousin of Jim's. The service was conducted at the fashionable church of St Ignatius Loyola on Park Avenue at 84th Street and attended, according to the *New York Times,* by more than 3,000 people. The bronze coffin was covered with a thick blanket of orchids which cost $2,000. A funeral cortège of twenty-five cars, led by Jessie and the two boys and surrounded by police outriders, made its way to Woodlawn Cemetery where the last eulogies were made. It was all quite disgracefully over-the-top, a supreme manifestation of the vulgarity Jessie tried so helplessly to keep at bay.

For a man through whose hands had run millions of dollars, Jim Donahue had let very little of it stick. His estate when he died was valued at $3.7 million ($36.63m), of which $2.94 million was Woolworth stock. By the time his brokers, including his brother-in-law Franklyn Hutton, had been paid the $1.77 million ($17.61m) they were owed there was precious little left. Wooldon Manor on Long Island, valued together with its contents at a mere $317,390, was willed back to Jessie, whose money had paid for it in the first place. In the wall safe, the bottomless well which he had plundered so often during his marriage to pay for his bets and his boys, there was found over $100,000. His bank account contained $250,000. And the *Japauldon*, created for Jim and Jessie just ten years before at a cost of $350,000, was written down for tax purposes to a value of $50,000. Its value might as well have been nil – without her Jim beside her Jessie would no longer ride into Palm Beach with ease in her caboose with the gold taps.

From this will, signed just two days before the suicide, Jimmy and Wooly picked up a small cash inheritance to be held back until their thirty-fifth birthdays. Though improvident to a fault, Jim at least hoped his death might instil prudence in his sons. In that, his last wish, he was to be as unsuccessful as he had been himself through life.

CHAPTER 3

MR BOJANGLES

Jessie's ambition to have her son educated in the manner befitting a Woolworth heir sent her in the direction of Choate, a grand and, at the time, somewhat self-congratulatory East Coast boarding school situated a couple of hours north of New York at Wallingford.

Though abandoned by the time Jimmy arrived, the old school song – 'Choate, Choate, we're the coming men of note' – was remembered in the corridors and occasionally hauled out. It summed up the general belief that here, in the wooded glades and the clapboard houses and colonial columns which dominated the hillsides around the east side of the sleepy Connecticut town, young men of the right stuff would be properly schooled and rise to lead their country. Choate boys went to Yale, Harvard, Princeton. Their fathers were not millionaires but multi-millionaires, if not billionaires. Andrew Mellon, outright owner of Gulf Oil and the Aluminium Corporation of America, liked his Choate schooling so much he sent his son Paul there. Between father and son they raised so many new buildings the campus began to resemble an Eton or a Winchester.

Jimmy arrived by chauffeur-driven limousine – a not unusual sight at Choate – in September 1931, just a few months after his father's death, accompanied by a black-clad and heavily bejewelled Jessie and faithful family secretary Leonard Haynes. A whole new uniform had been purchased, consisting of shop-bought tweed jacket, flannels and handmade shoes; the fees were paid out of the family account at the Chase National Bank on 45th and Madison.

Jessie declared to friends that her son was to be a Princeton man, even though the odds by this stage were quite clearly stacked against him achieving any measure of academic success. Despite the attentions of Mrs Olivier there was little evidence that Jimmy had taken the idea of schoolwork seriously in the grey, blank days since he left The Hun nearly four months before. But at least, now he was at Choate there was a chance he might be able to find friendship, camaraderie, team spirit and the sense of sharing which the school promoted as its ideals.

The headmaster George St John was there to greet the late-coming pupil, and though an awesome and frightening figure – his photograph shows compressed thin lips and a steely gaze exuding an Episcopalian fervour – to the Donahues, the likes of St John would seem like men from Mars. Though he raised tens of millions of dollars from parents and ex-pupils, St John would walk round the grounds picking up litter. So diligent was he in learning the names of his pupils that he insisted all new boys have a recent photograph provided by their parents, so he could pin the suitably captioned picture up in his house, where he would sit in the evenings studying it until the boy's name was committed to memory.

No school with an ambitious building programme was going to spurn the grandson of F. W. Woolworth, but as George St John sat at tea with his wife Clara, a Burne-Jones figure with a long face and Victorian style dress, the application form Jimmy brought with him must have made dismal reading. Against the questions 'What has he done in English?' and a dozen other topics including maths, geography, history, Latin, French, German there was an ominous blank. It was clear the boy, though possessed of a precocious adult charm, not only was lacking in academic attainment but had done nothing to round out his character with hobbies, passions or even interests. In English, observed St John bleakly, '[He] hasn't read a great deal and doesn't seem to like to'. While the senior staff scratched their chins over their new arrival, he was placed in Hill House and turned over to the care of housemaster George Steele.

Steele was already in possession of the chilly reference from James Hubball, headmaster of The Hun junior school: 'He has no ambition to achieve good grades in his school work and it is therefore necessary to give him a great deal of close supervision and checking-up in order to get him to do his work. Failure in his studies does not affect him in the least or spur him to greater efforts . . . he will not spend the necessary energy to attain a reasonably good record.' He added, rather bitterly: 'It is very difficult to give you a very accurate idea of Jimmy's preparation because the boy has missed so much time from school. At no time since he has been with us has he ever gone through a school year without being absent for long periods because of poor health or for other, *apparently unavoidable* reasons.' Hubball concluded that Jimmy was courteous, amenable to school discipline, and 'willing to co-operate with the school authorities', but in truth he was recalling a boy who had left his care more than a year previous and before the onset of puberty.

Those who had the opportunity to observe Jimmy in the first few days at Choate found him wary, shy and surprised at the warmth of his greeting. He had lived too along away from the company of his peers and was unprepared for their interest in him.

Returning from Choate, Jessie concentrated on the shell-shocked Wooly, who was to be dispatched in October on an 'educational' trip to Africa 'and around the world'. This trip had the effect of stabilising the boy, giving him a focus and reference point which stayed with him through his adult years. Witnessing his father's suicide altered him ineradicably.

For Jimmy, calming the troubled seas within proved harder. Nor were his problems made easier by continued physical problems of one sort and another. No sooner had he returned to school than orthodontic difficulties which he had suffered over the past eight years now reasserted themselves. The 'mal-relation of the jaws and the irregularity of the teeth' as his doctor, Edward Griffin, described them, would now require regular monthly surgery and bridgework. Soon after Christmas he was in hospital for 'a slight operation' and the school wrote to Jessie asking that whatever further work might be needed on the boy's mouth could be done before his return to school. Already the old pattern of illness and absence had re-asserted itself and Jimmy, after six months at Choate, was beginning to drift.

In this he was not alone. The term after he joined Choate another sickly boy from a rackety, apparently privileged background also arrived by chauffeur-driven car at the school. But if John Fitzgerald Kennedy had emotional problems too – deriving from a childhood plagued with illness – at least he had an older brother, Joe, already well-established at the school and regarded as something of a hero, to help calm them. Choate treated J. F. Kennedy much as they treated Jimmy Donahue – with polite interest and not a little suspicion.

The only thing that interested Jimmy was the school's dramatic club, which was in the early stages of planning a production of Gilbert and Sullivan's *The Mikado*. When Jack Kennedy later recalled his Choate days, he was to pour scorn upon the headmaster's apparent inability to choose anything other than these mild Edwardian musical satires.

However much it was Jessie's intention that her son should become integrated into Choate's society, she undermined these pledges by her continued irritation at the necessity for him to adhere to the school schedule. The Woolworth millions were capable of buying anything and silencing all gainsayers; yet here she was, at weekends and holidays, held to ransom by a group of schoolmasters whose honeyed words in their letters assured her of their continuing thraldom. Why, then, could she not have Jimmy when she wanted? Especially when the *Japauldon* was kitted out and ready to head for Florida? In March, with the Easter holidays approaching, sweet words between parent and teachers turned to a frosty stand-off: Jessie wanted Jimmy out of school early so they could get going for Palm Beach. A stiff note from Jessie's secretary Leonard Haynes asked the housemaster George Steele why Jimmy could not be let out early. Jimmy himself, on the telephone, had told Jessie he could get away early – what was the problem?

Unfazed by this big-gun approach, Steele informed Haynes with asperity that 'Jimmy will leave here on the noon train March 18', and reminded him 'the boys arrive back at Choate noon Sunday April 3'. The underlying message – no matter how rich you are, how discommoding this may be, the boys travel as one. In the end, however, the Woolworth millions won out. Jim baled out of school early, apparently suffering from a particularly debilitating form of sinus.

The *Japauldon* was a source of immense pride and schoolboy boasting, and it was Jimmy's habit to get up on the plate with

41

the train-driver and help drive the train south to Palm Beach. He was at Cielito Lindo while his classmates were still packing their trunks. Nonetheless an assignment sheet was sent down to him; he was behind with his studies, and showing an insouciant disregard for the peer pressure which usually makes schoolboys conform.

Out of a momentary sense of guilt, Jessie wrote on Jim's return to Mrs St John: 'I want to thank you for all the interest you have shown in my boy – it was indeed very kind of you and I did appreciate both yours and Mr St John's letters. Jimmy returned to school today in fine condition – he certainly had a healthy vacation – out all day in the sunshine swimming and fishing and no late nights. He has absolutely no sinus now.'

Those who knew Jessie Woolworth Donahue in her latter years observed that some steely carapace had strengthened her from childhood, shielding her from emotion's deeper wounds. The loss of her husband was consigned to a private place in her heart, but she knew when to unlock it to advantage. When she felt the need to see her boy again, within a fortnight of his return to school, she sent for him to come back to Six East 80th Street. She wrote to his housemaster: 'Thanks for allowing Jimmy to come down this weekend – you can't imagine what it meant to me to have one boy with me at this sad time.'

Her conscience, and maybe word from Jimmy of the one-upmanship in the school, prompted her to further action. Jack Kennedy's father Joe had presented the school with a movie projector. Now Jessie ordered a copy of the new hit film *Dr Jekyll and Mr Hyde* starring Fredric March and Miriam Hopkins. The film was a sensation, with strong sexual undertones: no wonder 500 of the school's 520 boys turned out to watch. It may have raised Jimmy's kudos in the eyes of his classmates, but next day he was back to extra lessons to try to catch up with the backlog of work.

No homework had been done while he 'recovered' from his sinus problems in Palm Beach and pretty soon it became clear that, even with all the coaching, the French exam he was due to take in the summer term simply was not worth attempting. As the school year ended that forlorn ambition to be a Princeton man was further away than ever.

A late decision was taken to withdraw him from the Latin class, and Mrs Donahue was advised that her son should have extra tuition in English. Despite his advancing years, his handwriting was pitifully unformed through lack of practice, and his grasp of the language's essentials shaky at best.

The masters alternately seethed and despaired. His algebra teacher H. N. Lewis reported: 'Jim has been to every compulsory and no voluntary conference I have held. With an extremely difficult job Jim left the task entirely up to me, with the possibility of Luck stepping in should I fail him, but with an entire disregard of the fact that without his doing his share – and even more than his share – there was no hope of his passing.'

His housemaster wrote in a memo: 'No academic urge whatsoever. Had to plead with his Mother to withdraw him from the school – practically demanding that this be his last year – interested in the stage – as a producer – I've tried to educate him somewhat along these lines pointing out to him how much (a) cultivated background would make him a patron of the arts – worthy life for one with such a financial background – but 'tis the tinsel of the Follies which appeals.

'No use to continue in the German class – would it be worthwhile if I took him alone in German – perfectly willing. As far as I know all goes well disciplinarily – and Jim has learned how to mix in the corridor – but naturally not with the stronger element.' He quit school with the other boys on 8 June and would not return for nearly four months.

Back in Palm Beach, which was still barely more than a village, his reputation as a prankster spread fast. Opinion was divided among the super-rich as to whether Jim Donahue's boy was amusing or beyond control. Jessie gave Jimmy a car which had, according to a contemporary 'a big spotlight on the running-board. Jimmy would go around at night flashing this into people's cars to see if they were doing anything! That was his sort of kick.'

All too soon, adult New York began to reveal its pleasures to Jimmy. When he was thirteen, his cousin Barbara Hutton had come to stay at East 80th Street while she attended Miss Hewitt's school in Manhattan, and it was through her eyes that he began to see the outside world. Jimmy became the sibling Barbara had never had. Though Wooly was the same age as Barbara, it was to Jimmy that she clung. Jessie took pride in mothering her and offering her lessons in life. In her diary Barbara wrote: 'Deep down I feel inadequate. I am ugly, fat, awkward. I am also dull. To be dull, says Aunt Jessie, is a cardinal sin. "Be mean, be stupid, but don't be dull!"'

Barbara used her cousin as a shield, sounding-board, escort and confidante. She was encouraged to attend parties at the socialite Cobina Wright's house in Sutton Place, where society and the world of entertainment mixed, and such figures as Cole Porter, Fred Astaire, Tallulah Bankhead, Arturo Toscanini and Jimmy Durante rubbed shoulders with the Chryslers, Vanderbilts and Astors. Jimmy came too, and his nascent love of showbusiness developed fast in such an atmosphere. Already prompted by his parents' friend Flo Ziegfeld to take an interest in the stage, he was now actually meeting people he had seen on the movie-screen back at Choate.

On other days Barbara and he would go to the Central Park Casino where they sipped orange juice and danced to the music of Eddy Duchin, or they would stay at home in East 80th Street playing records while Wooly went off chasing girls. The names of all three, linked in speculation as to their likely marriage paths, were already gossip-column fodder.

One item the columns did not pick up was Barbara and Jimmy's constant forays to Cartier. Newly-discovered, and with prices to frighten even the super-rich, it seemed quite the wickedest thing to go to the jeweller's and spend grandpa Woolworth's money. Philip van Rensselaer records an early foray into the Fifth Avenue store where Barbara took the teenager Jimmy in to buy him black pearl and diamond cufflinks with matching studs, a watch and a gold ribbed cigarette case with *pavéed* sapphires. The shopping spree continued with Barbara choosing a jade necklace and a rock crystal and diamond boudoir clock, and a number of other items. In an afternoon she disposed of $100,000 ($1.2m) but it was not so unusual. Indeed, retail therapy at this sort of level became a fixation with the cousins.

❧

The return to school after the summer break shows no increase in Jimmy's academic determination, despite his schedule for the year being reduced to four main subjects – English, French, algebra and physical geography. A month later, failing in his studies, bored and frustrated and friendless, Jimmy walked out of Choate. Now aged seventeen, worldly, and with sufficient financial resources to sustain whatever course of action he chose, he took off for New York and went missing for several days before he could be found.

He had met Bill 'Bojangles' Robinson, the sensational black dancer, in a bar, and had gone to New York to take dance lessons with him. 'The boys thought he was a pretty cool guy for doing that,' recalled one contemporary, though others, perhaps resentful of Jimmy's sophistication and his superfluity of cash, complained to masters of his woeful lack of team spirit.

Bojangles had become an overnight celebrity when at fifty years old he conquered Broadway with a dance-on part in *Blackbirds of 1928*. His solo spot in the show was credited with boosting threefold the revue's weekly gross. He became widely known for single-handedly saving Broadway shows which otherwise had little to recommend them. Forty-two years older than his new protégé, Bojangles's background could not have been more dissimilar from Jimmy's. An orphan son brought up by his grandmother who had once been a slave, Bojangles started his professional career at the age of seven in Richmond, Virginia as a boy dancer. His performances, most particularly his tap-dancing down a set of steps from which routine Fred Astaire borrowed liberally, were electrifying, and Jimmy was stage-struck. There and then, he decided he wanted to be a dancer too.

Soon Jimmy was back at Choate, under house-arrest and denied the privilege of home-leave for Thanksgiving. Despite a quite obvious need to discipline the boy – and the fact that mother and son had had their first serious row since the death of Jimmy's father – Jessie ingenuously asked if she could have him by her side at this family time. She received a brittle answer from the Head. The 'escape' was considered shocking, and St John wrote to Jimmy's housemaster: 'I had a talk (with him). At the end of it I told him I did not know what we could do – it depends on how understanding a school we have, what the reverberations are – above all, how Jim lives and works, and what he proves from this moment on. We certainly haven't left him under any misapprehension as to the impression he has made.'

To Jessie, St John wrote: 'At first I did not see any possibility of our going on living and working with Jim. I didn't see how we could consider anything except his withdrawal from the School. It is a testament to my tremendous interest in him . . . that I am clinging. Jim has left me little to cling to otherwise.'

Even at this stage St John sought not to offend the Woolworth millions and hid himself behind the shield of his pupils: 'If we are able to keep Jim here at school it will be because the boys are fine enough and grown-up enough and understanding enough to make such a thing possible. Certainly if the boys decide they can go on working with Jim they certainly would not put up with some second serious offence on Jim's part. Nor will they put up with negativeness on Jim's part.'

In essence it was an omen of what was to come; something of which St John no doubt was aware but wanted to put off – something too which Jimmy must instinctively have sensed. In any event the behaviour did not change. Classmate Roderick McCubbin recalls: 'The teacher of our German class was Albert Blume. Blume is the German word for flower, and I remember one day Herr Blume was at the board writing something in German and Jimmy got up, did a tap-dance all the way up to the front of the room, presented him with a flower he had picked from the school garden, then tap-danced all the way back to his seat, taking a bow before he sat down. Everyone fell about laughing. Herr Blume didn't get shook up about it, he just said something in German and left it at that.'

That master, well aware of the tragedy which was still raw in Jimmy's life, adopted the standard reaction used by other members of the faculty of not putting pressure on the boy. He reserved his frustrations for a letter he wrote to the headmaster concerning his vain attempts to one-to-one tutor Jimmy up for an exam: 'He made very little attempt to learn anything . . . his attitude was not much more than passive submission.'

Having sat the exam, the teacher reported: 'He did not try. He had threatened to spend only seven minutes on the exam if it were given to him on Sunday – Jim was evidently enraged over the fact that he had to spend the [Thanksgiving] recess in Wallingford.

'I am anxious to help Jim all I can. So far this year I have had to spend so much time in class-teaching Jim that I have been unable to do full justice to the rest of the class. In other words he will continue to be a hindrance to the progress of his division. He has not taken the trouble to learn how to study – why should he?

'This is in effect what Jim said the other day: "Why should I study? Some boys get five or ten dollars for each B they get. My mother wouldn't even say thank you if I got a 100% in a course. All she says when she calls up is are you still in school?"'

The Jimmy Donahue problem was assuming nightmare proportions. Jessie's over-indulgence, aggravated by her indifference to the minutiae of school life, was torturing the boy. On the one hand, she wanted him by her side when she rode proudly down to Palm Beach in the *Japauldon*, on the other she wanted him to succeed in school. She seemed incapable of assessing the damage her laissez-faire attitude was having on the boy. 'Above all,' one acquaintance said, 'Jessie held the view that it was vulgar to have a job of work. Therefore Jimmy's education was of secondary importance.'

As Christmas approached and as he collected his trunk to catch the noon train out of Wallingford for Christmas in New York, Jimmy thumbed his nose at the school, its teachers and pupils. The general feeling among his peers was that he wouldn't be back – he had said so himself, and the hint had been dropped by masters that Jimmy had been expelled. For the pupil, comparing the adult intoxications of Broadway with the stultified adolescent life at Choate, there was no contest. His shyness and his inadequacy at sport had left him rejected by his peers; thus he saw no reason to conform, and the shaky admiration he earned from his pranks and jokes and the occasional generosity of his mother was not enough to tie him to the place.

Roderick McCubbin recalls: 'He was a strange character, eccentric. He was likeable, a bit peculiar, but funny – there were a lot of people there who had as much money as he had and probably little family life. He larked about, I don't know if it was a question of ability, but he suffered an attention gap and didn't seem interested.'

George St John, who had problems with other pupils – not least Jack Kennedy, whose father was by now begging for the boy to be taken back after a series of misdemeanours – was determined not to alienate Jessie Woolworth, her millions, and her powerful friends. And yet he dreaded the return of his *bête noire*. Finally, on Boxing Day 1932 he wrote to Jessie: I have warned him of the . . . danger of a miserable life when he is older, with little respect from others and little self-respect inside, with only such friends as a shallow, foolish, uneducated person can make, they always watching to impose upon him and use him and his money for their own purposes. He is bound to be noticed . . . when he comes to manhood; and it would be a terrible thing to be covertly smiled at through life for childish ignorance and conceits. Jim needs, even more than a poor boy, to make himself a real person.'

This prescient portrait concluded with the advice that Jimmy should educate himself up to college standard or his life would fail its early promise; and that he should re-learn the respect he once showed his mother but which had worn thin during his time at Choate: 'I hope Jim will more often be a comfort to you by showing good sense and an appreciation of the best values in life, and by showing you a chivalrous respect and affection and an understanding desire to help.'

Whatever the pressures, Christmas passed smoothly enough. Wooly was abroad and Jessie confided that she sensed an improvement in her son. 'I must say although I had anticipated quite a little trouble with Jimmy during the vacation I found him much improved,' she wrote. 'He was out with me quite a good deal of the time – he also seemed to be more reasonable and tried not to upset me. His one idea of vacation is to stay out as late as possible and then brag about it. He fabricates a great many stories to the older boys to make them believe he is a great sport. What I am trying to tell you is that I did find an improvement but still think he is a strange boy and hard to understand.'

Nowhere in this is there any self-doubt or questioning of the way that she had brought up her son. The years of indulgence, of apparent illness, of the shock of his father's suicide and the very long leash which his mother's money had let him out on – none of these were acknowledged in Jessie's letter. Analytical she was not; or possibly she did not want to open questions into her own parenting.

The boy's unhappy saga of afflictions continued. Warts on his foot caused discomfort and created further need for him to be excused games on his return to Choate. While other boys rowed and did athletics, Jimmy was driven by car into nearby New Haven to see Dr John Lane, recommended by Jessie's own GP John Harris. The only bright light on the horizon was that he had been selected to play a part in the school production of *The Pirates of Penzance*.

The lure of New York, of Bojangles and his stimulating crowd, was all-consuming. Allowed down to the city on a Monday to see Dr Harris, he did not return until the following Sunday. Also Jimmy was enjoying his first sexual encounters. His proclivities were exclusively homosexual, though he had been self-contained enough to keep it from his colleagues at

Choate. Jessie was in Palm Beach and knew nothing of her son's extra-curricular activities.

A letter from his doctor demanding that Jimmy be returned to New York for further treatment of his warts was the final straw for the Choate staff. At first Jimmy's housemaster George Steele played the request with a straight bat: 'I know how inadvisable it is for him to be in New York alone and particularly while his mother is in the South,' he noted bitterly and Harris's plea met with a bleak rejoinder saying that if Jimmy had to travel to New York he, Steele, would be forced to travel with him.

George St John determined that the Donahue problem had got out of hand. The predictions he made before Christmas – that he could not control his pupil, nor did the pupil wish to submit himself to the conventions of Choate – were coming to pass. The problem might yet have been overcome, but a group of senior boys in the school petitioned St John, telling him that Jimmy's unruly behaviour was ruining the boys' morale. On 14 February 1933, St John wrote to Jessie in Palm Beach: 'It hurts me awfully . . . it has gradually become common knowledge that Jim ran away to New York, and further than that, it is known that Jim has been smoking here at School since. The boys feel very strongly that Jim is not a boy whom they can rightly allow to stay in the school. They feel, and I fear rightly, that Jim's negativeness and commonplace point of view lowers the whole morale and standard of any group of fellows he is in.'

He instructed Jessie to arrange her son's withdrawal from the school the following day, adding: 'I think he needs this action to stab him awake.' A telephone call from St John asked the usually imperturbable Jessie to tear herself from the delights of Palm Beach and head back to New York to meet her son off the one o'clock train from Wallingford. Meanwhile he was to be kept under house arrest in Hill House, the final alienation from his peers.

The timing of Jimmy's expulsion could not have been more inconvenient for his mother, however. Still bravely determined to make a splash in Palm Beach, even without a husband at her side, she had planned a series of parties to encourage the great and good to look upon her as something more than just a rich woman with inherited millions, but a great society hostess too. St John's letter arrived at Whitehall, the massive stone edifice in Palm Beach where she was temporarily roosting while Cielito Lindo underwent some costly and entirely unnecessary refurbishment, on the morning she was due to give a socially-enhancing dinner for a hundred. Among her guests were the Duke and Duchess of Sutherland, the Earl and Countess of Warwick, Countess di Zoppola, and a raft of Palm Beach eminences including Pulitzers, Munns and Wideners dragged there to witness how she could entertain European aristocracy with her silver which was gold. The idea of having to race northwards to cope with her younger son's latest mishap was frustrating and embittering. In addition Woolworth had hooked himself up with an heiress, Dorothy Fell, and she was keen that she also should be impressed with the dinner. Now was not the time to be abandoning her plans: Jimmy would have to be fetched from school by a secretary.

Aged seventeen, Jimmy was on the educational scrapheap, despite the fact that, with the Woolworth millions very much in mind, The Hun School wrote rapidly to Jessie to offer him a place back at his old school. They did not have the courtesy of a reply, for Jessie decided he had had enough schooling. Jessie returned her attention to the gaming tables of Palm Beach and to the task of re-opening Cielito Lindo.

Jimmy did not even bother to come home to mother. Escorted back to New York, he went to stay at the family suite of rooms at the Hotel Pierre. Since his father's suicide Jessie had not set foot inside the house on East 80th Street and workmen were now preparing her new home, a triplex apartment at 834 Fifth Avenue, said by some to be the largest apartment New York had ever seen.

After consulting with friends and family, Jessie worked out a three-month plan to send Jimmy as far from the fleshpots of the city as she could. A place had been booked for him on a ranch in Tucson, Arizona, to keep him busy, toughen him up and give him an outdoor outlook. But the outbreak of warts on his left foot worsened and he was hospitalised while they were removed. Having to resort to crutches for a month after his release effectively put paid to Jessie's Wild West ambitions for her son. Instead he finally travelled down to Palm Beach with Jessie 'to sit in the sea for a few weeks', she wrote wistfully.

As soon as his foot recovered the Wild West plan was once again enacted; but far from ending up on a dude ranch in Tucson, Jimmy found himself in the statelier climes of the Arizona Biltmore hotel in the state capital, Phoenix. By the time he and Jessie arrived they found it was too late in the season to enjoy the ranch's range of activities to the full and, in any event, he wrote to his old housemaster George Steele: 'The place looked very shabby so we decided to come to this hotel and it is very nice here.' Though the Arizona Biltmore featured a cowboy astride a bucking bronco on its headed paper, it was as far removed as possible from the ways of the West. Indeed, it was the state's plushest hotel and mother and son felt comfortable enough there.

With the Palm Beach season at an end, Jessie returned to New York and Jim travelled to join Barbara in San Francisco.

New York Society was in a state of flux by the 1930s. It was the richest, and on the way to becoming the most culturally aware, social grouping in the world. But having established and marshalled itself at the turn of the century, it felt nervous about allowing in newcomers of dubious ancestry. Certainly the family of an Irish animal fats-renderer with a factory on West 39th Street had little chance of making headway, but even the Woolworth clan, who had given the city its tallest building, stood in a kind of no-man's-land. The families of Jessie Donahue and her two sisters were richer than most, yet because of the source of their wealth – humble five-and-dime stores – society's doors still did not easily yield to their touch.

The rules had been laid down by a man called Ward McAllister, who had earned his stripes as a member of New York's elite after he enjoyed the ennobling experience of dining with Queen Victoria's chef. He was the man who decided who was who, and who could be invited where. To his way of thinking, there were 400 people, and no more than 400, worth cultivating. With the connivance and support of Mrs William Backhouse Astor he decided that was it; and it became law. The press referred to Society as 'the 400' and the name stuck.

Within a few years the writer Igor Cassini was able to observe: 'The way high society operated, up to World War I, is dead as a mackerel. Its *modus operandi* has changed vastly, and the pomp, circumstance, and lavishness of the past are gone with the wind.' Yet despite this levelling process the Woolworths and the Donahues never, ever, made it into the 400.

If the Woolworth riches cushioned them from this blow, they did not cushion them from them all. Jimmy's cousin Barbara had vowed to wreak revenge on the stuffy, insular world of the 400 and rise above, to walk with kings and princes, in fact to become royalty itself. Already she had made her debut with a party for a thousand guests at the Ritz-Carlton, showering them with champagne at a time of Prohibition and serenading them with the music of three orchestras – Rudy Vallee, Meyer Davis and Howard Lanin. The *New York Times* used up two-and-a-half columns listing the names of the guests, most of them unknown to Barbara. As a social debut it was, as her biographer Dean Jennings observed: 'a cheap investment at thirty-five thousand dollars or more'.

Escorted by Jimmy, she also had her cousins George and Louis Ehret in tow, but already Louis had taken a dislike to Jimmy: 'He was bright as a dime and very witty but his sense of humour was the washroom variety, full of cloacal references and four-letter words. He never stopped talking about orifices, of what went into and came out of them. But Barbara was titillated by his talk. Even at that age he was queering half the big-name homosexuals in New York, people like Maury Paul, the gossip columnist. And he wasn't too discreet about it.'

Jimmy, though now Barbara's chief confessor, had been left behind in the States when she made her debut before King George V and Queen Mary at Buckingham Palace on 19 May 1931. But she wrote to her cousin about meeting the Prince of Wales, and to another she described the prince: 'He was deft and light on his feet, a good dancer. He was also very cheerful, almost too cheerful, a bit tipsy maybe. It's hard to imagine him as the future King of England.'

That the Prince of Wales had chosen to dance with one of the world's great heiresses came as no surprise, but though he issued an invitation for her to join his party in Biarritz the following month his interest had already focused elsewhere, on another American woman fifteen years Barbara's senior – Thelma Furness.

If the Woolworth clan, most particularly Jessie and Barbara's father Franklyn Hutton, nurtured hopes of Barbara ensnaring the Prince, their timing was off. Earlier that year the Prince had dropped in on a cocktail party given by Lady Furness at her home in 21 Grosvenor Square. Also present was Wallis Warfield Simpson, the wife of an Anglo-American shipping broker and former Guards officer, whom Cecil Beaton described thus: 'She looked coarse. Her back was coarse, and her arms were heavy. Her voice had a high nasal twang. She was loud and brash, terribly so – and rowdy and raucous. Her squawks of laughter were like a parrot's.' Lady Furness, perhaps understandably given that she was about to be usurped in the Prince's affections, recalled Wallis Simpson's hands: 'they were large; they did not move gracefully'.

It was the fashion that year, apparently, for Americans homing in on the royal court to be less than completely graceful. Barbara was all too aware that she was overweight, bearing what the writer and socialite Elsa Maxwell described as 'pendulous' breasts. But if she herself felt like a fish out of water in the too-rarefied air of Buckingham Palace, with its awful lighting and snobbish servants – she was to describe it as 'a quick trip to Hades' – her accounts to her cousin-confessor did nothing but spark in him the desire to emulate her in some way. But it is a sad fact that while eligible and nubile heiresses may make their way with ease to the side of princes of Wales, no such path exists for their male counterparts. Jimmy's early ambition was to break that rule and meet the Prince of Wales, and to this end he tried to persuade Jessie to buy a London house.

Soon the *New York Evening Journal*'s columnist Billy Benedick, in reporting that Jessie would not be returning to the East 80th Street house and would continue to live at the Hotel Pierre, added the news that she had signed a long lease on a house in Mayfair. Wooldon Manor and Cielito Lindo had lost their charm, and London society would shortly be opening its arms to receive her, he predicted. But the writer clearly knew little of Jessie's obsessive gambling. The gaming laws in London at the time made her daily pastime virtually impossible to pursue, and yet she was tempted to relocate for at least part of the year for she, too, had forged an ambition to meet the Prince of Wales.

Right now, however, another prince was to occupy Jessie and Jimmy's thoughts. Twenty-eight-year-old Alexis Mdivani was one of three princely brothers from the Russian state of Georgia who shared good looks, skill on a polo pony, vaulting ambition and a ruthless streak which had secured the first two lucrative marital arrangements. Now Alexis, already married to an heiress Louise van Alen, encouraged Barbara in what she herself wanted, to be married to him. The fact that her friend was currently married to him seemed not to be an obstacle. Despite the fact Barbara was barely twenty-one, she saw it as an escape route from the obsessive control of her father Franklyn Hutton as much as anything else: 'I was always lonesome, I wanted a companion. I thought I would have more freedom.'

On 29 November 1932 Mdivani was divorced and Jessie and Jimmy were summoned to appear in Paris for the nuptials on 22 June 1933 at the Russian Cathedral of St Alexander Nevsky on the Rue Daru. Mother and son embarked on the SS *Normandie* and arrived at the Ritz Hotel to take up residence with their much-feted relation. The pictures of Jimmy, taken with his mother at this event, show a beautifully turned-out young man – tall, tanned, with an impeccably cut morning-coat and carrying a bowler hat. Jessie, dressed as she saw fit for the occasion, was described as a marshmallow with snowman's eyes. Other sartorial solecisms of the day included the bride's father, successful manager of her fortune who had raised its value to $40 million ($408m), bringing in an income of $2 million ($20.4m) a year – Franklyn Hutton wore spats and too large a buttonhole. The Rolls Royces queued in the Place Vendôme to drop their ineffably rich passengers including the tall and tanned Woolworth, back from his African odyssey and typically with a cigarette in one hand and a woman in the other.

The ceremony went off satisfactorily enough, with the two Donahue brothers holding aloft the traditional Russian Orthodox ceremonial crowns above the bride and groom. Serenaded by a heavenly choir, Barbara and her prince stood surrounded by a cloak of heavy incense, kissed icons, walked in circles around the altar and sipped sacred wine. Jimmy was ahead of them – before the ceremony he had consumed six Brandy Alexanders. His face, a picture of innocence in the wedding photographs, masked a deeper darkness. That night in Paris he appeared at Bricktop's *boîte*, standing at the top of the stairs naked, apart from a *cache-sexe* improvised from a red and white checked napkin. Was it bravado, or despair, that drove him to do it?

CHAPTER 4

HOT AND BOTHERED

Jimmy's thirst to get himself noticed was compulsive. One day he persuaded a friend to join him in a practical joke. They would dress as nuns, get in a car and drive across the bridge to West Palm Beach, and go to the cinema. What the friend did not know was that Jimmy's plan was rather more elaborate. Halfway across the bridge which spans Lake Worth – the major route between mainland and Palm Beach – Jimmy stopped the car, got out, pulled up his nun's habit and squatted in the middle of the road. The subsequent act of defecation had the required effect and several cars collided with each other.

Jean Flagler Matthews, daughter of the colony's founder, arriving in the resort mink-clad, in a cortège of cars carrying staff, family, luggage, animals and friends, incurred Jimmy's ire. The next morning he telephoned her house declaring himself to be from the West Palm Beach Water Supply company. 'You are going to have to turn your water off because we're fixing the mains,' he told the housekeeper. The woman assured him they would comply, and Jimmy packed his bags to go racing at Hialeah. The following day on his return he was reminded of Mrs Matthews' plight and called to tell the housekeeper: 'I thought I called you and said not to use the water.' The woman assured him that, so far had they followed his instructions that Mrs Matthews has just left the house to use the bathroom in the Everglades Club. 'Well that's very funny, one of my men has just got a load of shit down from you.' Maybe not so funny now, but it made Palm Beach rock with laughter at the time, since the pretentious Mrs Matthews was not universally adored.

Mrs Matthews had the chance to find out about Jimmy for herself when he arrived at her door and purloined the fur coat she had cast aside (and rightly: the temperature was 80 degrees), dressed himself in it and executed a tap-dance across her hall.

Jimmy invented a family called the Livingston-Livingstons and had their entirely fictitious parties reported in the local newspapers, publications which were all too eager to report the doings behind doors which were shut to them. The joke ran for several weeks. On another occasion, he sat in the writing room of the Breakers Hotel with Mary Munn (later the Countess of Bessborough) and penned a sweetly-phrased note to Mrs Harry Hays Morgan, mother of Gloria and Thelma Furness, saying how much the resort missed her and, at the page-turn, scrawled in capital letters: 'SO GET YOUR FAT OLD WRINKLED ASS DOWN HERE.'

Back in New York Jimmy went to see a friend, Mary Sullivan, who worked in the bookshop at the Waldorf-Astoria. Spying two old ladies browsing among the shelves he bore down on them with a solicitous inquiry, having first taken off all his clothes. His friend was sacked and he bought her a set of sables by way of compensation.

Behind the jollity there was a rising desperation. He hated being alone and found it difficult to sleep. Marooned one day in the new family home at 834 Fifth Avenue, where Jessie had provided him with his own suite of rooms – as much to keep him at a distance as an acknowledgement of his adulthood – he filled a bag with gold boxes and trinkets and prepared to run away. But there was nowhere to go, and the idea fizzled out before he even reached the front door. 'It was a very cold, austere house,' recalled a friend from that time. 'There was no love in that house, and all Jimmy wanted was love and affection. He used to do those things just to get attention.'

Through the summer of 1933 a pair of producers, Morris Green and Frank McCoy, sought financing to stage a new musical comedy, *Hot and Bothered*, with an eye to it coming into Broadway. Choosing as their star a veteran of the silent movies, Oscar Shaw, and hiring the writing team of Harlan Thompson and Louis Gensler, they earmarked the 2,500-seat Boulevard Theatre in Jackson Heights, a corner of the Queens district of New York, and hired a cast and dance troupe. The custom of the day required that while the shows should be slick and spectacular, a strong story-line was not a priority. A good band, a chorus-line with great legs and acceptable faces, and a few one-line gags were more important than plot or substance.

Green and McCoy hired a dozen chorus-girls and among the twenty-strong cast auditioned two actresses called Dorothy Dilley and Dorothy Vernon. Dilley, a friend of Jimmy's, arranged for him to audition for McCoy and he duly landed the smallest part in the show, that of Second Detective. The whole cast were required to hoof it to Gene Salzer's 'orchestra' and if Jimmy was a little weak on delivering lines, he made up for it with footwork. Elated by this sudden step on the ladder to stardom, he renamed himself Jimmy Dugan.

The show was doomed to failure. Originally slated to open on 17 July, its was postponed until the 24 July. A new announcement said it would open in September. A further date of 9 October was followed by a definite date of 23 October. Finally a date was arrived at: 30 October. But on that night, the show once again failed to open. By the following day cast, band, crew and management were ready to chance it.

Brave words were uttered by the management about the show beating house records, but *Hot and Bothered* was a dire entertainment. On the second night, Jessie Donahue arrived in jewels and her Rolls Royce, with her sister Helena McCann. Unused to their surroundings, for Jackson Heights is no Palm Beach, they did not like what they saw and when Jimmy arrived home late that night, flushed with the audience's applause for his modest contribution, he was told in no uncertain terms by his mother that his future was not as an actor. Ignoring the fact that Jimmy had probably put more effort into preparing for this one small part than Jim Donahue had done in the whole of his career, Jessie exercised the power she was to wield for the rest of her life over Jimmy – that of financial excommunication. If he wished to pursue a career in the theatre, then it should be as an impresario.

Though he was subdued by this threat, the issue was resolved by other forces, namely the public's sublime indifference to *Hot and Bothered*. It suffered the same fate as the shows which bracketed it at the Boulevard theatre – *For God and Country* and *The Divine Drudge* – and after ten days it was consigned to theatreland's furnace. The gossip columnists, paying slightly closer attention to events than their theatre critic colleagues, raked the ashes and managed to suggest that during its short run Jimmy had enjoyed close relationships with both Dorothys as well as a dancer, Lois Spreckles. But in fact he had no time for these imagined multiple heterosexual dalliances.

He was already living a triple life: in the theatre, with his boyfriends, and as an eligible bachelor-about-town. While the rest of the *Hot and Bothered* cast laboured at rehearsal, he was photographed, smoothly turned out in silk-faced tuxedo, at the opening party of the Fall season at the Central Park Casino, on the arm of a suitable heiress, Antoinette Johnson. The columnists waited in vain for the announcement of their betrothal.

After nearly fourteen years, Prohibition had finally been repealed and Jimmy celebrated by throwing a party at which, with heavy irony, only non-alcoholic drinks were served. In the aimless weeks leading up to the end of 1933, Jimmy sought some other role. It was awaiting him.

By common consent, one honeymoon was deemed not enough for the world's richest girl. A short foray through Europe taking in Lake Como, Venice and Biarritz had been fine, but at the beginning of 1934 the Prince and Princess Mdivani decided upon a grander tour, more becoming to their status. Jimmy, at the invitation of Barbara, was ready to go, too.

The journey started at Grand Central Station, where Barbara's private railcar the *CurleyHut*, connected to the rear of the 'Overland Limited' train, awaited its mistress, her husband, her cousin, her retinue of staff and her sixty trunks. At midday on 5 January the honeymoon express puffed out of New York, and straight into trouble.

Alexis Mdivani's two brothers, siblings of a similar stripe, had both married rich women and together founded the Pacific Oil Company. In due course it was discovered that in setting up the company with their wives' money the intention had been to drill, not for oil, but for cash; and a fortnight before,

Prince David and Prince Serge Mdivani had been indicted on fourteen counts of fraud and grand larceny.

The news that Prince Alexis had been subpoenaed to appear at his brothers' trial greeted the honeymooning couple as they steamed into Chicago the morning after their departure from New York. Inevitably the information was brought in person by reporters hoping to carry away further gleanings, and in this they were not disappointed. Hoping for an interview with Alexis, or preferably Barbara, they had to make do with Jimmy, roused from his bed by Barbara's secretary Nancy Allard and sent out to deal with the reptilian horde.

Jimmy came out onto the observation platform, shivering in blue silk pyjamas, a gaudy yellow silk robe, cravat and slippers. Asked about his supernumerary status on a honeymoon, he countered that he had been invited along because of his brilliant wit: 'I'm the court clown – without a court. They tried to get Ed Wynn[1] but he couldn't make it. Actually I'm Barbara's bodyguard,' he added, and to demonstrate the point brought out a handgun from his pocket, challenging: 'Anyone care to argue the point?'

This was a defining moment for Jimmy. Until now he had been famous by association – because of his mother, his grandfather, and his cousin. Now for the first time, as he saw it, he was being extensively interviewed by the press, in his own right – not realising that the fourth estate's time-honoured means of entrapment is to exhaust an interviewee with questions until the guard is dropped and an unexpected truth pops out.

Goaded on in this manner, Jimmy waxed lyrical about his days at Choate, about his departed father and his role in *Hot and Bothered*. He signed autographs 'Jimmy "Dugan"

---

1 Popular radio and TV comic

Donahue', implying that his showbiz career was far from over. The reporters learned little more about the activities of Prince Alexis but they had found a new darling, for Jimmy's wit, charm and inheritance made him a suitable subject for their paragraph-making. A magical symbiosis had occurred which had nothing to do with the young man's ability as a hoofer.

The invisible Prince Alexis aimed to keep it that way, having no intention of becoming embroiled in his brothers' trial, and when the *CurleyHut* steamed into Reno, Nevada, he quietly slipped off the train and headed for the airport. The press were left with little to write about except to revisit the details of the $120,000 carriage in which the trio were travelling: two bedrooms of rich gilt-weaved yellow fabric, hung canopies over the beds, and tapestries of blue and gold brocade over the period furniture of the observation room.

Jimmy and Barbara continued the honeymoon voyage alone, the eighteen-year old consoling the twenty-one-year old as their gilded prison trundled west towards San Francisco; two young people trapped by too much money and too few resources to cope with what it brought.

The cousins arrived in San Francisco to a hostile crowd, with police and investigators waiting to quiz them about the whereabouts of the runaway prince. Now it was Barbara's turn to experience the novelty of facing the press, encouraged by Jimmy whose happy Chicago encounter was still fresh in memory. But the reporters, always sanctimonious when they felt they were faced with common criminals, raucously demanded the story of Alexis' flight. Neither Barbara nor Jimmy was equal to the onslaught which followed them wherever they went.

Whether it was bravado, a calculated distraction, or simply his eternal wish to be noticed, Jimmy decided he would reveal more of his showbiz intentions to the accumulated reporters. He put a record on the turntable of Barbara's portable gramophone, found a bare section of floor and went through his dance routine for them. One, Ralph Jordan, summed it up in three words: 'Spirited, but lousy.'

Finally the entourage, including Jimmy, Barbara, her companion Ticki Tocquet and secretary Nancy Allard, boarded the Japanese steamship *Tatsuta Maru* bound for Honolulu and the Far East. Though there were few enough of them, virtually the whole of C deck had been acquired, including the royal suite and every cabin on the starboard side. The voyage provided a time for reflection and, according to Barbara Hutton's biographer Philip van Rensselaer, Jimmy counselled his cousin to drop her husband, even though they had been married only four months and she had just celebrated her twenty-first birthday. He suggested marrying a real title, the Duc de Valençay from France, or Britain's Duke of Argyll, though he can have known little or anything of either of these aristocrats. Jimmy's argument was that the Mdivani princedoms were almost certainly bogus and that though each of her many pieces of luggage carried a princely coronet Barbara was not, in fact, a princess.

'My fantasy is to see you as the Duchess of Westminster, living in a palace like Blenheim,[1] surrounded by thousands of acres of rolling countryside. Like a Gainsborough!' van Rensselaer quotes Jimmy as saying, adding that Barbara then asked her cousin if his ideal was to be an English country gentleman. 'I would like to be best friends with the Prince of Wales,' Jimmy said, momentously.

For the moment, Barbara and her *faux* prince were reunited when the *Tatsuta Maru* arrived in Japan. Alex had flown ahead

---

1 In fact it is the Dukes of Marlborough who live at Blenheim

to meet his wife and the threesome now embarked on a lengthy tour starting in Tokyo, then moving on to Kyoto, Kobe, Shanghai and Peking. None of them had toured the East, or read much about it, but on the basis that money buys knowledge, they forged noisily ahead, surrounded wherever they went by hordes of pressmen. The knowledge of the world which Choate was unable to give him was now being delivered to Jimmy first-hand. Though still short of his nineteenth birthday, he played a pivotal role during this lengthy, cash-consuming odyssey, for already the signs were that the marriage would not last. As Barbara unburdened herself to him he became an increasingly important element in her life.

The honeymoon party moved on to India, disporting themselves with maharajahs and visiting a Bombay orphanage before all were struck down with amoebic dysentery and forced to head home via Paris and London. In Paris, Jimmy stopped off long enough to visit once again Bricktop's in the Rue Pigalle, and within days the word circulating in New York was that he had found a job there as a crooner. The story went that he was singing every night for pocket money and that this was another bid to become an all-round entertainer, but in truth his performance in front of the microphone was singular, perfunctory and uninvited; drunk again. A staff news correspondent short on scoops, and a nightclub short on publicity did the rest.

Back in New York, Jimmy posed as his own valet to give an interview to the *Daily News* in which he laid down his marker to his mother: 'No, no, he's not giving up his theatrical career, he's only been taking a vacation,' said the 'valet'. And though the question had yet to be resolved as to which direction this career would go – dance, stage, even Hollywood – on one thing the valet was firm: Mother approved. 'That's all been thrashed out. Mrs Donahue will not interfere.' But in truth the pursuit of greatness as a dancer was half-hearted: the acid put-down delivered by Ralph Jordan was no help, nor despite the brave words to the *Daily News* did he find his mother any the less receptive to his showbusiness ambitions.

He arranged a lavish party at 834 Fifth Avenue, in part because he enjoyed parties and in part because he wanted to draw attention to himself, but in this latter ambition he was unsuccessful. His cousin Barbara stole the headlines the following morning for having worn a million-dollar diamond necklace. News of her recent twenty-second birthday party at the Ritz in Paris, with two thousand guests and assorted shopping sprees, brought the Woolworth family riches into focus at a time when the Depression was at its worst. Blithely, Jimmy chose the occasion to adopt a Hitlerian moustache.

During his late teens Jimmy spent much of his time with, or waiting for, Barbara Hutton. As her self-proclaimed court jester, and as someone with a lot of time on his hands, there were worse things to do. As Philip van Rensselaer told this writer, 'Jimmy wanted to *be* Barbara – she was notorious, she was admired. She attracted headlines and attention. Above all she had become glamorous, and Jimmy wanted to be all those things.' Another person agreed, observing: 'Barbara was being made love to by princes and Jimmy wanted that, too.'

He worked up an act from Irving Berlin's hit show *As Thousands Cheer* with singer and dancer Marilyn Miller. They tap-danced their way through a couple of numbers at the Antibes Ball at the Ambassador Hotel on Park Avenue to polite applause, but it was rapidly coming home to him that, rich and talented though he may be, he was at one with the poor boys beating on agents' doors, discovering few breaks and lots of heartache.

Jessie's words about the nature of his continued relationship with the theatre were finally heeded and in the winter of 1934, as his mother ostentatiously bade farewell to New York and headed with a group of friends towards Palm Beach aboard the *Japauldon* to open up Cielito Lindo, he was sent to the producer Gilbert Miller to begin work as an assistant manager on Miller's show *Ode to Liberty*.

Jimmy's lordly title disguised the fact that he was an assistant stage manager, the lowest form of life in the theatre. Quite soon he discovered that fetching a star like Ina Claire her cigarettes was a significant part of his duties: 'he is just a messenger boy' sneered the New York *World Telegram*. He made up for it by seducing as many members of the cast as he could.

His nights, when not occupied with this less glamorous arm of theatre, were spent at El Morocco, New York's jazziest nightclub. It was there Jimmy came to know Libby Holman, the doomed torch-singer who was to remain close to him for much of his life. They had originally met in Palm Beach, and by 1934 she was a major Broadway star, oddly vaulted into the pantheon by the murder two years before of her husband Smith Reynolds, heir to the Reynolds tobacco fortune, who had been shot dead, probably by Libby herself. Because of the power wielded by the Reynolds family who did not wish to see their dirty linen washed in public, Holman was able to evade being charged; but she walked through the rest of her life trailing a long dark shadow, condemned by the press and public. It made her dazzlingly appealing in Jimmy's eyes.

She was eleven years older than her admirer – Jimmy always preferred older women, if he preferred women at all – and was engaged in a so-called 'Boston marriage' with a strawberry blonde named Louisa Carpenter, a member of the Du Pont family. The *ménage* included Libby's small son Christopher and Louisa's adopted daughter Sunny.

Though of different generations, Jimmy and Libby had many things in common – both famous, both rich, both trying to break into the theatre, because Libby Holman had thus far been acknowledged only for her singing. She spoke for both of them when she said: 'Some day I'd like to play Juliet, then sing at a nightclub after the performance.' How Jimmy wished that for himself!

At about the time Jimmy started work on *Ode to Liberty* his friend starred at the New Amsterdam Theatre on 42nd Street in a quasi-operatic entertainment called *Revenge with Music*. The audiences loved to hate Libby, speculating in the intervals as to just how she had managed to shoot her husband and get away with it; and her hit song of the night, 'You and the Night and the Music', had the distinction of being banned on the radio – the lyrics, and the way Libby sang them, were considered risqué and immoral. Jimmy revelled in her almost satanic notoriety, and trailed around after her as she cut a swathe through New York nightlife, drinking at the Chapeau Rouge where the owner, Pepe d'Albrew, wore a wriggling white mouse in his lapel, and dining at 21, the Colony and the Central Park Casino. Later they would visit the Stork Club, owned by former bootlegger Sherman Billingsley, or drop by their favourite, El Morocco.

By the spring of 1935 Jimmy was back in London with Barbara, shadowing her as she cast off her princely husband and went about acquiring a new one. On 23 March the Woolworth entourage boarded the SS *Bremen* and sailed for the United States, Jimmy wildly claiming to waiting reporters that he carried a revolver for Barbara's protection. Word had reached New York of the marital split, and Jimmy was given the job of keeping newsmen engaged on A deck while Barbara scuttled down the crew gangplank. Finally the entourage met up again and made for Jimmy's home at 834 Fifth Avenue. Next day he drove her, in the supposed anonymity of a cheap sedan, to

Newark airport with Barbara's stepmother Irene Hutton in tow. Playing cops'n'robbers with the press was an amusing diversion even if his cousin's emotional life was in tatters.

Less than three months later Prince Alexis Mdivani was dead, decapitated when his Rolls Royce crashed at 100 mph, but by then there was no longer a princess to mourn him. Barbara was already, following a Reno divorce, the Countess Haugwitz-Reventlow. Jimmy had followed her to Nevada for the wedding, which took place in the borrowed home of a local physician. When Barbara and her count travelled to San Francisco to begin their honeymoon, Jimmy went too.

No doubt this second husband of the world's richest woman found her cousin's presence as perplexing as had the first, and he grew to despise him; but there was no separating Barbara from Jimmy at times as emotionally taxing as a honeymoon. Her first marriage had been in large part a ruse to wrest herself from the iron grip of her father Franklyn Hutton. Her second, a conscious attempt to obliterate from her mind the two wasted, fruitless and emotionally barren years immediately behind her. Love did not necessarily come into it when it came to husbands, but Barbara did love Jimmy.

When the honeymoon party arrived at Hardenberg Castle on the Danish island of Lolland, Reventlow's ancestral home, Jimmy had become so used to this cosy propinquity that he became enraged at being relegated to a guest cottage – especially since Count Reventlow's brother, the head of the family, had renovated fifteen rooms within the house specifically for the use of his guests. Alone at night, Jimmy started to burn the cottage's furniture – tables, chairs, stools – in the fireplace along with more conventional materials. To the attendant press corps he imitated the count's stiff Germanic mannerisms. This went down terribly well.

So well, in fact, that he could not leave his newfound mimicry alone. By September the entourage had moved to Paris, then on to Rome and the royal suite of the Grand Hotel. Rome, by late 1935, was overrun by Mussolini's fascist mobs, dressed in their black shirts and terrorising the populace. Cars were torched, stores looted, passers-by attacked, all in the name of the new order. Beneath the tourists' balcony, on 28 September, a seething mob gathered in the plaza by the Via Vittorio Emanuele Orlando to celebrate Mussolini's invasion of Ethiopia. Shouting slogans and waving placards, they seemed a ridiculous bunch to Jimmy who was, in the warmth of the early autumn evening, drunk. Stepping out onto the balcony and raising his arm in a fascist salute, he adopted Il Duce's hectoring tones and swaggering posture to bellow: 'Viva Ethiopia! Long Live Haile Selassie!' To improve the shining hour, he unbuttoned his trousers and urinated on the mob below.

Were it not for the instant intervention of the city police, the honeymoon party would have been violently attacked. Instead a police captain came knocking on the door of the bridal suite and demanded entry. One of Barbara's entourage recalls now: 'Jimmy had come in from the balcony and they suddenly heard the police knocking on everybody's door. Jimmy crawled under the bed. The police were allowed in – Barbara was in bed – and asked if she had seen a man answering Jimmy's description. She said "I'm sorry I don't know what you're talking about, I never saw anybody" when suddenly there came this voice from under the bed – "*She's not telling the truth!*"'

The police dragged him out, arrested him and escorted him to police headquarters, later coming back with an expulsion order for Barbara and her husband, and with the promise that, were Jimmy to stay, further violence would ensue. Simultaneously the royal suite suddenly became unavailable, and ex-King Alfonso of Spain was suddenly produced to bolster their case for the honeymooners' downgrading.

After prolonged questioning, Jimmy was driven to the railway station and an express train headed for Ventimiglia on the border. He was accompanied, for good measure, by the hotel manager and two armed plainclothes men. Press reports concentrated on two black eyes he had apparently acquired. Such was the volatile temperature in Rome that a government official was forced to issue a statement on what by now had become an international incident: 'The Italian government has been assured by Count and Countess Haugwitz [sic] that they had nothing to do with the Donahue incident, and they expressed deep regret to the Italian government. Both feel Donahue got just treatment in the circumstances.' Another source said that Jimmy recognised the incident was an affront to Italian feelings but 'he did not appear to be worried'. The source continued that Barbara and her husband said they liked Italy and were admirers of Premier Mussolini.

As Jimmy boarded the train he was asked if he had enough money. 'Certainly,' he grandly replied, 'I even have a house in Paris and I will go there.' In the event he headed for the Ritz, where he occupied a suite on the same floor as his uncle, the appalled Franklyn Hutton, who pointedly ignored him. Next day he set sail on the SS *Normandie* for America, entering via Canada in the hope of evading reporters. When they caught up with him he denied he had yelled anything; had never mentioned Ethiopia; and had left Italy of his own free will. No one believed him for a minute.

He arrived back at 834 Fifth Avenue to find it empty. Jessie had taken his brother Woolworth to Europe, and their ships had crossed in mid-Atlantic. By the time Jessie returned on the *Europa* Jimmy had already made plans to return to London.

Later that year, according to Bill Robertson, Barbara Hutton's aide, Jimmy tried a reprise of his balcony escapade, this time in Germany. 'He shouted "Down with Hitler", which in that country, at that time, was most foolhardy. They chased him round and round the revolving doors of his hotel and, once again, he was expelled from the country. He was very lucky to get off so lightly.'

If Count Haugwitz-Reventlow thought he was at last rid of his cousin-in-law, a rude surprise awaited him when the bridal couple reached London in late 1935. The umbilical link between the cousins remained. It was almost as if Barbara feared her husband and needed brotherly protection, and Barbara encouraged Jimmy to come and join them. In the weeks running up to the birth in February 1936 of the couple's son Lance, Jimmy became a permanent house-guest at the couple's home, a rented Regency house at 2 Hyde Park Gardens owned by a Mrs Wakefield-Saunders. He acted as the couple's unofficial press spokesman during the unusually complicated pregnancy and birth, and causing a sensation on one occasion by bursting into tears as he uttered: 'I'm afraid this is very serious. That is all I can say.' It was, of course, a Jimmyesque joke.

But during this period, in the aftermath of the birth of Lance Reventlow, first Barbara, then Jimmy, were introduced to Seconal as a recreational drug by Barbara's former sister-in-law Roussie Sert. It was an introduction whose consequences would be serious, even deadly.

⚜

If there was one thing that George St John at Choate had taught him, it was that, with the fortune available to him, with his undoubted intelligence and with his flair, Jimmy should use these gifts to create something – and for Jimmy that something meant the theatre. For one who had sat in Palm Beach at the feet of the great Flo Ziegfeld, listening to his anecdotes of a lifetime's dedication to creating magic on stage and on celluloid, Jimmy decided this was the career for him.

Flo Ziegfeld had grown rich in the past twenty-five years on the annual production of his Ziegfeld Follies revues, which featured extraordinarily elaborate staging, a wide variety of performers and choruses of beautiful women. In between these *bonne-bouches* he created a raft of Broadway hits including *Show Boat* and *Bitter Sweet* and had been used to including among his backers Jim Donahue. In the summer of 1932, when Jim's son had just turned seventeen and Ziegfeld's latest Broadway show *Hot-Cha!* had got under way, the maestro suddenly developed influenza which soon turned to pneumonia. He died unexpectedly of pleurisy on 22 July, and the continuing vacuum left by his death finally determined Jimmy that he would be, if not a dancer like Bojangles Robinson, then a producer like Flo Ziegfeld.

This ambition, when voiced to Jessie, had a more sonorous ring. The only chorus-line dancers she had known of were those who attached themselves briefly to her late husband, driving a wedge deeper into their marriage; whereas she was positively dazzled by Ziegfeld, his achievements and, naturally, his money. The idea that Jimmy, unqualified for anything by virtue of his fractured education, might find a career on Broadway was warming indeed.

The star of *Hot-Cha!* was Lupe Velez, an actress noted for having given her boyfriend Gary Cooper a nervous breakdown and who was to become known in the newspapers as the Mexican Firecracker. Velez was a dangerous and uncontrollable voluptuary whose uninhibited behaviour was to have a profound effect on Jimmy. Seven years her junior, Jimmy was in awe, not a little in love, and ready to absorb the influence of this glamorous, exciting, outrageous figure. Lupe's biographer Floyd Conner notes how, during the run-up to the opening of

Hot-Cha! the star so hated being confined to her costumes that she would rehearse in the nude, and such was her unconcern for convention that she would make the trip from the hotel to the theatre each night in a mink coat and slippers, with nothing underneath.

He co-star, Bert Lahr, noted that she never washed: 'When she'd go to the Mayfair or somewhere she'd put on a dress. Nothing under it. Nothing. So when I'd be clowning with her on stage and I'd notice her dirty hands I'd say, "You've got your gloves on again."' Velez would respond by chewing gum onstage and letting it hang out of the side of her mouth so that Lahr could see but the audience could not.

Velez observed that people liked her because she had 'pep', but *Collier's* magazine saw it differently, with a lampooning article headlined 'The Girl With One Talent'. That particular talent drove one admirer to seek her backstage during the run of *Hot-Cha!* to present her with a bracelet, two-and-a-half inches wide and encrusted with diamonds and twenty-one large rubies. Though she married Johnny Weissmuller, she maintained a passion for Cooper and when she described the star's new escort, the Countess di Frasso, as 'nothing but an old whore', the countess retaliated by tossing a glass of wine in her face.

Later she toured with another influence in Jimmy's life, Libby Holman, in a production of Cole Porter's *You'll Never Know*, blacking the singer's eye one night in New Haven. Holman's biographer Jon Bradshaw describes how Velez screamed at Libby: 'You bastard, you son-a-bitch, I *keel* you with *thees*,' brandishing a huge diamond ring given her by Weissmuller. She would also show it to the director, threatening: 'Thees is the ring I'm going to murder that Jewish beech with.' Following these outbursts, she would kneel down in the wings, cross herself, and pray. Later still her hatred caused her to urinate in the wings in the hope that the shortsighted Holman, who followed her onstage, would slip in the puddle and fall.

Being around Lupe Velez was an induction to a whole new world, one where glamour and squalor stood face-to-face in intriguing configuration. Having been fired by the death of Flo Ziegfeld, Jimmy started to search for a vehicle in which his wayward friend could star and by December 1935, five months after his twenty-first birthday, Jimmy was set to carve a new career by entering negotiations with a former racing driver, Felix Ferry, whom he had met through Ziegfeld and who was intent on producing a new revue.

Through a swiftly-acquired agent – a very necessary prop for any upcoming Broadway producer – Jimmy announced that he would be making his debut as backer and co-producer in a show called *Transatlantic Rhythm*. Written by Irving Caesar, veteran creator of such hits as *No No Nanette!*, and starring Lupe Velez with a cast of sixty including crooner Dixie Dunbar, the Four Yacht Club Boys – picked up from Barbara Hutton's twenty-second birthday extravaganza a couple of years before – and a large troupe of American showgirls, it also attracted a late signing, the singer Ruth Etting, America's *soi-disant* 'Sweetheart of the Air'.

To those who knew him and those who merely read the gossip columns, this looked like the first work Jimmy had ever undertaken. 'Yes,' foghorned the agent, 'he is really going to work. He'll be good too. When he's in town he spends every night in the theatre – never misses an opening, everything from Shakespeare to burlesque.' While a deep interest in the Bard may be a little fanciful, it was true that Jimmy had finally found a fraternity outside the dullards and bluebloods, as he saw them, with whom he had grown up; a fraternity where his good looks, youth, exceptional charm and, of course, money allowed him to feel equal if not superior.

In Palm Beach, or on Fifth Avenue, his compatriots were better-born, were college-educated, had jobs. But on Broadway, Jimmy was a star even without having to try. As the *New York Daily News* reported: 'Joan Crawford and Franchot Tone have a real rival among the autograph-seekers – and their rival is no less a person than Jimmy Donahue, who seems to be almost as well known to the general public as the Hollywood stars. During the intermission of a Broadway premiere last week Jimmy stood at the outskirts of the lobby in the midst of a milling crowd of autograph fans. He signed his name scores of times ... and always with a flourish and a funny face.' It was not just among the great unwashed that Jimmy enjoyed his admirers: the bonus was the never-ending supply of chorus-boys on tap.

Jimmy approached his role in all seriousness, calculating that if he could get it right, he could quite swiftly fill the gap left so recently by Ziegfeld. He had the one thing it took to mount a Ziegfeld-style production – money – and he had an able director in Felix Ferry. He had as his star the newsworthy name of Lupe Velez as well as Lou Holtz, described as America's most bankable comedian.

Velez, though an undoubted star, was no longer finding it so easy after twenty-five films to attract the attention of Holly-wood producers; and had decamped to England, where she was still a front-rank star. Within the space of a year, she was to make three movies. This suited Jimmy's plan: sensitive to the fact that this was Woolworth money backing the show and with his own lack of experience as a producer, he was keen for the project to be tested outside the ambit of Broadway's ferocious critics. Since Lupe was in England, that might be just the place to polish up the show before bringing it back to Broadway; no matter the cost in shipping cast, costumes, sets and technicians across the Atlantic. Rehearsals began in the early summer of 1936 while Lupe was completing the worst movie of her career, *Gypsy Melody*.

※☙◊❧※

Jimmy arrived in Britain against the backdrop of growing gossip about King Edward VIII and Mrs Simpson. The former Prince of Wales had been monarch since his father's death in January of that year, and since 1934 had been in love with the twice-married so-called Baltimore Belle. The British press had taken upon themselves a vow of silence, leaving all but the innermost grouping around Buckingham Palace and Downing street in complete ignorance of the growing constitutional crisis. Among the less well-informed there was a hope that the affair would blow over, as the Prince's other liaisons with married women had done. To air the King's dirty linen in public would to be to trigger an unprecedented schism between monarchy and populace. By the time Jimmy arrived in London, the King was already hosting dinners at St James's Palace with Mrs Simpson his *de facto* hostess. Her name was starting to appear in the Court Circular, and the American press, unfettered by the misguided loyalty of their British counterparts, homed in on the couple.

An ideal opportunity presented itself when the King and a sizeable entourage set out on a cruise of the Dalmatian coast on a large chartered yacht, the *Nahlin*. Wherever the royal party went, they were met by laughing, shouting mobs and the gentlemen of the Press. Daily, the King and Mrs Simpson were photographed together – passing through Salzburg, driving through Athens, bathing in the sea, and on one occasion being spied on in a small boat, her hand on his arm and the King looking down at her. Lady Diana Cooper, one of the party, tired of Mrs Simpson's charms after ten days: 'her commonness and her Becky Sharpness irritate,' she observed, adding, 'The truth is, Wallis is bored stiff with the King.'

Witnesses reported that already Mrs Simpson had acquired the knack of reducing the new monarch to tears, despite the fact that she was receiving an income from him of £6,000 a year as well as being showered with jewels and the other trappings of royalty. The King's official biographer, Philip Ziegler, questions whether she loved him at all, or whether she merely exploited him. A courtier, Ulick Alexander, described the King as being possessed by 'the sexual perversion of self abasement' and that it was clear that he was frightened by her, and enjoyed being frightened by her. What Wallis got from this arrangement, at a sexual level, is harder to define. None of this however was evident, even to the most persistent American reporter, as the couple was trailed around Europe.

By the middle of September, when this curious bunch of holidaymakers returned home, Jimmy was already hard at work on pre-production of his musical. Conceived as a straight take of a Ziegfeld spectacular, *Transatlantic Rhythm* required a full orchestra and a cast of one hundred, who would wear between them nearly 500 costumes a night. The idea was that a pre-London run would start in Manchester, and the city's Opera House was booked for a fortnight in September.

But no matter how much money Jimmy threw at the show, it seemed never to be enough. Moreover, Felix Ferry was found to be wanting as a director; costumes were slow in coming through, as were the sets. Conceived as it was, it was a colossal undertaking and considerably more than either man was capable of handling. The Manchester opening, on 8 September 1936, was cancelled and rescheduled after through-the-night rehearsals had failed to pull the production together into cohesive form.

The arrival in Britain of this glamorous juggernaut had

Lovers in the spotlight … Jimmy and the Duchess face the press, New York, 1952.

Love rules the waves … Jimmy and the Duchess aboard the *Sister Anne* in the Mediterranean, 1951.

Happy families: Jimmy (aged six), Jessie, Jim and Woolworth, Palm Beach 1922.

The coming men of note … Woolworth Donahue, aged seven and his brother Jimmy, four-and-a-half, together with Shrug on East 80th Street, January 1920.

Born to lose: Jim Donahue contemplates his massive gambling losses, 1924.

Uncharacteristically shorn of her jewellery, Jessie Donahue poses in New York, 1925.

A little piece of heaven: the Donahue mansion Cielito Lindo became the second largest establishment in Palm Beach after Mar-A-Lago, stretching from the Atlantic Ocean inland to Lake Worth.

Despite its colossal size, the Donahues' attempts to win their place in Long Island society with the acquisition of Wooldon Manor met with failure. After two seasons they never lived there again.

Guilty? This photomontage was used by the *New York Journal-American* to indicate the belief, which the laws of libel did not permit them to state openly, that it was Jim Donahue who had stolen his wife's jewellery in New York's biggest ever heist.

At Choate, the headmaster would pin up photographs of new boys in his study until he had learned their names. Jimmy at fourteen.

Hot and bothered – but that was just press speculation about his love-life. Aged eighteen, Jimmy bows to the society columnists' wishes and dances with an eligible girl.

In the shadow of Ziegfeld: Jimmy's doomed effort at theatrical production, *Transatlantic Rhythm*, opened in London's West End, but never made it to Broadway.

Programme for *Transatlantic Rhythm*, 1936; Jimmy's failed attempt to become the next Flo Ziegfeld.

Chaperone with a gun – or so he claimed. Jimmy escorts cousin Barbara Hutton back to New York on the SS *Europa*, 1934.

Dancing in the dunes: Jimmy in the Sahara, 1935.

The last dance ... Jimmy with Marilyn Miller practise their act for the Antibes Ball, April 1935. It was the last time he performed in front of an audience.

The Woolworth dynasty attends Barbara Hutton's first marriage in Paris, 1933. Woolworth Donahue, Mrs Franklyn Hutton, Jimmy, Jessie, the bride, Franklyn Hutton.

Finest hour – Jimmy in his pilot's uniform of the Civil Air Patrol, 1942.

Hangover and humiliation – Jimmy's forced induction as a private soldier, New York 1944.

caught the attention of the press. Though supportive articles showing Lupe pastiching the film stars Gloria Swanson, Claudette Colbert, Katharine Hepburn and Dolores del Rio were of help, the continued presence of reporters trying to discover just what was going on backstage was not.

A report in the London *Daily Mail* paid tribute to the company: 'Physically and mentally fatigued, the players – the majority of whom are making their first appearances in this country – are nevertheless preserving wonderfully good spirits. They are loyally determined to give every support to their producer in what has proved to be one of the most difficult tasks ever attempted in a Manchester theatre.'

Two weeks later, with *Transatlantic Rhythm* now transferred to the Adelphi Theatre in London in preparation for its West End debut, the same newspapers reported that the dress rehearsal had been abandoned after the orchestra, their wages unpaid, walked out in a body. Earlier, the actors had called in representatives of Equity; and Ruth Etting, also starring in the show, delivered a statement to the press that she would not go on unless paid. The cheques Jimmy had written to Ruth and Lupe had bounced. 'At the time I understood there was sufficient money in the bank to meet the cheques,' he limply explained, but the truth was that at this crucial moment Jessie had withdrawn her financial support.

Frustrated at the continued absence of her favourite son, and with the prospect of a long London run keeping him away for the rest of the year, she sensed that the easiest means by which to bring Jimmy home was to simply shut her purse. She went back to giving dinner parties for the likes of the Countess of Abingdon and William Randolph Hearst, taking great comfort in reading about them in the next day's press, learning, for example, from the New York *Journal American*, 'Jessie who is petite and blonde, one of the very few natural blonde types

here, is looking prettier and younger than ever this season.'
There may have been no extra money for Jimmy, but her press
spokesman got a bonus that day.

This financial abandonment came as a shock to Jimmy, and
as an act of betrayal to Ferry and the stars and cast of the
show. Chaos ensued. During the day of the opening night,
conference followed conference in the theatre's boardroom,
where Jimmy's wealth, Jimmy's family and Jimmy's commitment to the theatre in general and this production in particular
came under close and critical scrutiny. Despite his worldliness,
his unerring charm and his boundless optimism, Jimmy's
twenty-one years were no match for the disappointed and angry
men and women ranged before him.

In order to preserve some sense of decorum Jimmy and Felix
Ferry belatedly divided their shared responsibilities – Ferry to
the production side, Jimmy to the finance side – but by now
there was so little money left in the kitty that Lupe Velez theatri-
cally heated some oil lamps to cook steaks while awaiting the
outcome of the day's events. There was so little space backstage
that the cast fought among each other – and with the myriad
outsiders who casually strolled in to witness the turmoil – to
find their change of costume.

During the afternoon, there came a visit from two representatives of the Lord Chamberlain's office, custodians of the
nation's morals, with a directive that a suggestive sketch called
'America's Sweethearts', which featured a negligee-clad Lupe
as a newlywed, be cut from the show. Members of the company, some in tears, some on the verge of hysteria, stood about
the passageways already made-up for the stage. Many were
in their dressing-gowns as their costumes still had not been
delivered. Finally, with ten minutes to curtain-up a decision
was taken to proceed, even though no dress rehearsal had
been held at the Adelphi, and the cast had only the previous

week's performances at the Manchester Opera House to rely upon.

'Colonel' Snyder, Ruth Etting's tough-guy husband and manager, insisted that Jimmy or Felix Ferry go onstage and confess to the audience that the company was appearing without payment. Neither was inclined to agree, but an arrangement was reached where none of that night's box-office cash would be touched by anyone until a common share-out could be agreed the following morning.

The press scented a crisis of unprecedented proportions being enacted backstage at the Adelphi. The *New York Times* reported that such was the unrest among the company that Lupe Velez had sung a number 'to quiet the hollering showgirls'. Reporters noted the extra police called in to keep the theatre from being mobbed by curious Londoners.

When the curtain finally went up *The Times* could hardly wait to cast the first stone. 'After so much extra-theatrical excitement, the show itself came as something of an anticlimax. It turned out to be brilliantly hollow entertainment,' was its verdict. This critique merely echoed the fashion of the day, which was to deride Hollywood stars who brought shows to London expecting a culture-starved nation, with few stars of its own, to fall at their feet. The reviews, lukewarm at best, did little to dispel within the company the upsurge of unrest and hostility, though all forbore to mention the nightmare which took place onstage at the end of the first act. The climax of this part of the show was the arrival onstage of a giant airliner, from which descended members of the chorus; the plane was then due to depart from the stage to make way for Ruth Etting. Inexplicably, the plane became stuck and could not be budged offstage, which drove Etting and Colonel Snyder into paroxysms of rage.

Though passably amusing and arguably better-delivered than

any similar show on the West End stage, *Transatlantic Rhythm* looked as though it would not make a second night. Ruth Etting, perhaps the most fractious of the cast, quit the moment the curtain came down and Lupe signalled to Jimmy that, despite their friendship, she was not prepared to continue working indefinitely with a cast which remained unpaid.

Nevertheless she walked onstage the next night and declared: 'I am sorry to say Ruth Etting is ill, and I will be singing her part. I'm not as good, but I'm twice as loud!'

Despite desperate wires to New York, Jimmy was unable to reach his brother Wooly or anyone else who might help his cash-flow difficulties. The obvious source of extra funds – his cousin Barbara – was at hand in London but for once was unable to help. She had an income of slightly less than $2,000,000 a year before taxes, and during the first year of her marriage she had spent more than $4,000,000 on jewellery alone. There was no further finance forthcoming for Jimmy, and by now it looked as though his great dream of becoming a theatre impresario was over in a single, glorious, West End night.

By the morning, predators had begun to circle. Realising that the show's notoriety alone would keep the audiences flocking for weeks, and that the expenditure was over, it was now time, with a little bridging finance, to reap the rewards from fat box-office returns. Jimmy too was aware of this, but in the face of Jessie's implacable determination not to help, there was nothing he could do. His grandfather Woolworth had left behind one of America's great legacies, yet Jimmy had barely enough to pay his taxi fare to the theatre.

With an hour to go before curtain-up on the second night, and with the audience not knowing whether there was a show for them to see, a deal was struck with one of the circling predators, Al Cohen. He promised to guarantee the show's debts in return for taking whole ownership. This was still not enough to save Ruth Etting or Lupe Velez.

A week later, a disconsolate Jimmy was found by a reporter on the boat-train platform at Waterloo Station, his bags packed, *en route* for Southampton. 'I lost some money,' he admitted, 'but I am not going to say how much. It really does not matter.' He added: 'I think I have learned something. The next show I finance I will do on my own. It will be my show and nobody else's.'

There was to be no next show. Belaboured by the bad publicity which exposed his ineptitude as a producer, demoralised by the reviews, and beaten by the drubbing he had taken from his director and the company, it came to Jimmy that he could enjoy the life of showbiz, its glamour and its sordidness, its stars and its chorus-boys, without a hands-on involvement. *Transatlantic Rhythm* cost him at least $150,000 ($1.48m) in cash, but that was not the loss. It was that his first major venture, indeed the only major venture in life, had ended in such ignominy and failure; and that it was finally brought home to him that he would never have control over a portion of the vast fortune his grandfather had left. Unlike cousin Barbara, he would have to exist for the rest of his life on the generosity of his mother, a tap that could be turned off at a whim.

⁂

Jimmy returned swiftly to the US, aboard the SS *Normandie*, where, on the passenger list, he discovered a bitter Lady Furness, who had not long been displaced as King Edward VIII's *maîtresse en titre* by Mrs Wallis Warfield Simpson. It was only a handful of years since Thelma Furness, married to the shipping magnate Lord Furness, had consummated her love for the Prince under the wide skies of Kenya. Later she wrote:

This was our Eden and we were alone in it. His arms around me were the only reality; his words of love my only bridge to life. Borne along on the mounting tide of his ardor, I found myself swept from the accustomed mooring of caution. Each night I felt more completely possessed by our love, carried ever more swiftly into uncharted seas of feeling, content to let the Prince chart the course, heedless of where the voyage would end.

Lady Furness's presence on the *Normandie* gave rise to much witty talk among the *cognoscenti*, for it was aboard this ship on the high seas, two years before, that she had cooked her goose with the Prince of Wales. She had taken the young Prince Aly Khan into her stateroom and, after years of unsatisfactory sexual play with the future king, engaged in a week of passion which had the result when she stepped ashore, according to one writer, that she was 'looking ten years younger'. The Prince got to hear about the encounter and 'all the Prince's colonial racist snobbery was aroused along with his wounded pride'. Within days, Thelma had been supplanted in the Prince of Wales's affections. Her erstwhile friend Mrs Simpson had become the future king's favourite. As the scandal of the King's love for a divorced woman was about to break in the press, Lady Furness was leaving Britain with her sister Gloria in search of calmer waters.

Some speculated that it was on this voyage that Jimmy learned the secrets which were to unlock Wallis's passions more than a decade later; but it seems unlikely. Even though London society had all but ditched Thelma to stay onside with the new royal favourite, as the former mistress of the King, Lady Furness occupied a rather different position in society's stratosphere from the lowly, and failed, twenty-one-year-old theatrical producer. She did not cast him a glance.

CHAPTER 5

THE GREAT ESCAPE

If he seemed like a helpless ingénue among the sharks prowling the waters of London's theatreland, back in New York Jimmy quickly regained his jaunty *savoire-faire*.

Though his predilections were exclusively homosexual, he nonetheless enjoyed the company of prostitutes – for the stories they told about the johns they'd had, and because they had easy access to drugs. One friend recalls a night in New York where Jimmy commandeered his mother's chauffeur and limousine, drove over to Lucille Mallon's brothel on the East Side, and took out the entire staff, including *madame*, for an evening's drinking. 'The car stank of this sweet-smelling stuff they were smoking,' recalls the friend now. 'No one knew what marijuana was in those days.'

Some of Lucille's girls became intimate friends, and one night Jimmy bribed one of them to let him take her place. 'He made himself up beautifully, put on a gorgeous dress and high heels, and went out with this hayseed salesman from the mid-West,' recalls another friend. 'They spent the evening drinking and dancing, and this man thought he was a helluva guy for buying himself a hooker for the evening. Just imagine the surprise when they got back to his hotel!'

Another favourite haunt was Polly Adler's, perhaps the swishest bordello in New York. Polly, daughter of a Russian immigrant tailor, ran her business from a twelve-room apartment on 55th and Madison before moving to even smarter quarters on Central Park West. She counted among her clientele most of the more priapic males of the Social Register, together with an interesting seasoning of other classes – the gangster Dutch Schultz, for example, was often to be found lording it in the Louis XVI drawing-room, taking full advantage of the fare offered by the two cooks as well as the girls.

'The more desperate the times, the more men seek the great escape of sex,' Madam Adler once observed, and none could challenge her expertise in that particular department. Certainly Jimmy's behaviour in early adulthood, a mixture of promiscuity, exhibitionism, sadism and apparent benevolence (usually in payment or atonement for some further excess) derived from such desperation.

One close friend from that time observed that he could not go into a nightclub without wrecking it: 'Then he'd pay for everything, smile that delightful smile and fade into the night. He never slept. He had no relationships of any real merit. I once accused him of not being a true friend and he replied that he could have a hundred new friends that night, meaning they could be bought with a hundred-dollar bill. He didn't understand the concept of friendship, and I think you have to blame the parents and in particular Jessie, the ice-maiden.'

Jimmy became intimately involved with Francis Spellman, the Cardinal Archbishop of New York, a notorious homosexual predator and friend of Jessie. St Patrick's Cathedral was a great cruising ground, particularly late Mass on a Sunday, and the cardinal was rumoured to have deflowered many young men. Jimmy once welcomed him to his mother's apartment at 834 Fifth Avenue wearing a ball-gown and high heels.

During this period of re-acclimatization, he was sent by Jessie up to Wooldon Manor. The mock-Tudor mansion was now abandoned, and Jimmy had not set foot in it since before his father's suicide. Jessie had felt unloved by Southampton society, which took slowly to new money, and the way new money had of renaming its houses, and she had rarely visited Wooldon Manor in the ten years it had been in her possession. At the time of Jim's death the pipes which led to from the pool to the ocean had still not been installed and the pool had not been filled in a decade.

An acquaintance recalls: 'The Donahues, much to everyone's outrage, bought this house in Southampton. They put up massive iron gates – it was just a simple country house which they bowdlerised. People thought they were vulgar and nouveau riche, and they refused to let them become members of the Southampton clubs. It happens in a small resort like that.' So the Donahues were cold-shouldered for having too much money and for not having the grace to disguise it.

In the wake of Jim's death, Jessie had set out to become Queen of Palm Beach by issuing invitations to beach parties, dinners, dances and entertainments at Cielito Lindo and aboard her yacht *Freedom* berthed on Lake Worth. Her orbit now was New York, Palm Beach, Biarritz and Monte Carlo; Wooldon Manor, replete in its sumptuous magnificence, was a ghost house and had to go. President Roosevelt gave it the once-over as a possible summer White House, but nothing came of it. Ever-hungry newspaper columnists, ravenous for the titbits fed to them by hired press agents of the super-rich, wrote successive articles extolling Wooldon Manor's virtues, adding almost as an afterthought that if someone were to approach Jessie with the right price, the place could be theirs. But either Jessie did not bribe these scribblers sufficiently, or the readership of their columns was not as well-heeled as they claimed. Either way the place remained unappealing and unsold until finally the decision was taken to auction it.

Too late the columnist Nancy Randolph, whether at the behest of Southamptonites or not, issued a siren-call to Mrs Donahue through her *Daily News* column: 'It is highly possible that, if Jessie were to return with her fortune, she would be welcomed by the very social powers who turned so cold a shoulder on her in the past. Southampton would be scrupulously polite, I have a hunch, to anyone who'd foot the bill for a little large-scale and lively amusement. From being the most giddy and glittering summer resort in America during the halcyon days of 1928–9, it has plunged into desuetude.'

But this very public appeal fell on deaf ears. Wooldon Manor was now decayed, with rusted shutters and flaking paint, and Jimmy was given the melancholy task of sorting through the remainder of the family possessions and awaiting the dire result of its sale. The place had cost Jessie more than $1.6m in purchase and renovation, but was disposed of to the highest bidder, who never lived there, for a trifling $137,000. It was to be demolished in 1941 to save the payment of tax.

For Jimmy, saying goodbye to his childhood memories was yet one more step on the path towards the isolation he was to feel for most of his adult life.

꧁꧂

The seismic rumblings emanating from Buckingham Palace and Fort Belvedere now made themselves felt in America, where New York society joyously speculated at the outcome of the anguished machinations within England's royal court. Though 1936 was a year which had seen the occupation of the Rhineland and the outbreak of the Spanish civil war, the consequences of these were as nothing by comparison with the possibility that an American woman might become Queen Empress. Frances Alda, who had encouraged Jessie Donahue to take singing lessons from her, did brisk business in the Colony Club restaurant one day taking $4 bets that Wallis would ascend the throne. Following her lead, the *New York Journal-American* ran a headline 'King Will Wed Wally'.

Once Mrs Simpson had decided to divorce her husband, she had taken a house in London's Cumberland Terrace, a stone's throw from Barbara Hutton's mansion in Regent's Park. Their respective residences could not be more dissimilar: Hutton's Winfield House had been bought and remodelled at a cost of $5m, and decked with Canalettos, whereas the Duchess was living in a draughty stuccoed terrace on a short Crown lease. In the event she stayed a relatively short time while the swift but perilous stampede towards the King's abdication took place.

About the time Jimmy landed in New York to re-start his life after the failure of *Transatlantic Rhythm*, Wallis, having returned from a brief stay at Balmoral with the King, was travelling to Felixstowe on the Suffolk coast to prepare for her divorce from Ernest Simpson. By 27 October, the date of the hearing at Ipswich court, both British and American pressmen were eager to air Wallis's name in print and she was besieged by reporters and photographers. The judge, fully aware both of the background to the divorce and what was going on outside his courtroom, took a hostile stance towards her, granting the decree nisi with the stony words: 'I suppose I must, in these unusual circumstances.'

Wallis returned to London and went to stay with the King

at Fort Belvedere. By now he occupied a dressing-room directly off her bedroom and it was assumed by all within the royal circle that a full sexual relationship was what bound the King to his mistress. But her stay at the Fort became untenable as the wheels of bureaucracy forced the King towards the inevitable rout. The prime minister, Baldwin, had advised him that he had three choices: giving up his idea of marrying Wallis; marrying against the advice of his ministers, who would then be forced to resign, prompting the biggest split between crown and state since the execution of King Charles II; or abdication.

Faced with this horror of monumental proportions, on 3 December, Wallis left the country for France, leaving the King to negotiate an unnegotiable position. He told his prime minister: 'Mrs Simpson is the only woman in the world and I cannot live without her' – a phrase that was to come back and haunt those who remained close to him in the years ahead.

The crisis broke on 11 December, and finally the ex-King, as now he was, spoke to his people, saying, 'I have found it impossible to carry the heavy burden of responsibility and to discharge my duties as King without the help and support of the woman I love.' The die was cast and Wallis was left to carry the burden – often quite lightly, it must be said – of this historic rending of Britain's royal fabric.

In New York the broadcast was greeted with whoops and hollers in El Morocco, where Jimmy was hosting a party for his new-found friend, the singer Ethel Merman.

Christmas 1936 was a chilly affair on both sides of the Atlantic. The newly-fashioned Duke of Windsor sat out his enforced six-month separation from his beloved Wallis – it was deemed they could not meet until the divorce was absolute – at Schloss

Enzesfield, the home near Vienna of Baron Eugene de Roths-
child, where there was plenty of service but not much warmth.
Wallis remained at the Chateau Candé in the Loire Valley
owned by a friend, Charles Bedaux. For Jimmy, Christmas
consisted of a evening party at 834 Fifth Avenue with Jessie
and a few of Jessie's friends – but none of Jimmy's. From his
mother he received his Christmas present, a writing desk made
for mad King Ludwig of Bavaria, and new carpeting for his
rooms. Wooly, so inured to the lack of festive atmosphere at
834, did not even bother to attend, and sent his valet over to
pick up his Christmas presents. The maid received a pair of
diamond earrings and was happier than anybody.

Nor did the New Year promise gladder tidings. While keeping her sons on a relatively tight rein, Jessie herself had been
overspending wildly – on the refurbishment of Cielito Lindo,
on the upkeep of *Japauldon* and, mostly, on herself. Her acquisition of priceless jewellery continued apace, so did the ceaseless
ebb of large sums over the gaming tables at Palm Beach, Monte
Carlo and Biarritz. In January 1937 she sold ten per cent of
her inheritance – 60,000 shares in Woolworth stock – to finance
the overspend. It did not mean she intended to spend less;
indeed she opened the year as she meant to go on – with a
spectacular dinner at Cielito Lindo with festoons of coloured
lights and spotlights on the new swimming pool and lily pond.
Among the stranded gentry she managed to collect around her
that night were Princess Cora Caetini, the Marquis di Selina,
the Earl of Sefton and Viscount and Viscountess Adare.

Jimmy was not invited. By now his predilection for pranks
meant that when Jessie was in 'tugboat' mode – tying up to a
peer or two – he was purposely excluded.

Travel is the ultimate delusion of the super-rich. The discussion of where one has been, or where one is going, the
people who are there to greet or bid you farewell, the respective

merits of schlossen, castelli, châteaux and castles and the various demerits of their owners, are sufficient to convince all concerned that a fulfilled life is being actively pursued. Work, jobs, were never part of the conversation in the middle years of the twentieth century but the furious pursuit of travel demonstrated a worldliness and a zest for life.

For Jimmy Donahue, therefore, the simplest way to obliterate the lack of direction in his life was to travel. During the mid-1930s he crossed the Atlantic sometimes six times in a year, commanding staterooms, dressing in black or white tie with the inevitable gardenia, gossiping with the dowagers during the day and disappearing below-stairs after dark. Ocean travel appealed to many things in him – sex, wanderlust, recognition of his status which came with the purchase of an expensive ticket, and the somnambulistic trance of ocean travel which otherwise could only be achieved with a Seconal pill.

As Britain and the Empire recovered from the tremors of the abdication – where Church, State, the Throne and the people had been pulled in different directions – Jimmy blithely sailed back to England on the *Bremen* to join Barbara Hutton at Winfield House in Regent's Park.

By the spring of 1937 a new order had emerged at Court, and the rush from royal failure to royal success, from the photogenic David to the deeply uncharismatic Bertie and his dumpling wife Elizabeth, was loathsome to perceive. Best recorded in the poet Osbert Sitwell's verse *Rat Week*, society's wholesale flight from one king to the next was not unique in history, but none the lovelier for all that. For American citizens in Britain it meant little except that, for a time, their accents were less noticeable in Mayfair's salons. But with Americans including Sir 'Chips' Channon, Nancy, Lady Astor and Emerald Cunard providing such buttressing to upper-class life in the metropolis, any anti-Americanism could not last long. And with people like Jimmy spending money at Anderson and Shepherd in Savile Row, at Sulka in Bond Street, and at the Ritz in Piccadilly, everyone wanted to forget the abdication.

In the country, away from London, the bruises lasted longer; but Mayfair inclined, in the end, to the New York view that the Duke and Duchess of Windsor made glamorous exiles and were rather like a folly on a huge country estate, a glorious ruin of no practical value but of intense visual interest. Within a short span the nation got what it wanted, a coronation, and if the man enthroned was not the one they had expected, it mattered less as the days went by. *Le Roi est mort, vive le Roi!*

Barbara Hutton, as the Countess Haugwitz-Reventlow, languidly took part in the celebrations as Society saluted its new leaders, and as she made a stately progress through the Queen's Ball, the Chelsea Flower Show, the Covent Garden Mozart Festival, the Derby, Wimbledon and Royal Ascot, Jimmy tagged along too.

He then set off for Biarritz to join Jessie. One newspaper breathlessly reported: 'The proximity of the Spanish civil war holds no terrors for Jessie and Jimmy Donahue, who have leased Mrs Gilbert Miller's villa in Biarritz, formerly owned by Jean Patou, for the summer.' As if the movements of these super-rich were of moment while a civilisation was being torn apart an hour's drive away, a further half-column went on to describe how for the past ten years Jessie had graced the gaming tables of the seaside resort and how she would now sit alongside Amleto Battisti – the 'Uruguayan gambling man with the mind of a mathematician and the memory of an elephant' – whose aim it was to win back the $1 million he had lost eight years previously. During the intervening years Battista had returned to Uruguay to study the mathematics of chance and now was in Biarritz for revenge, bankrolled not with his own money but by a syndicate of Cuban, South American and French adventurers. History does not record whether Battisti was successful in his venture but one thing was sure in Biarritz that season: that Jessie would lose, as she always did, heavily.

When Jimmy's cousin Barbara decided, for tax purposes, to renounce her American citizenship in favour of the Danish nationality of her husband, Jimmy accompanied her back to New York on the *Europa* to complete the necessary declaration. Neither was to foresee the short- and medium-term effects of what was conceived as a simple way to save Barbara hundreds of thousands of dollars a year. On 16 December 1937 she renounced her rights to American citizenship and triggered a colossal row: as the *Europa* sailed away again with the cousins on board, Woolworth stores workers went on strike and paraded the streets of New York with placards reading: 'Babs renounces citizenship but not profits' and 'While we're on strike for higher pay, Babs takes her millions and runs away.'

Because neither cousin was capable of making the connection between the money they spent, gleaned from Woolworth dividends, and the workers who made the profits which provided the dividends, they were oblivious to the fact that, for some time, shop workers had been agitating for a living wage. Barbara confessed she never read the papers – 'There's quite enough ugliness in the world' – and Jimmy read only the gossip columns. But the row started to take on monumental proportions, with columnists fanning the flames, acting as *agents provocateurs* in time-honoured fashion. The force of criticism was levelled against Barbara, but Jimmy felt its draught as well. By now Jessie was counselling her niece that she needed a public relations outfit to sweeten her public image, and within weeks of Barbara's tax-avoiding act of repudiation, she was advising a return to American citizenship. Ever a more friendly voice than that of her father Franklyn Hutton, Barbara listened to Jessie, and complied.

Encouraged by the success of public relations man Steve Hannagan and his assistant Ned Moss, Jessie chose at this juncture to have herself profiled in the popular press. The result was an embarrassing slab of hagiography: 'She is very shy, and despite her vast worldly possessions maintains a simple attitude towards life,' the piece in the *Journal-American* began. 'She has been blessed by an abundance of grey matter . . . if she lost every penny tomorrow she could win fame and fortune on the concert stage with a singing voice that thrills all those privileged to hear it.' The piece, written by the venal Maury Paul who was known to take backhanders in return for favourable puffs, went on to report that Jessie was one of the US's largest individual taxpayers who eschewed avoidance schemes because of her love of the mother country, and that she gave endlessly to charity.

When the article turned its focus on to her social life, those who knew Jessie threw back their heads and roared with laughter: 'Titled foreigners bore her, name-flingers nauseate her and grandeur leaves her colder than an icebox. Her jewels are superb but are not worn ostentatiously. Likes to try her luck at the gambling tables and usually wins.'

All this was a paltry disguise. Jessie Woolworth Donahue was making a belated attempt to be accepted as one of the 400, and to have her name included in the Social Register. In every other respect life had handed her everything she ever wanted; but though she entertained royally, some doors – the most important doors – remained shut to her. 'There was too much of money about her,' recalls an old acquaintance. 'Other people in her sphere were rich but there wasn't about them a constant reminder of their wealth. With Jessie, everything she did, or said, or wore, spoke of the money she had inherited. And to be honest, if the money hadn't come from five-and-dime stores but somewhere like Cartier, maybe people wouldn't have felt quite that way. I am afraid people, even at the highest level, can be prone to snobbery sometimes.'

Jessie pushed the family's lengthy lineage, claiming to be able to trace her ancestry back to pre-Revolutionary days, and pointing out she was eligible for membership of the Daughters of the American Revolution and the Colonial Dames of America. But most people were more familiar with the Frank Woolworth version, of how he had started life milking cows in Jefferson County.

Regularly in the columns during the 1930s pieces would appear in praise of her, as she furthered her bid for acceptance: 'If there is a more kindly or more charitable matron in the whole of New York . . .' wrote one scribe in 1937, '. . . the other night Mrs Donahue sailed for the Old World on her usual summer vacation. But before motoring to the pier she spent several hours signing cheques that were later sent by her secretary to the many poor and needy families on Mrs Donahue's private charity list – and whom she was anxious to protect from want during her absence.' Another time a journalist felt it proper, for reasons known only to himself, that his readership should know: 'Mrs Donahue is the one member of the Woolworth-Hutton group who definitely and genuinely dislikes publicity. She does not care two straws about seeing her in the society columns.' The piece appeared in just such a column.

Later, after the war, one more attempt was made to launch Jessie into society's stratosphere. "When the rumour spread like wildfire around Newport that General and Mrs Eisenhower were coming to visit Mrs Donahue, together with former Ambassador and Mrs Joe Davies, Newporters turned themselves inside out trying to be nice to Mrs Donahue," ran one report. "Suddenly she discovered she had become the most popular and sought-after lady in Newport. The rumour spread that some of Newport's best people had got together and decided that a joint proclamation be sent to the Social Register demanding that she be inserted." It came to nothing. Miss Bertha Eastmond, the autocrat who decided the acceptability of all new applicants, saw no reason to alter her earlier judgement of Frank Woolworth's daughter. Though Jessie may consort with kings and princes, the harder she tried knocking, the more firmly Miss Eastmond's door remained shut.

Though many other doors remained shut and membership of the 400 remained elusive, nonetheless there was a certain loftiness about Jessie's progress through life. Oblivious to the *Anschluss* in which Austria shamelessly ceded its sovereignty to the Third Reich, and to the consequences which were visible to all, the following summer she took Jimmy with her to Salzburg, where she rented the thirteenth-century Schloss Kammer, a massive edifice with walls so thick whole rooms could be contained within them, and where in the courtyard a gigantic pool was built in a series of ramps. A large retinue of servants waited upon the Donahues, and guests were ferried about the lake in a gondola propelled by a boatman, and rewarded for their minimal exertions with large glasses of slivovitz.

Back in New York, Jimmy resumed his friendship with Libby Holman, whose show *You'll Never Know* opened on Broadway in September. He followed her around the provincial run, living at second-hand the life that would now never be his, yet still taking the rewards in the shape of chorus-boys. The show itself, Cole Porter later confessed, was the worst with which he had ever been associated, but the cast blamed the notoriously mean Shubert brothers who were producing it. In order to save overtime, the Shuberts would order stage-hands to begin packing up the props while the actors were still onstage. One night in Philadelphia, Libby Holman made her entrance late in the second act to discover that all the pictures and some of the furniture had been removed from the scene. Libby looked round the barren set, then ad-libbed to her co-star Rex O'Malley, 'I'm terribly sorry you lost your inheritance and had to sell all your pictures.' Those backstage, including Jimmy, broke into hysterical laughter, even if the audience didn't get it.

Jimmy was with Libby the night she bumped into the increasingly unhinged film-star Tallulah Bankhead who, like Libby, was a bisexual extrovert. Something about her appearance, or Jimmy's, as they entered the elevator made something snap inside Tallulah and she began shouting obscenities and cursing the singer. Libby was startled but said nothing, getting out at the next floor. Jimmy rode on, saying: 'Tallulah, why were you so rude to Libby?'

'I don't know, I thought she was deaf and wouldn't hear.'

'She's not deaf,' said Jimmy, 'she's blind.'

'Oh,' said the star, airily, 'I knew it was *something*.'

Libby gave a party for her son Topper's sixth birthday, hiring at Jimmy's suggestion Benny Goodman, Gene Krupa, Lionel Hampton and Billie Holiday, simply because the boy had suddenly developed a taste for jazz on the radio. Her biographer Jon Bradshaw recorded: 'As the part progressed Jimmy Donahue performed a hilarious striptease, Mrs Clark Gable cried continually because Gable had deserted her for Carole Lombard ... the band played on and, at nine in the morning when the party ended, Lionel Hampton was found asleep in Libby's bedroom, embracing what Billie Holiday described as 'a big-assed bottle of vintage champagne'.

'That was one a hell of a party,' said the singer, 'the way a party's supposed to be.' It was the best review Jimmy got in his all-too-short showbiz career.

For a time the gilded cousins, Jimmy and Barbara, who had been so close since childhood, now drifted apart. Barbara pursued a highly social life based in London but taking in Paris, Venice and other assorted watering-holes. Jimmy returned to New York and submerged himself in the world of showbusiness which he had come to see as his haven and bolthole.

As the Palm Beach season of 1939 opened up, Jimmy was to be found escorting Jessie to various entertainments including a first night in the resort's tiny movie house, then the races at Hialeah, and a series of dinners at Cielito Lindo featuring once again a sprinkling of aristocracy ('titled foreigners bore her') which included the Duke of Marlborough, the Earl of Dundonald and Lord Charles Hope.

Jessie cannot have read *Fortune* magazine's article that year which explained the strange attraction rich Americans and British aristocrats had for each other:

> British Society is much more quickly and directly purchasable by Americans (not by their own kind) than is New York or Southampton. The reason is that the British cannot take seriously the fantastic idea that an American (or any other colonial, including the Australian Bushman) could have a social position. They regard Americans as simple-hearted savages with a penchant for providing free lunch for their betters.

At this time Jessie was employing a staff of over one hundred at the main house and, as one guest from that time pointed out 'if she didn't like the way it went that night, they'd all be fired'. The gossip columnist Cholly Knickerbocker got it absolutely wrong when, after such a display of extravagance, he reported to his readers: 'She has lost her taste for Palm Beach. It's an open secret that Jessie Donahue would willingly hand over her magnificent Cielito Lindo to anyone offering a certified check for half of what the place cost her.'

Jessie revelled in Palm Beach, Jimmy less so. His homosexuality, perfectly acceptable in New York, did not amuse his contemporaries in Florida. After a brief sexual encounter with one of the black servants at the Bath and Tennis Club, some friends got to hear about it and next time he was in the club had one of the servants walk round ringing a bell with a message on a board 'Paging Mr NIGER'. There were howls of suffocated laughter as Jimmy stamped out in a rage.

In due course Jimmy, Jessie, Wooly and the Donahue caravan, oblivious to events taking place in central Europe, headed for Monte Carlo and ultimately Biarritz. On the Côte d'Azur there was much talk of, but little belief in, an impending war. They entertained from a rented yacht moored at Cannes. At dinner one night with the columnist Elsa Maxwell, Jimmy bumped into his erstwhile Choate contemporary Jack Kennedy, whose bootlegging, *arriviste* father had defied the snobs by becoming US Ambassador in London. Kennedy indicated that war was imminent, but was pooh-poohed by Jimmy and Wooly. The social season continued on its gay way until 23 August, when the news that Germany had negotiated an agreement with Russia 'burst like a bombshell in our midst', recalled one present in Cannes.

By that stage Jimmy and his mother had moved on to Biarritz, once again to stay at their customary villa. But France, whose memory of the last invasion was still fresh, swiftly started to prepare itself for the worst. On 3 September, Britain declared war on Germany and the second conflict in less than twenty-five years to be played out on the European mainland was under way.

Barbara arrived in the coastal resort. More realistic than most during the 'phony war' period, due mainly to a briefing she had been given by Joe Kennedy at the London embassy, she had ordered Winfield House to be mothballed, sending her gold plate, her Louis XV furniture, her Meissen dinnerware and her Canalettos to a warehouse in the country. Depositing much of her jewellery at Coutts bank she had come south to meet her husband, now separated from her, to retrieve their son Lance before returning to America. In a remarkable transaction, Count Reventlow handed over the boy for $500,000. The deal having been secured in Biarritz, Barbara made plans to quit France, securing tickets for herself, her son, and staff on the *Conte di Savoia*, which was due to sail from Italy in a few days' time.

Stung out of their lotus-eating torpor by Barbara's example, the Donahues similarly packed their bags and arranged by telegram that they, too should have berths on the same ship. All around were signs that the old way of life was about to be suspended: banks refused to cash Jessie's cheques, the shops, their windows suddenly empty in the mid-afternoon heat, started to shut early. The staff at the Hotel du Palais, built by Napoleon III for Empress Eugénie, grew stiff-lipped at the family's extravagant demands.

Finally, in a large grey Rolls Royce, the family Donahue headed east across France towards the Italian border, with Jimmy and Wooly taking turns at the wheel. At Cannes, where they had so recently dined with Elsa Maxwell, they found chaos. The streets were jammed with taxicabs, dilapidated buses, even little donkey carts in which farmers were offering to drive people to Paris. So great were the traffic jams, the roads were virtually impassable.

Most holidaymakers, including Elsa Maxwell, were instinctively heading towards the capital city, though many were soon to discover that the north Channel ports of France, their final destination, had no ships to take them out of the country. On the road, too, were the Duke and Duchess of Windsor, forced to abandon their new home, the Château de la Croe at Antibes, and travelling in convoy – one car for the royalties, one for the luggage, one for the staff – towards Paris.

At one stage it was estimated by Miss Maxwell that 60,000 Americans had amassed in Paris prior to departure, but though the west-east route seemed unorthodox, it was at least towards certain embarkation. The mood in France altered rapidly during the three days it took the party to get from Biarritz to the Italian border. At their departure from the coastal town, there had been smiles of regret, the customary courtesies, the formal compliments. By the time they reached the border, attitudes had hardened, and the Donahues were forced to submit to the humiliating process of having their luggage minutely, and slowly, inspected. Then officials demanded to inspect their wallets and other bags containing money and, claiming the rules of war, confiscated all their French currency. For the first time in their lives all three Donahues – Jessie, Jimmy and Wooly – were penniless.

The ride into Genoa was completed in sour silence, and as they arrived at the dockside they witnessed scenes of near-panic as 2,156 passengers, most of them American, struggled to get aboard the *Conte di Savoia*. Under the captain Alberto Ortino the ship finally sailed, docking briefly at Naples where the Donahues were treated to the unexpected sight of Barbara and her entourage walking up the gangplank. Misled as to the point of embarkation, she had travelled the length of Italy at breakneck speed in order to catch the ship. Left behind, at Genoa and Naples, were two Rolls Royce limousines and assorted back-up cars, none of which were ever seen again.

⚯

During the voyage each of the well-heeled passengers, including Prince Francis Joseph of Spain, had a chance to tell their story. A fashion model, Selma Freeman, described how she left Paris by taxi, telling the driver only when she reached the city limits that she wished him to take her to Bordeaux, 400 miles away. From there she traversed France in an easterly direction, taking six days to complete a journey which would have taken a few hours had the French trains still been running. There was little to do on the lengthy voyage except play cards and, in Jimmy's case, engage in below-decks encounters with the sailors.

The *Conte di Savoia* finally berthed at New York on 23 September 1939, nearly three weeks since the declaration of war. Though none of the passengers had encountered gunfire or conflict, the atmosphere on board ship remained tense. On one day an announcement, cool and terse, came over the loudspeaker system that the *Athenia* had been hit by an enemy torpedo and had been sunk. The voice politely apologised for the interruption, and the short statement was followed by music. As they disembarked, the Donahues, were left in no doubt that they had come close to the conflagration which was starting to rage in Europe.

By comparison, New York was *en fête* – all but for a small grouping of disgruntled shop-workers who, hearing that Barbara Hutton was disembarking, surrounded the Pierre Hotel where she had a suite of rooms. As Jimmy and his mother were driven past the Pierre *en route* for their own home, a stone's throw away at 834 Fifth Avenue, they were able to see placards which angrily read: 'Barbara Hutton! Is eighteen dollars a week too much?' Another read: 'Babs Hutton flees Europe's War. Seeks peace. But how about peace with the Unions?' There were many more. Jessie, equal legatee of Frank Woolworth's great fortune and with a greater chunk of Woolworth stock, averted her eyes. Largely unknown outside her own society and those who feasted on the gossip columns, her low-profile was in sharp contrast to her niece's consummate inability to avoid the headlines.

During the voyage, Jessie had discussed the future with Jimmy. Now aged twenty-four, and a recently qualified pilot, he was the ideal age to enlist and he might have considered such a course. The stumbling-block lay in the incomplete, utterly woeful, education which had denied him a place at college; for without a college education it would be extremely difficult to become a commissioned officer – and to his mother's way of thinking, a war career in the ranks was unthinkable. Yet Jimmy, unlike his brother Wooly, had become a high-profile figure, just the sort that the gossip columnists could pick on with a 'We hear Jimmy will shortly be enlisting' story when they knew full well he wasn't. Jessie did not want another Woolworth grandchild to be vilified, as she had just seen her niece vilified, and she consulted her public relations men to see what could be done.

By way of consolation for having so successfully killed his theatrical ambitions, Jessie had bought Jimmy a Grumman Goose G-21A amphibious plane for his twenty-fourth birthday. It cost her $33,000 ($393,000) and was delivered the same weekend Neville Chamberlain declared war on Germany. Ugly but stable, it carried six passengers and was a handful for a newly-qualified pilot; but Jimmy usually travelled with a co-pilot as a safety measure. It cruised at 180 mph at 5,000 feet and had a range of 825 miles. Of the hundred or so produced by Grumman, most were put straight into war use by the US Navy and US Army Air Corps, but one or two individuals including Marshall Field Jr and Lord Beaverbrook (who bought two) used them for private transport. It was a huge status symbol.

In the light of this, the PR men came up with the answer

and the *Daily News* obliged them by running the piece. 'If you see a big grin on the cherubic pan of Jimmy Donahue, it's because the Woolworth heir has at last won Momma over. Until a few days ago Mrs Jessie Donahue had consistently refused to set foot in an airplane.' The lickspittle piece described how Jimmy had taken his mother on an air tour of Long Island after persuading her to set foot in his personal airplane, which was housed at nearby Roosevelt Field. The piece pointed out that Jimmy had been flying for a year, and that he would be taking part in the Civil Air Patrol scheme. Shortly after, it was reported that he was attempting a new parachute record at an air meeting at Colorado Springs. In a Ryan Brougham monoplane he was climbing to an altitude of 24,500 feet but had to bail out early, nevertheless taking nineteen minutes to make his descent. All in all, the picture was painted that here was a young man preparing himself for the rigours of war, albeit so far in a civilian capacity.

There followed a similar article, this time in the *Mirror*, which trumpeted: 'No longer do cocktail parties, nightclubs and screen stars interest him. He takes flying lessons at Morrison Field here in Palm Beach and he will develop into a first-class pilot. His big ambition was to fly the Atlantic solo.'

The first thing Jimmy had done on getting his pilot's licence was to enrage his Palm Beach neighbours by flying under the Lake Worth bridge separating the island from the mainland, not once, but three times. Given the shallow draught of the bridge it was some achievement – but that was as far as Jimmy's aerial ambition went. 'The truth was that Jessie did not want either of her sons in the armed services and she went out of her way to make sure it never happened,' says a contemporary from that time.

Nonetheless, a story soon appeared in one newspaper saying: 'Mrs Donahue will soon be in a position to point, proudly, to two sons in the armed forces of the USA.' Of Jimmy it said: 'He is anxious to get in the naval aviation forces, and has spent much time in Washington endeavouring to unravel "rules and regulations" red-tape.' The story pointed, for the first time, to the difficulties Jimmy faced without a college education, but helped, *inter alia*, to explain the arguments against his being accepted as an officer.

What did not appear in the official history of Jimmy Donahue, pilot, was another prank, now related by a Palm Beach friend, which got him into deep trouble: 'He was so proud of this Grumman seaplane and Jessie, as usual doting on her son, paid a fortune to have it brought over on a freighter from San Francisco to Honolulu so he could fly it about while they were out there for a visit. He obviously got bored and decided to buzz a US aircraft carrier which was patrolling off Honolulu and the admiral got very mad. As a result Jessie had to call him up and entertain him and Jimmy had to, given this was wartime, report to the admiral's quarters and explain himself.'

⁂

During the early stages of the War little changed for the rich. Much lip service was given to the plight of the poor Europeans, and patriotism became more fervent. Early in 1940 a luncheon for the first lady, Eleanor Roosevelt, hosted by William Randolph Hearst and his wife included in its small number Jessie and Jimmy. It was in aid of French soldiers. But following a disagreement with other charitable ladies which resulted in several fund-raising do-gooders being shown the door at 834, Jessie's well-oiled publicity machine was trundled out to record: '(She) goes to great lengths to keep the public from learning of her many kindnesses to those less fortunately placed in life. And notwithstanding the fact that she gives an aggregate of a small fortune, annually, to this and that charity, her donations are made with the strict understanding that they be listed as "anonymous".'

The columnist – once again the venal Maury Paul – then went on to list the various charitable donations Jessie had lately made, including the purchase of 300 tickets for a charity night at Radio City Music Hall; turkeys, cigarettes and other items to US soldiers; and various other war efforts.

After yet another broadside from Maury Paul eulogising this most charitable of women, Ethel Merman, Jimmy's great friend, hooted scornfully at the way his mother was being portrayed in the press; but then, as later, Jimmy had no desire to reproach his mother. She continued to see him, and his brother Wooly, in adulthood as attractive adjuncts to her comfortably upholstered life. Early on she had formulated the plan that they should never be financially independent of her, and in her presence the brothers remained, to the end of their days, polite, deferential and obliging.

War donations or no, she was running through her money faster than it was coming in. In the summer of 1941 she dumped another 30,000 Woolworth shares on the market, raising $500,000 and reducing her personal holding by ten per cent, a repetition of her earlier fund-raising act in 1937. She also gave 20,000 shares to Wooly, who after a lengthy and colourful bachelorhood was getting married.

The object of Wooly's affection was Gretchen Randolph Hearst and, unlike every other woman who had come Wooly's way – and there had been many, from Dorothy Lamour to Hedy Lamarr to Joan Bennett and with a liberal sprinkling of less well-known but equally toothsome names – she earned Jessie's respect by virtue of her lineage. She was a great-great-granddaughter of General 'Stonewall' Jackson, and had had a recent but brief marital attachment to a member of the Hearst family. Wooly had engaged himself eight years earlier to another eligible, Dorothy Fell, who walked out just days before the wedding, saying, 'He is not my kind', and sending back her ten carat diamond ring. Since then the nearest he had come to the altar was an attachment to British actress Wendy Barrie, whom Jessie loathed. Miss Barrie's drawbacks, according to the matriarch, started with the fact that she was an actress, went on to the fact she had no money and culminated with the criticism that 'no one knows who her family are'. During the liaison Jessie allowed herself the observation that she would be taking her son abroad 'to escape actresses'. Like a lamb, Wooly complied.

Finally, and with Jimmy as best man, Wooly abandoned bachelordom at a hastily-arranged ceremony at Cielito Lindo on 28 January 1940. 'Sum' Woolworth, brother of the famous Frank and last relic of a forgotten generation, gave the bride away. The couple borrowed Jimmy's Grumman Goose to fly to Jamaica for their honeymoon and a row ensued when Jimmy, who had already bought the couple a present, insisted on charging them $500 for the privilege. Wooly refused and the couple were forced to come back, tourist class, via Pan-Am, leaving the newlyweds fuming. Four months later, Gretchen entered hospital in Washington for an unspecified abdominal operation and three months after that, the marriage was revealed to be over.

Jimmy meandered back to New York and gave luncheon at 834 to the Marquess of Milford Haven, nephew of Lord Louis Mountbatten. The Marquess, who Jimmy considered a dull sort, found himself surrounded by a bright, beautifully-turned-out young crowd of six ladies and six gentlemen. It was not vouchsafed to him that the people with whom he was sharing a sumptuous repast were all prostitutes. After luncheon, Jimmy asked the Marquess if he would care to see his mother's famous bronze collection which was in the next room. Lord Milford Haven, who knew nothing of bronze, assented and the door was opened. There, before him, were half-a-dozen black men, oiled and standing naked in provocative poses. Just another of Jimmy's little jokes.

CHAPTER 6

MUMMY MIGHT HEAR

In a space of months, the war had completely altered the sexual make-up of New York. Until Pearl Harbour and mass mobilisation, the gay culture had remained a fragmented and isolated affair – a secret garden to be enjoyed by the few, while the many who felt themselves to be 'different' were still without vent or expression to their feelings. Now with many men in uniform removed from the straitjacket of home-town life and cast into the melting-pot of New York, there was a sexual explosion which allowed Jimmy, with his money, his charm and his good looks, a new and liberated *laissez-passer* through the homosexual clubs and bars – like Tony's in Swing Alley on West 52nd Street where Mabel Mercer sang – which were springing up weekly in the city.

Homosexuality was still illegal, however, and with the New York Police Department pursuing its almost pathological vendetta against gays, often by means of entrapment, the gay community remained an inward-looking group with its own rules, mores and manners. One member of that community, quoted in Charles Kaiser's book *The Gay Metropolis*, described it thus: 'Everybody you met had a style of elegance. It was not T-shirts and muscles and so on. It was wit and class. You had to have [white tie and] tails and be polite. Homosexuality was an upscale thing to be, it was defined by class.'

When in New York Jimmy now pursued a cultured life, going to the theatre and the Metropolitan Opera – a favourite pickup joint – and ending up typically at El Morocco and '21'. Then a group of friends would be taken back to 834 Fifth Avenue, where the party, often developing into an orgy, would continue past dawn. Friends of Jessie Donahue swear that, to her death, she knew nothing of Jimmy's other life; but a more dispassionate interpretation of the facts would be that she simply looked the other way. She identified in her son what she had seen in her husband and, as with Jim, she chose not to confront it. By creating a separate suite of rooms for Jimmy at 834 and maintaining an iron grip on his finances, she knew he would never leave her. What he did out of sight and earshot was his affair.

On one occasion when Jessie was in Palm Beach, Jimmy bought the whole of Lucille Mallon's cast of characters from her bordello back to 834 and served them all a formal dinner, with footmen, waiters and much champagne. On other occasions when his guests were exclusively male and invited to his own quarters, Jimmy would treat the whole thing as a huge joke, whispering, 'Ssssh! What if Mummy were to hear?' as they started to party. But in truth, given the size of 834, she was unlikely to be aware of such gatherings even if she was in residence.

In between partying Jimmy continued to fly out of Roosevelt Field when in New York and Morrison Field when in Palm Beach. At Morrison Field he was able to witness the massive and near-instantaneous build-up of troops and supplies since the airfield became the main supply base and jumping-off point for the US Air Transport Command, flying out B-17s and B-24s virtually around the clock. But despite mixing with combat officers Jimmy felt no compulsion to hasten his own contribution to the war effort. While he languidly prepared for war, ordering a new and well-cut CAP uniform before submitting to the portrait photographer's art, the Duke and Duchess of Windsor were in Europe suing for peace, even though the Duke's message of appeasement ran counter to the policy adopted by the British government.

Returning to France as an Allied liaison officer, the Duke had quickly been identified as a security risk: he and the Duchess had too many friends who spoke to the enemy. The Duke's military role was designed to put him in uniform, then sideline him, a stratagem which worked effectively as he was sent on obscure errands within France. As the Germans advanced, the Duke abandoned his Paris posting, heading for Biarritz and La Croe, his house on the Côte d'Azur. He was, in effect, a deserter. Later, in order to minimise the embarrassment his return to Britain would occasion, King George VI made his brother Governor of the Bahamas. The deal was that he would not return home to Britain, nor would he set foot on American soil, until he had established himself in Nassau, the Bahamian capital. He had been found what was considered, all round, to be the safest posting; safe, from the Windsors' point of view because of its distance from the conflict, and safe from the British government's perspective because the Duke, an increasingly erratic figure, could do little political harm there.

The Duke and Duchess arrived disgruntled, discommoded and disappointed at Nassau on 17 August 1940. The quasi house-arrest under which they had been put was not to last for long. Despite their instructions to stay away from the American mainland, almost immediately its allure, by comparison with the suffocating provincialism of Nassau where the population was a mere 15,000, proved too much. The American coastline was 200 miles away; London was more than 4,000. By December the Duchess, with an infected tooth, had sailed to Miami for treatment, and the heady welcome she received encouraged her to persuade the Duke they must return forthwith. He needed little encouragement.

The Windsors' trip to the mainland was not entirely social. The Duke was desperate to engage Sir Edward Peacock in a series of money-talks. Peacock, besides being a director of the Bank of England and an intermediary in Anglo-American financial disputes, was also an unofficial financial adviser to the royal family. He was too busy to come to Nassau and waste an extra day in travel, but was prepared to make himself available in Palm Beach to discuss the Duke's morbid and abiding belief that he was within an ace of bankruptcy.

By April 1941, after many false starts, the Windsors prepared to land at Miami, disembarking from the liner *Berkshire* to the ecstatic applause of 2,000 onlookers. Palm Beach was ready to proudly claim the exiles as its own.

Palm Beach had a fascination for the Duchess, in its high concentration of the rich and the well-connected, but also because as a girl she had experienced its heady charms when visiting Indiantown, where her uncle S. Davies Warfield built the Seminole Inn; Warfield Boulevard and Warfield Elementary were named after him. Her childhood visits were as a poor if well brought-up girl. Now to return as the focus of attention to the world's richest resort, though nearly all the colony's residents were richer than her, was an unimaginable victory.

The colony's social round had continued, unabated by war. One resident recalls: 'All the men here then had inherited wealth and none of them worked. Most of them played tennis and

golf and went to Colonel Bradley's. Everyone went to The Patio
– it had a sliding roof and a nightclub and delicious food, and
stayed open until three or four in the morning. No one went
to bed early – we would go back to someone's house and go
swimming and have breakfast. You didn't know there was a
war on – you got all the gasoline you needed and there were
eight or nine fancy markets which delivered, and you could get
everything you wanted. There were still parties every night.'

A three-day round of luncheon parties and dinners for the
Windsors started at Jessie Donahue's house, finally fixing that
elusive jewel in her social crown. Though Palm Beach boasted
finer, older, names – the Amorys, Munns, Phipps and Stotesbu-
rys – it was to this widow of a homosexual Irish adventurer
whose family owned a hide-rendering factory that the ex-King
prepared to hasten. All Jessie's angling to become one of the
400 disappeared into the ether with this one visit. She had
finally arrived.

How Jessie came to execute this coup went back to before
the outbreak of war. In France, she had befriended the Duke's
ally and former Lord-in-Waiting, the Earl of Sefton, who like
Jessie was incalculably rich, but unlike Jessie, could trace his
lineage back to the twelfth century. Sefton did not know Palm
Beach particularly well, but he did know Jessie, and soon he
was a house-guest at Cielito Lindo. Though he had found it
difficult to acclimatise himself to Wallis – 'We Molyneux came
to England with William the Conqueror,' he once complained
early on in the relationship: 'and Mrs Simpson still treats me
as if I were a serf!' – when introductions were called for, he
had no hesitation in suggesting, as a hostess to the royal visitors,
his old friend Jessie. Cielito Lindo, he explained, was as much
a royal palace as anything that could be found in the New
World.

In addition the Windsors, especially the Duchess, had made

friends with Barbara Hutton who extolled both the virtues of Palm Beach and of her aunt Jessie. Thus Palm Beach was made for the Windsors and, to a lesser extent, the Windsors for Palm Beach. Here, there were perfect manners and an unsurpassedly sumptuous backdrop. Back in Nassau it was hot as hell, humid, and the populace was less adoring. A favourite joke there about the Duke and Duchess was 'He used to be First Lord of the Admiralty – now he is third mate on an American tramp.'

So Palm Beach prepared, as only Palm Beach can, for their exiled royals. At the Donahue house everyone, including Jimmy, waited nervously for the royal arrival. Shimmering in the mid-April heat, Cielito Lindo had never looked lovelier, its walls of old ivory and roofs of rose-coloured tiles shimmering gently in the vast gardens of blue, emerald and mauve, the colours of the tropical sea twilight. As the Duke and Duchess arrived they were greeted by Jimmy and Wooly, dressed in tropical light suits, and after a brief conversation were taken to meet Jessie, waiting for them in the drawing-room by the Renaissance fireplace.

Though her house was exquisite, Mrs Donahue was somewhat less so: 'She had a sort of runaway face, she wasn't at all goodlooking,' recalls a close friend of the Windsors. 'She was a squattish woman without very much figure, in fact she couldn't have been less distinguished in appearance. She had very little chin, but a very fine skin. You could see she was very rich – she wore an awful *lot* of jewellery, and always expensive clothes, but by no stretch of the imagination was the woman goodlooking.'

Her sons, however, were. The Duke took an immediate shine to Wooly who, on being told that this was the Duke of Windsor, piped up, 'And I'm the Duke of Cork' – a reference to his Irish ancestry. The Duke loved it. The group then moved into the garden where under the banyan trees and coconut palms the twenty-five other guests were assembled.

This, surely, was Paradise. For too long the Windsors had been on the run, living a disordered life out of suitcases, too anxious about the future, too bitter about the past. To them it was now clear that Nassau – this shameful no-man's-land – was to be their home for the war's duration, but the Governor's official residence was in a state of chaos, belatedly being refurbished to accommodate them, and the local populace had yet to take to the idea of an ex-king ruling them. Discomfort abounded, both actual and psychological, but here, to the accompaniment of tropical birdsong and the muted popping of champagne corks, the Duke and Duchess finally took their ease.

Luncheon was served in the Italianate dining room by a platoon of footmen, one assigned to each couple. The Duke sat at Jessie's right hand, the Duchess sat next to Jimmy. The long casement windows were open, the gentle Atlantic breezes wafted in. Palm Beach, especially those members of its society there present, had reason to be grateful to the royal couple, and the gratitude was mutual: it was a true high-water mark for all present. Jimmy's eyes concentrated on the Duke, who until this moment had remained a childhood hero. He had long wanted to meet this historic, romantic, tragic figure, and an immediate connection was forged between the two men – not, as some of Jimmy's more wicked friends later claimed, at a sexual level, but merely at a respectful distance.

Jimmy nevertheless entertained the Duchess with a mixture of jokes, gossip, war news and scandal. He was twenty-five, the Duchess was forty-four and in her prime. The Nassau sun had gently burnished her, and her clothes, hair, make-up and jewellery were now, after eight years in the Duke's company, flawless. She wore a simple dress by Mainbocher, with her famous jewelled flamingo brooch of sapphires, emeralds, rubies and diamonds on her left shoulder. Jimmy was dazzled.

The Windsors, as other members of that family are wont to do, were impressed by the Donahues' money, houses, servants and royal lifestyle and felt extremely comfortable, though far from awestruck, in their presence. It might be said that *Fortune* magazine's observations were, in this case, not so very wide of the mark.

Later that night the Windsors were guests at the nearby home of Wesson Seyburn, of Detroit, a party which Jessie and her boys attended. Then followed a round of celebrations including cocktails for 300, an evening with Douglas Fairbanks Jr, a golfing day for the Duke and the rediscovery of a host of old friends including Captain Alastair Mackintosh, who had been close to him during the Freda Dudley Ward epoch and was one of the Duchess's first friends in London, as well as childhood friends of the Duchess. Wallis broke her invariable rule of avoiding airplanes – she had seen too many crashes when, married to her first husband Win Spencer, she were stationed at an airfield – and ascended from Morrison Field in Harold S. Vanderbilt's air transport plane.

April was the end of Palm Beach's season; but so entranced were the Windsors by their stay that it became a favourite time for them to visit in the years to come. Soon the resort adapted to the royal ways and created a 'little season' to accommodate them. For now, the party over, they returned with heavy hearts to their duties in Nassau.

A few months after Pearl Harbour, U-boats suddenly appeared in the Caribbean and off the Florida coast, preying on tankers and ore boats coming up from South America. Enlivened by the visit of the Duke and Duchess, Jimmy was serving a moderately useful purpose in the Civilian Air Patrol, living a curious life in a single room in the by now shuttered and abandoned Cielito Lindo.

Jimmy's role was simply to spot for submarines and report back. It involved long and boring hours in the air, patrolling up and down Florida's Gold Coast, often seeing nothing except Allied aircraft taking off from Morrison Field. One friend from that time recalls Jimmy confessing that on one rare occasion he did actually spot a submarine which may possibly have been a U-boat, but did not bother to report it because to do so would have made him late for a cocktail party.

Two hundred miles away, the Windsors were doing their best to re-acclimatise themselves to life on 'Elba', as the Duchess sourly described Nassau. The tedious round of small-town events was too stifling for her, and as she told the American journalist Adela Rogers St Johns: 'Believe me, I would rather have been the mistress of the King of England than the wife of the Governor of the Bahamas!'

Even the combined efforts of Churchill, George VI and the former Foreign Secretary, now Ambassador to the US, Lord Halifax, were not sufficient to contain the footloose couple and, just six months after their inauguration into Palm Beach society, the Windsors made a semi-official visit to America in the autumn of 1941. From Miami to Washington to Wallis's home in Maryland, they were greeted by thronging crowds, and by the time they arrived in New York a ticker-tape welcome was waiting to greet them.

Mrs Rogers St Johns, well-connected and a wise counsel, had given the Windsors a list of Dos and Don'ts in preparation for their visit. The Don'ts included:

Go to a big New York hotel
Bring much luggage!!!!!!!
Have too many servants
Wear jewellery
Attend any parties unless guests are carefully checked
DO NOT GO to cafés or restaurants.

In every respect her advice was ignored. The Duchess's biographer Stephen Birmingham commented: 'They arrived in America that winter – New York, of course – like two bulls in a china shop. They ensconced themselves in one of the biggest, flashiest, most publicity-conscious hotels in town, the Waldorf-Astoria, where they took an entire floor. They brought more trunks and suitcases than harassed customs officials could count. With them came the Duke's valet, two maids for the Duchess, a secretary for each, all four dogs, and *all* Wallis's jewellery. Immediately they were taken up with enthusiasm by what was then known as café society, the playboys and play-girls of the era, the newly-rich and the would-be rich, the second-rate and lower-than-second-rate pretty and handsome and silly and gay.'

Into this harsh categorisation fell Jessie Donahue who, exalted by her triumphant encounter at Cielto Lindo, sought to repeat her success at 834 Fifth Avenue, grandly timing her descent of the marble staircase to coincide with the arrival, at its foot, of the royal party. Later, when the Windsors again dined at 834, Jimmy was to rig up a recording-machine with a microphone in the downstairs lavatory so that he could regale guests afterwards with the sound of 'the Royal wee'. But on this occasion, dressed in his CAP uniform and looking devastatingly handsome, he acted, impeccably, as host for his mother.

The New York leg of the Windsors' American tour was not

an unqualified success. Despite a high-profile public programme which included visiting the British War Relief Society,
a home for unmarried mothers, the Brooklyn Naval Yard and
the Red Cross, the press were looking for something else. They
found it in the endless packages which arrived at the Waldorf-
Astoria from the designer Mainbocher and from Bergdorf
Goodman's store: 'I haven't been in a shop since May 1940,'
complained the Duchess, 'before I left Paris. I'm [here] trying
to collect money for a clinic, but I hope you don't mind if I
buy one or two dresses.' The focus shifted to her hats: it was
said she had bought thirty-four. The Duchess claimed the
number was nearer five, adding: 'Since I am actually shopping
for a year, I don't think anyone could consider this outrageous.'
What, then, about her luggage? It was said the Windsors had
brought with them 106 pieces which were so bulky they
required a railroad car of their own. 'I've never counted them,'
she said tautly. 'But if you wish to, I'm sure we could arrange
it.'

The New York press, looking for a new angle after the acres
of eulogy printed by their provincial counterparts, decided to
bite. Headlines were critical, the tone of the body-copy was
sour, the concentration was on frippery. One biographer,
Michael Pye, observed: 'If only they had moderated their style,
and if they had not had the peculiar magic of royalty, they
would have done honourably. They went along with the
acclaim and privilege of royalty; they did not take the full
measure of the responsibilities.' The couple felt aggrieved and
humiliated by the raft of criticism levelled at them, but in Jessie
Donahue they found a sympathetic ear. Had not Jessie, Jimmy,
Wooly and Barbara Hutton all had more than their fair share
of woe from the unwashed and untutored who wrote the city's
tabloid newspapers? Jessie's sympathy and practical advice
earned Wallis's and David's gratitude and friendship, so much

so that soon Jessie and Jimmy travelled to Nassau as guests of the Windsors, flying in on a Pan-American seaplane, and duly signing their name in the visitors' book.

During the remaining war years, as the Duke and Duchess found their passage eased between the islands and the mainland now unfettered by governmental restriction, they took full advantage of it. The proximity of America, sighed the Duchess, was 'one of the distinct benefits of life on this otherwise lousy little island on which we have been marooned for far too long'. The aluminium millionaire Arthur Vining Davis made his yacht available to them, and quite soon the Duchess was back in Palm Beach 'to look at soup vending machines for my servicemen's canteen'. After that the Duchess became a familiar sight in the shops on Worth Avenue as well as in New York and Washington. Friends from Palm Beach, including 'Doc' Holden and the Donahues, paid brief visits to Nassau.

The Windsors were back in Palm Beach for Christmas 1941. They had endured riots in Nassau and an influx of Allied troops; what had been a sinecure had turned into a real job for both, one which they both took seriously. Though the scandal-mongers made much of the Duke's links with the Swedish businessman Axel Wenner-Gren, who in turn had close links with the Nazis, the general impression was that they were doing a good job in Nassau. Palm Beach welcomed them as returning heroes; once again Jessie opened up Cielito Lindo and Herbert Pulitzer, son of the newspaper magnate, also entertained them.

⚜

The presence of his cousin Barbara was very much missed by Jimmy. After their flight from France in 1939, their paths had diverged. Barbara became involved with, then married,

123

Cary Grant (the columnists delighted in calling the couple Cash'n'Cary), but the union was bound to fail. Grant was, to most people's thinking, homosexual or at best bisexual and, as a hugely successful Hollywood star with a ruthless dedication to his work, was ill-at-ease with his new wife's louche lifestyle. One of his friends said, 'Barbara surrounded herself with a consortium of fawning parasites – European titles, broken-down Hollywood types, a maharajah or two, a sheikh, the military, several English peers and a few tennis bums.' Grant said: 'If one more phoney earl had entered the house, I'd have suffocated.' By the end of 1943, the marriage was over bar the signing of the divorce papers and Barbara was once again casting her eye around.

Her gaze fell briefly on a charming, patrician-nosed US cavalry officer named Oleg Cassini. Cassini, later to become renowned as the fashion designer who created the Jackie Kennedy 'look', had arrived in America from Italy before the war and had married the actress Gene Tierney. In one of her more irrational moments, Barbara engaged Jimmy to win Cassini round to the idea of divorcing Miss Tierney and marrying her instead.

Her method was to invite Cassini and his wife to dinner, along with Jimmy and a number of others. Each found an expensive present by their plate – in Cassini's case, a gold watch. Later, after dinner, she cornered the soldier and said: 'Oleg, you are a cultured man. You are not as handsome as some of the other men in my life, but you do have a certain quality and I could even fall in love with you.'

Some days later Cassini was approached by Jimmy who said: 'You know, Barbara is very impressed with you. She likes you very much, and things aren't going too well with Grant. You might do well here for yourself, and for Barbara.' To Cassini's surprise, Jimmy then gave him an address in Hollywood and a time for a rendezvous: 'Barbara would like to see you privately,' he said. The couple barely knew each other.

At the meeting Barbara proposed taking Cassini and his wife to San Francisco, where she kept a permanent suite at the Mark Hopkins Hotel. The trip took place without incident. Back in Los Angeles, Cassini and Barbara met once more and she told him that Grant 'has a terrible temper and we have basic differences . . . and anyway, Oleg, it would be much better if you and I married.'

Cassini blinked. Of his wife, Barbara continued: 'I don't think she understands you as well as I do, and this might be the best solution for everyone. I will give her a million dollars, then you and I will be married.' To this day Cassini cannot work out who was madder, Barbara for hatching this unlikely plot, or Jimmy for supporting her in it. Given that Jimmy later told Cassini that he had once taken great pleasure in making love to a cadaver, it is perhaps not difficult to draw a conclusion.

<hr />

Since the bombing of Pearl Harbour it was becoming evident to Jimmy that sooner or later he would have to enlist. Wooly, having contracted blackwater fever on one of his African safaris, was declared 4-F and exempted from service; but Jimmy was not. Though army life as an idea was repugnant to Jessie, Jimmy was at ease with his piloting skills and felt that if necessary they could be put to good use. In addition, most of his contemporaries from Choate, the Hun School, and from Palm Beach had either enlisted or were talking of it. It was the proper thing for a gentleman to do. By the end of the War eighty-two former Choate boys would have given their lives to the cause of freedom.

The difficulty remained, however, that Jimmy had flunked school and not gone to college, and without a college education becoming a commissioned officer would be a virtual impossibility. If he could not be an officer, he declared, he would not join up. With the Grumman Goose commandeered by the US Army Air Force, Jimmy was a pilot without an airplane. His war work had ceased and he was exposed and vulnerable to conscription. In war, the armour-plating of vast wealth is as nothing.

Jimmy managed to convince Jessie that she must help, if necessary by using her money to buy the right responses. A campaign was launched to put a spin on his abject academic failure, and old contacts were tapped for a suitable reference. Given the largesse each of Jimmy's schools had received, surely it was perfectly possible to say how brilliant their former charge had been and what an excellent officer he would become? Jessie called John Hun at Princeton, but his response was to play with an entirely straight bat, writing a cordial letter to Jimmy at the Lord Baltimore Hotel in Maryland but attaching a 'To Whom It May Concern' which, though charmingly phrased, would prevent any selection board from taking seriously Jimmy's bid for officer status. 'At no time during his stay with us did he ever go through a school year without being absent for long periods because of illness or other, apparently unavoidable, reasons,' wrote Hun dryly. 'In addition to this, Jimmy did not have very much interest in scholastic work, and I don't think he was particularly excited about entering college. The result was that his energies were dissipated to some extent along other lines while he was with us.' Damning his former pupil with faint praise, he described Jimmy as 'reliable' and 'courteous'.[1]

---

1 Some months later, in June 1942, Hun wrote a letter to his former pupil begging for contributions to keep the school – undergoing a financial crisis – in business. Jimmy did not reply.

A similar bid to gain support from Choate and its headmaster St John met with the same forthright response: 'He, quite frankly, found the restrictions of a boarding-school rather difficult; in fact, so much so that, eventually we asked him to leave because of his uncooperative spirit,' he wrote. St John's own faint praise employed the words 'trustworthy' and 'disarming'. Jimmy's attempts to obtain officer status by the back door were not to succeed.

For the time being Jimmy managed to stay out of general service by joining the Army Air Force reserve inactive list, a quid pro quo for their having commandeered his Grumman Goose. After taking advice, Jessie discovered that by buying a piece of land near Morrison Field it could be argued that Jimmy, in developing the site as a civilian airstrip, was contributing to the war effort. How far this stratagem progressed in reality is not known; but for the time being it seemed that Jimmy was doing useful war service and therefore should be exempted from call-up.

He made attempts to find a more useful role outside the clutch of the military, including lending his piloting skills in a civilian capacity to a group of USAAF test-pilots who were trying out new aircraft at a secret airfield in the North-West. However secretive their activities may have been up until that point, everything changed when Jimmy arrived. The columnist Cholly Knickerbocker got to learn of his sudden appearance at the obscure North-West airstrip: 'They almost went into a mental tailspin when, as they sat in their barn-like bunkhouse one evening, playing a spot of poker, in walked Jimmy Donahue, their newest volunteer, accompanied by a very correct and wooden-faced valet, carrying a golf bag crammed with expensive golf clubs and followed by a taxi-driver laden down with luggage,' he wrote. 'The young, pink-cheeked Donahue wasn't even temporarily nonplussed at the concerted chorus of guffaws that greeted his P. G. Wodehouse-style entrance. Being a true chip off the old Woolworth block, he took his cue from the general hilarity, introduced his valet all round, and was on back-slapping terms with his new buddies in no time at all.'

The Windsors came back to Palm Beach in May 1943. They had revisited the States the previous year but a crowded schedule had kept them away from the resort; now they returned with relish for another round of sun-dappled parties among the people they liked best, the super-rich. Once again Jessie, Jimmy (on self-proclaimed furlough) and Wooly played host at Cielito Lindo, creating a party for one hundred at the sumptuous beach-house which was reached by an underground tunnel running under South Ocean Boulevard. The Windsors went on to stay nearby at the house of the financier Robert R. Young; on their return to Nassau they read in the newspapers that Win Spencer, Wallis's first husband, had been found bleeding on the porch of his house in San Diego, California, a knife protruding from his chest. He announced he had been 'peeling fruit' but the Duchess's biographer Charles Higham takes the view that it was probably a botched suicide attempt.

Jimmy was nervous about joining up. The army's attitude towards admitting homosexuals was hardly encouraging: a list of proscribed professions included dancers, window-dressers and interior decorators, and among the questions new recruits were expected to answer was 'How do you get along with girls?' To say that the army's knowledge and understanding of homosexuality was rudimentary at this time would be a colossal understatement. By the end of the Second World War around twenty million Americans had joined the armed services, but despite the huge numbers of gays who slid around the army's 'positive' vetting and were clearly playing a vital role in the prosecution of the war, the official attitude was still one of fearful disapproval. Homosexuality was viewed as a mental illness, one which in time might be 'cured'.

Worse than all this were the horror stories which came back to the gay bars in New York of the atrocities endured during basic training by members of the fraternity, and this was what concerned Jimmy most. At boot camp, no amount of money would alter his status as a private soldier and the prospect of being beaten up, and far worse, appalled him. It was no surprise that as the war dragged on he continued to avoid joining up for as long as he could.

Finally, the game was up. For some time the army's powers-that-be had had their eye on Jimmy – his resistance, in their view, a cross between cowardice and the abuse of privilege – and were determined for whatever reason to make an example of him. He had been discharged from the USAAF reserve list in May 1944, thereby making him open to conscription. By June he was facing an induction board in New York which passed him 1-A fit for service. Colonel Arthur McDermott, the New York City Service Director, was more than happy to expatiate on Jimmy's case to the press. An appeal, based on Jimmy's alleged development of the Florida airfield being essential to the war effort, was firmly and swiftly rejected. By November it became clear there was no further escape and the chairman of the Local Board 31, based conveniently close to 834 at Delmonico's on Park and 59th, happily reported that Jimmy would be inducted into the army on Friday 10 November.

Among the small number of draftees due to appear that morning was Gene Kelly, the actor and dancer, who was already a star with such films as *For Me and My Gal, Thousands Cheer, Dubarry Was a Lady* and *The Cross of Lorraine.* Kelly, it might be argued, was a far bigger fish than Jimmy, yet there was something about the way Jimmy had so skilfully resisted the draft for so long that irked the serving soldiers. Captain Waldemar Grassi, the Local Board chairman, was more than ready to tell the waiting press where, and at what time, Jimmy would meet his nemesis. It was a strong message from the Army that no one, rich or poor, was above serving his country.

Even so, the event did not go off without a last-minute struggle from a by now deeply traumatised Jimmy, who asked that his Selective Service records be transferred to Florida, in the hope of a further delay and perhaps a more sympathetic hearing from those who knew his work in the CAP and, maybe, had been to dine at Cielito Lindo. He lingered in Palm Beach, afraid and unable to make the journey to New York.

'In our opinion,' thundered the Board in advance of his Friday date, 'the return of James Paul Donahue from Florida for induction in New York would entail no extreme hardship' and, acknowledging at last there was no escape, Jimmy flew in to the city on the Thursday afternoon. He spent the night at 21 and El Morocco and did not go to bed. He arrived at Delmonico's, a five-minute walk from 834, shaven but too casually dressed in sports coat and turtle-neck sweater, and posed uneasily for photographers outside the Local Board offices.

There was worse to come before the day was through. He was appointed temporary corporal of the group of five other inductees and was ordered to march them the mile or so to the main induction centre at 460 Lexington Avenue, accompanied by press reporters and photographers and a baying crowd who sensed the significance of the occasion even if they were unaware of the identity of the principal player involved. The *New York Times* reported: 'Hundreds of persons along Park Avenue watched the procession, accompanied by newspaper photographers, but there were none of Mr Donahue's café society friends in the crowd apparently. He said it was too early for them to be up.'

This quip masked a deep foreboding. Jimmy and the other inductees entrained for Fort Dix, the boot camp in New Jersey, and his training as a private soldier began. On the radios a favourite Irving Berlin tune was being constantly played, sung by Judy Garland. It might have been written for Jimmy:

> This is the army Mr Jones
> No private rooms or telephones
> You've had your breakfast in bed before
> But you can't have it there any more.

CHAPTER 7

LIBERATION

Towards Christmas 1944 rumours started to circulate about Jimmy in New York and in Palm Beach, rumours which were to swirl about him for the rest of his life and to cloud his memory long after his death. Later the scandal-magazine *Confidential* got hold of the story and the legend spread like wildfire.

That Jimmy had become involved in rough sex, and was by now mixing with rent boys and lowlife queers, could not be denied. Army life had coarsened him and, to an extent, he took revenge for his brutal military indoctrination on boys who could be ill-treated, then paid off. Sexually he had moved permanently outside his social circle, never to return.

The scandal erupted after Jimmy took his first home leave, nine weeks after joining up. Returned to the warmth and elegance of 834 Fifth Avenue after the raw experience of a bitterly cold Fort Dix, he took a bath, changed into civilian clothes, and prepared for an evening cruising New York's gay bars.

Soon he was in Cerutti's, on Madison and 59th Street. Truman Capote[1] recalled the event thus: 'Cerutti's was a wonderful place. It was in two different rooms. The first room was all servicemen, and the second room had a marvellous pianist named Garland Wilson. It was there that Jimmy picked up this soldier. I was there on that night. Jimmy was giving a party at his mother's apartment on Fifth Avenue and he came into Cerutti's with Fulco di Verdura, the jewellery designer, and they made a dragnet of the bar. They picked up all these servicemen. They had a fleet of taxis waiting outside. They got them all into the taxis and took them back to the party. One of the servicemen passed out in the middle of the party. They put him on a couch and took off his pants and then got out the shaving cream and a sharp razor and they were shaving off his pubic hair.

'They thought it was hilarious. They were all drunk and stoned. He came to in the middle of it and someone accidentally cut off his prick. Anyway, they said it was an accident. What then happened was that there was a great panic and they wrapped this guy up in a blanket and put him in Jimmy's car and dumped him somewhere on the 59th Street bridge. When the police found him he was in shock. They got him to the hospital and managed to save his life. All he could remember a few days later was the name Cerutti's. The police went there. The bartender said yes, the guy had been there with Mr Donahue. Fulco and Jimmy got into a lot of trouble over this. But Fulco had nothing to do with it. As I understand it, it was all Jimmy Donahue.'

This became the accepted version of events, and since neither Jimmy nor the victim ever bothered to deny them, the story

1 Quoted in David Heymann's *Poor Little Rich Girl*.

became carved in stone, adding in later years to Jimmy's carapace of dangerous allure.

But Capote, not for the first time, had elaborated events; the
truth was less gory. The evening did, indeed, start at Cerutti's
and a group of men, led by Jimmy and Fulco di Verdura – a
Sicilian duke and jewellery designer – together with an Argen-
tinean, Francisco Murature, went back to di Verdura's apartment at 156 East 56th Street. The victim, George Henry
Williams, was not a sailor or soldier but a thirty-two-year-old
salesman who lived on the East side and was unknown to his
assailants. During the party which followed, Williams became
drunk to the point where he passed out, whereupon Jimmy
and Murature proceeded to strip his off clothes and shave his
head, chest and pubic region. At some point during the horse-
play, probably while sex was taking place, part of Williams'
left ear was bitten off.

Jimmy, assisted by the others, then dressed Williams, putting
on his trousers back-to-front, took him out of the apartment
and shoved him in Jimmy's car. It was one-thirty in the morning
and rather than dump their hapless victim back near his home
– he lived five blocks away – they careered off over the bridge
to Long Island City, fifteen minutes' drive away. At the junction
of 43rd Avenue and 23rd Street the car drew up and Williams,
minus hat, coat, shoes and socks, was tossed into the gutter.
The temperature was below freezing and Williams was only
semi-conscious. He was found twenty minutes later by a passing patrolman and driven to St John's Hospital, where he was
treated for concussion sustained during his fall from the car,
for his injured ear, and for multiple abrasions caused by the
shaving.

Williams gave scant details of the assault while in recovery,
and next day feigned amnesia. Nonetheless a police investigation was initiated which led eventually to Jimmy and one

other man being arrested. It took three months for them to be hauled before assistant District Attorney Jim Clark, head of the city's complaints bureau. Clark had the authority to curtail the inquiry, but disliked intensely what he heard from Jimmy, and sent the matter to the Second New York County Grand Jury.

During this time, Jessie had not been idle. The whereabouts of the unfortunate Williams had been discovered, and he was informally interviewed by her representatives. A sum of $200,000 ($1.8m) was deemed sufficient to buy him a new set of clothes and a hat big enough to disguise the mutilated ear, and thus his silence was bought. When it came time for the grand jury to deliberate, they chose to throw the charges out. 'Williams lived off that money for the rest of his life,' said someone who saw him occasionally in later years. 'He was pretty much low-life, but he didn't at all mind the fact that people thought he'd been castrated. That, and the money everybody knew he'd been paid by Jessie, gave him a certain cachet. Without it, he was a nobody.'

Apart from the belated feature in *Confidential*, the whole incident went largely unreported in the press. It was claimed that Jessie threatened to sue anyone for libel who wrote about her son in connection with Williams' rape. However, others believe that the manner in which she silenced Williams was liberally employed elsewhere, both in the police department and the press. Jessie had learned, from the theft of her jewellery all those years ago, that the Woolworth millions could be put to good use in sustaining the family reputation.

Whatever the view of the grand jury, the army – notwithstanding its ignorance of the details of the case – decided they had had enough of Private Donahue and shortly after the jury's deliberations to Judge Owen Bohan in April 1945, they decided it was time for him to go.

While Private Donahue was making his ignominious exit from the US Army and preparing to scuttle for cover, former Field Marshal the Duke of Windsor and his lady embarked on the peripatetic career which would cause them to become known as the Wandering Windsors. They all had something they wanted to escape from.

The Windsors had visited Palm Beach again in August 1944, reinforcing in their minds that this was a place where they could happily be left alone. They stayed with their friend Robert Young, and dined at Cielito Lindo with Jessie, Jimmy and Wooly. Frustrated and out of steam, the Duke now tendered an early resignation as Governor of the Bahamas and, after King George VI had formally signed off his brother's release, the Duke and Duchess of Windsor set sail for the last time from Nassau for the American mainland.

Because of his too-close involvement in the botched investigation into the murder of a prominent British businessman, the baronet Sir Harry Oakes; because of his financial involvement with the Nazi sympathiser Axel Wenner-Gren; and because of his forceful suppression of bloody food riots, the Nassau episode is usually written as the Duke's epitaph insofar as public service is concerned. A more balanced approach would be that, by encouraging outside investment and acknowledging the rights of the native population, he set in train a movement which turned the Bahamas into the successful archipelago it is today. But that is an unfashionable view, and when the Windsors left Nassau five months short of their five-year term it was under a cloud. 'His Second Abdication' was a typical headline in the mainland newspapers.

The Duchess, who had suffered stomach pains for most of the Nassau period, was admitted to the Roosevelt Hospital in New York and was operated on for cancer. The operation was a success, and by the middle of September she was ready to begin a lengthy convalescence at the Waldorf-Astoria. Their tour of duty complete, the couple returned to New York in the spring of 1945. Jessie welcomed her royal friends at 834 Fifth Avenue, but her charming, harum-scarum son, recently discharged from service, was absent – ordered to stay as far away as possible from these crucial guests. Barbara Hutton had, during the war, established a house in Mexico, and Jimmy was sent down there to stay out of harm's way.

Meanwhile the Duchess made a gracious visit to the headquarters of the Salvation Army decked out in sables and wearing pearls, a diamond clip, and aquamarine and sapphire earrings; a combination that even glittering Jessie Donahue would have found hard to upstage. The hard-bitten columnist Walter Winchell took exception; and when finally the Windsors quit New York in September, embarking on the United States troop-ship *Argentina* for their home in France, he pulled no punches. Calling them 'the Dook and Dookess' he bade them farewell: 'Good riddance to them both – the snobs.' It was not the last they were to hear from Mr Winchell.

Jimmy stayed away from Palm Beach and his mother for a time. From Barbara's home in Mexico he flew back to New York. With the war at an end things were changing fast. He went to see his old friend Libby Holman at Treetops, her estate in Connecticut, but by this stage in her life she had developed an ulcer which did not fit well with her heavy drinking. Slowly friends began to fade away under the onslaught of her increasingly vicious tongue; on one occasion she went to visit her oldest friend Clifton Webb. As the evening wore on and Libby became drunk, she sat and listened as Webb, not for the first time, maundered about how his mother Mabelle had abused him as a child, and how she pried into his life and meddled with his affairs. 'Cliftuary, Mabelle's *ruined* your life,' was her response. 'Why don't you chloroform the old cunt?' Of her husband Ralph Holmes she rasped, 'Poor Rafe, poor Rafe. He's got the biggest cock in Connecticut, but no ass to push it with.' With similar abandon, she elbowed Jimmy out of her life.

There was always about Jimmy a jaunty, jolly air, no matter the emptiness within. On VJ Day he walked down Fifth Avenue, tossing off his clothes as he went, until he was naked. A few days later in the St Regis Hotel at luncheon, he once again started to denude himself. The waiters brought screens and, having surrounded him, permitted him to continue. On another occasion, having paid a visit to a butcher's shop, he walked down Fifth Avenue with a cow's udder protruding from his flies. When halted by a policeman, he took out a pair of scissors and snipped it off while, according to an eyewitness, ladies of gentle birth fainted dead away at the sight.

The Guinness heiress, Aileen Plunket, whose more famous sisters were Maureen, Marchioness of Dufferin and Ava and Oonagh, Lady Oranmore and Browne, recalled: 'Jimmy would be dining at some madly grand dinner in New York. It would be black tie, tiaras for the ladies, chandeliers, all that sort of thing. Jimmy would suddenly take his plate off the table and put it on his knee. Then he'd unbutton himself and pull out his cock. You couldn't believe it. He'd lay it out on top of all his food so that you could see it lying in his potatoes and his gravy and his sauces looking like some pink sausage. And then he didn't stop there. He'd start waving to the butler who naturally looked as though he were about to faint. He'd hand the wretched man a knife and fork and say he wanted his meat sliced very fine! Jimmy could be outrageous but I have to admit the horrified expressions on the faces of the people he wanted to shock used to be quite funny and enjoyable to see.'

But there were darker moments, too. The author Charles Higham quotes an informant who claimed that Jimmy and a friend cornered a waiter at the Waldorf Towers and tried to rape him. When the man resisted their advances, they castrated him. Given the fuss over the earlier incident which did *not* end in castration, this seems an unlikely conclusion to what was otherwise indubitably an accurate story. According to the Duchess's biographer Stephen Birmingham, when a male prostitute failed to satisfy Jimmy's requirements he was made to eat an excrement sandwich. Another male prostitute, called round to 834 to provide his services, chose not to go but instead sent his room-mate who, being fat rather than the muscular specimen Jimmy was anticipating, drew a howl of rage. As soon as he had taken his clothes off they were seized by Jimmy, who then called in his valet and ordered the man to be put out in the street, naked.

The socialite and photographer Jerome Zerbe took a fundamental dislike to him and was not afraid to say so. In the early hours of one morning he received a call from a woman called Toni Johnson who said she was at 834 with Jimmy, and Jimmy was complaining that Zerbe didn't like him; would he not come over for a glass of champagne and try to patch things up? Zerbe arrived, and Jimmy repeated the question, 'Why don't you like me?' The photographer replied, 'It's not that I dislike you. But I disapprove of you. I don't like the public spectacle you make of yourself – it's not fair to your nice mother. Nobody gives a fig what you do in your private life, but when you make a public display of it, it's disgusting.' Jimmy listened to this lecture with contrition and promised that he would try to become a better person. He escorted Zerbe to the lift. When it arrived and the door was opened by a handsome young elevator boy, Jimmy cried out, 'Oh, he's *gorgeous!*' and fell to his knees to kiss the startled young man's crotch.

A friend from that time says: 'He got away with it because he possessed great charm. He could burn your house down and turn it into a joke. You'd get so damn mad at him and then you'd forgive him – he would act like a little tiny boy.' Another friend said, 'He was a mischievous imp. But he was very kind in many ways.'

In New York he was eager to remind one and all of his presence, he turned his attentions to the figure of Sam Lurie, a not entirely wholesome character who fed the gossip columns stories which were sometimes right and sometimes wrong. Lurie was a self-important fellow, who once got knocked down by a young man in a lavatory for speaking to him while they were both in the stalls. As he lay on his back on the bathroom floor, Lurie squealed, 'You know, *this will ruin you socially*' – a phrase which reverberated round New York's smarter bars accompanied by much hilarity.

Jimmy had taken against Lurie for some slight, real or imagined, and decided to test his honesty. With a friend he cornered Lurie and mentioned, a complete fabrication, that his cousin Barbara intended to return from France and establish a nightclub in New York, the like of which would be unequalled the world over. Having passed on his exclusive 'story' to a tabloid newspaper, Lurie took off for California.

'Jimmy was remarkable,' recalls the friend who was involved. 'He could imitate anyone's voice having listened to them for a few minutes only. He called up the superintendent of Lurie's building on 39th and Lexington and said, 'This is Mr Lurie, I'll be detained in California for business reasons for some months. I have arranged for my furniture to be put in storage.' Jimmy called the Mayflower moving company and emptied the apartment. Then he set about relinquishing the lease. When Lurie came back a fortnight later, there was no furniture and no apartment.'

By now, Jimmy had tried his hand at two careers, theatre production and piloting, and both had fallen apart through no fault of his own. Unlike his father, mother, cousin and brother

Jimmy had made his attempts to break out of the money-trap and forge a career. If Jessie had not snapped her purse shut, it is likely that *Transatlantic Rhythm* would have made a successful transfer to Broadway[1] and Jimmy may, indeed, have seen himself stepping into Flo Ziegfeld's shoes. If it had not been for Jessie's abrogation of parental responsibility in the matter of his schooling, he would have been accepted as a commissioned officer and, instead of an ignominious discharge, would have served a useful war role as a pilot. If, if . . .

Now, at thirty-three, he chose to abandon himself to a life of unabated hedonism. He had created a character for himself, that of a mad prankster, and he set out upon a career of making mischief. He abandoned his accomplishments – one friend recalls: 'he could speak French and Italian beautifully, but he refused to do so. And after the war was over, he lost all interest in flying' – and settled down to a life of mayhem, rising late each day and living through the night. Whatever resentment and anger he felt for the way he had been thwarted and emasculated by events, he never shared his thoughts. He turned away sympathetic and indulgent comments with a joke and a laugh and never spoke of his disappointments.

The money continued to trickle down to him from Jessie, derived from her vast income from her Woolworth stock and other investments, but it was now clear that Jimmy would never get his own capital. The author Philip van Rensselaer remembers Jimmy bewailing this state to his cousin Barbara Hutton: 'She gave him a million dollars, just like that.'

Jimmy remained her one true confidante, even though they had barely seen each other since her marriage to Cary Grant.

---

1 After his departure *Transatlantic Rhythm* had a successful West End run and turned in a profit.

Now that, too, was crumbling and she sought a quick end to it by a Mexican divorce. But Jimmy, by now well-versed in the ways of that country, advised her that Mexican divorces were not recognised in many states and persuaded her to change her mind. Instead they trooped up to the courthouse in downtown Los Angeles and disposed of three years' marital commitment in as many minutes. She and Jimmy toasted each other in champagne and Seconal, shook the dust of California from their feet and headed back to New York: three husbands down, several yet to go.

Both were restless, both longed for the travel and the taste of Europe which had been denied them so long during the war years. Both decided to go to Paris, Barbara flying from La Guardia, Jimmy travelling by the *Queen Mary*.

Of all the capital cities in the world, Paris after the Liberation was the place to be. Freed from the shackles of occupation, a devil-may-care attitude overtook its elegant boulevards which had remained almost unblemished by conflict. Paris had declared itself alive and well and the city filled with British and American writers, soldiers, diplomats, artists and eccentrics. Gradually there returned plentiful supplies of food and wine, and drugs – Britain's ambassadress Lady Diana Cooper later confessed that if she felt a diplomatic reception was likely to prove sticky, she laced the cocktails with Benzedrine – and a party atmosphere prevailed.

At Ciro's, Charles Trenet and Edith Piaf took it in turn to sing, and the grander restaurants – Prunier, and the Méditerranée in the Place de l'Odéon – were soon serving fresh seafood. Having bricked up their wine cellars just as the Germans marched into Paris, Louis Carton in the Place de la Madeleine were now able to offer fine vintages once again. The nightclubs, including Monseigneur in the Rue d'Amsterdam, an ornate and expensive establishment with Russian violinists serenading the clientele, started to re-open. Paris was vibrant from the artistic talent which flooded back to its boulevards: Picasso staged an exhibition of his work painted, then stored, through the war years. Truman Capote and Arthur Miller shared the same hotel in the Rue du Bac where Jean Paul Sartre and Simone de Beauvoir drank in the basement; Camus and Colette and Gertrude Stein and James Baldwin all met and mixed, though needless to say, their world was very far removed from the bejewelled existence of the Rue Faubourg St Honoré and the Place Vendôme. It was especially true of the young Gabriel García Márquez, who sipped the champagne air of the capital city but drank *vin ordinaire* and shivered in his unheated garret, far removed from the tropical warmth of his South American homeland.

Oblivious to this thrilling artistic wave, the Windsors arrived back to find their house at 24 Boulevard Suchet untouched and set about re-establishing their pre-war routine. But though the Duchess courted the city's approbation by stating that she hoped to join a relief organisation helping war victims, the couple continued to be dogged by the same bad press they had left behind in New York. Paris possessed no Walter Winchell, but reporters duly counted the 134 pieces of luggage unloaded on to the platform at the Gare du Nord. Later the Duchess was heard to remark that Paris now offered the most expensive discomfort she had ever known.

Before the war, the choice of this city as his residence by the world's most glamorous ex-King had flattered the French. Now, with all that had happened in the intervening years, the Windsors' presence was not so compelling. Some argued, snobbishly, that the Windsors were *déclassé* and no longer welcome in the city's leading salons. Certainly they were not embraced by the official British presence there; arguing that the Duke would be better off in America, Duff Cooper, the ambassador, wrote to King George VI's private secretary Sir Alan Lascelles: 'He can do no good in this country. Neither of them have ever liked the French or will ever begin to understand them.' The frustration which had seized the couple from the very moment of their exile nearly a decade before now bubbled to the surface, and the Duchess cornered Cooper's military attaché Brigadier Denis Daly with the rebuke that the Duke had been treated disgracefully by the ambassador. Daly was inclined to see her point.

'At fifty,' wrote Jacques Dumaine, 'the Duke remains the royal Peter Pan ... his wizened jockey's face, his fair hair and his debonair appearance contribute towards his persistent youthfulness and make one understand the note of novelettish sentimentality in his abdication.' The *New Yorker* diarist Janet Flanner commented that the lines on his face were the result of too much sun, and not too much thought.

No sooner, it seemed, than they had arrived in Paris than they were packing their bags again – 155 of them this time – and heading back to New York. They had been warned by the owner of their house in the Boulevard Suchet that she intended to sell the property, but the Windsors were in no hurry to vacate: their American visit was to last nearly five months, during which time they made no attempt to have the house packed up.

Jessie's friends and neighbours in Palm Beach, Robert and Anita Young, were at the dockside at Pier 90 to greet the royal couple and for the last two months of 1946 and the first two of 1947 they pursued a sybaritic path, dining and visiting, posing for photographs, ordering clothes and jewellery and linen. Relieved of the care of duty, jobless and directionless, the Duke wavered between a yearning to serve his country and the greater desire to serve his wife. They set up home at the Waldorf Towers, a serviced apartment block attached to the hotel and one of Manhattan's smartest addresses, and decorated the place with royal portraits and other memorabilia. They visited 834 Fifth Avenue for luncheon, and dined with Jessie at the Colony.

According to the Duchess's biographer Charles Higham, it was at this point that she met Guido Orlando, a publicist, and confessed that the Duke was worried that in the microscopic dissection of the war which was now taking place, the Duke's visits to Germany in 1937 might be perceived as pro-Hitler. Then, he had visited a beer hall, drunk three pints of beer, put on a false moustache, joined in a sing-song and made an impromptu speech saying how much he loved Munich. What may have started out in all innocence as a vain attempt to create some status for himself, post-Abdication, as the defender of the common man, came crashing about his ears as he was roundly condemned by the Press in Britain and America for his unquestioning espousal of the Nazi cause. His official biographer Philip Ziegler refers to an interview given at this time to a *Daily Herald* reporter which, in the end, was suppressed, but in which he stated 'if the Labour party wished, and were in a position to offer it, he would be prepared to be President of the English Republic'.

Now, a group including Lord Hardinge of Penshurst – who had been his private secretary when he was king in 1936, but who had transferred his affections, like so many others, to the new king upon Windsor's abdication – had convinced itself that, had Hitler managed to get access to the Duke during the early stages of the war, he would have been happy to become a puppet head of State in the event of a successful invasion of Britain. Orlando came up with a 'patriotic' scheme to counter any suspicions which may have been held against him. A party would be held at Delmonico's Hotel for a hundred Purple Heart veterans, and the Windsors would grace it with their presence.

Photographs would be taken and, at the end, the veterans would present Wallis with bouquets and notes of thanks (the bouquets to be paid for by the Windsors). The party was a success, except for the moment when the official hostess, Mrs Sailing Baruch, was confronted by Jimmy who teased: 'I understand the Duke likes you very much. He always did have a weakness for sailors!'

This visit was designed to establish in the eyes of the world that the Windsors belonged to no one country, and owed nothing to anyone. While the first part may have been true, the second was less so: many New York traders who dealt with them came to regret the bills they failed to settle. Nor were they immune from occasional finger-pointing. One columnist noted with relish the Duke sitting in El Morocco, with his ex-mistress Thelma Furness placed just a few tables away, trying desperately hard not to notice her. The Windsors spent March in Florida, at Palm Beach and elsewhere, and returned to Manhattan to formally open the New York Book Week. Jimmy also attended, the irony being that these three had probably read fewer books between them than any individual attending the event: the Duke once proclaiming happily: 'I'm not much of a reading man'. They set sail in May for France (only eighty-five bags this time).

In June 1947 the Duke and Duchess celebrated their tenth wedding anniversary. 'Ten years have passed, but not the romance,' proclaimed the Duke, beaming at his wife. 'It's gone on and on.' Certainly, it had been a roller-coaster ride, blessed by the fact that there had been little time in that decade for the couple to stop and examine their relationship. The Windsors stood together, *contra mundum* – that was the force that bound them together; that, and the Duke's obsessive love for his wife. But by now the Duchess was an oppressed woman – sidelined by the royal machine, hemmed in by her husband, separated from her blood family. She smiled, she waved; but her existence was daily becoming emptier. The chilly void of the future faced her, a future unchanged by improved fortune or romantic fulfilment.

In Paris, Barbara and Jimmy both put up at the Ritz Hotel, whose other occupants included Ernest Hemingway and Marlene Dietrich. With the war over the place was full to bursting, with a six-month waiting-list of the rich and not-so-rich. The franc was devalued and the dollar now went a very long way. Barbara occupied a second-story suite overlooking the Place Vendôme, Jimmy a smaller set of rooms which she paid for.

A particularly favourite haunt was Le Boeuf Sur Le Toit, 'the city's number one chic queer nightclub', according to one who visited regularly. 'At one time there was a lady fortune-teller out the back and one night Jimmy, totally in drag, sat down and consulted her. She didn't get it that he was a man – so he got up on the table, pulled up his skirts and showed his private parts. She saw then, all right.'

Soon Barbara took up with a young man of Lithuanian origin and no particular profession called Igor Troubetzkoy who claimed the title of Prince, which by no means diminished his appeal in her eyes; they went for a holiday in St Moritz, and by the time they returned to Paris they were married. Once again, Jimmy was playing court jester to his older, richer, better-known cousin. The press were out in force to cover the return of the newlyweds; just as they had been eager to record the scene when, wearing tennis shorts, bobby-socks and penny loafers, Barbara returned to the Ritz only to be turned away by the doorman eager to greet the arriving King of Cambodia. Announcing she had the same rights as any king, she pushed through the entrance doors. According to one account she was photographed being escorted away by an 'astonishing' number of police. The international press loved Barbara; they knew little and cared less about her cousin and Woolworth co-legatee.

Jimmy was present when Barbara publicly celebrated her fourth marriage a few weeks later at the Ritz. This was an opportunity once again to meet the Duke and Duchess, and he pressed Barbara to invite them. Dutifully, they came, along with the despised ambassador Duff Cooper and his wife Lady Diana; and Randolph Churchill, son of the recently-ousted Prime Minister. By now, though they had only met maybe half-a-dozen times, there was an intimacy and understanding between Jimmy and the Duke and Duchess. In a foreign land, where they felt unwanted and overlooked, the Windsors saw in Jimmy an envoy from a lovelier place, Palm Beach, where all doors opened, all women curtsied, and the sun always shone.

Soon after, Barbara became unwell and was operated on to alleviate an acute inflammation of the kidneys at the Salem Hospital in Bern, Switzerland. Another operation followed in which an ovarian tumour was removed. Jessie, who had taken a house in Newport, considered the matter serious enough to curtail her summer on Rhode Island and, wiring Jimmy, informed him of her intention to sail for France. Le Havre, where her ship docked, was conveniently close to Deauville and she spent some days in the rejuvenating surroundings of the resort's casino before heading south with her son to comfort her niece.

It was a long way for an aunt to come, but Jessie had long ago shouldered responsibility for Barbara in times of trouble. Even so, Jessie's version of comfort fell far short of the maternal. 'She was a very distant person,' recalled Dorothy Strelsin, who used to dine with her in New York and gamble with her in Monte Carlo. 'She was a pleasant person, but austere in many ways – there was no exuberance.' Barbara's husband, soon to be discarded like all the rest, talked of the lack of maternal affection in her life: 'She was haunted by a feeling of longing. The longing, though I doubt she knew it, was for a mother, any mother, to do the things for her she knew mothers did. Barbara was moulded by her affectionless, insecure childhood.' Prince Igor could have been talking of Jimmy.

Later Barbara was diagnosed by a psychiatrist, Dr Gerhart Freilinger, as suffering from anorexia nervosa. The doctor drew the conclusion that with one parent a suicide and the other often absent, she had been ignored as a child, and her refusal to eat was a way of drawing attention to herself. Jimmy, raised in exactly the same circumstances, chose to do it a different way, with mischief, and with sex. It was too late to unprogramme the mischief and even though, that spring, Dr Alfred Kinsey produced his *Sexual Behaviour In the Human Male* which claimed that 37 per cent of US males had had some homosexual experience, thereby creating a new train of thought about the legitimacy of sexual freedom, it was too late for Jimmy. He had chosen a dangerous path but now sauntered down it without a backward glance.

Having summered in Paris and at their old house on the Côte d'Azur, la Croe, the Windsors sailed west again that autumn, pausing briefly to be interviewed at Southampton by over fifty radio, newsreel and newspaper reporters on the forthcoming nuptials of Princess Elizabeth and Lieutenant Philip Mountbattten. Inwardly coldly furious that they were not to be among the 2,200 invited guests, they merely mouthed platitudes and headed onwards for New York. Later they were to hear a most curious story concerning the lieutenant in the days leading up to the royal marriage. It was said that he had been invited, without really knowing her, to spend the weekend in Cornwall with the novelist Daphne du Maurier. He had arrived at the local railway station and as their eyes met down the length of the platform, an instant understanding arose between them. They spent the next two days alone but when it was time for the navy officer to return to London he told Miss du Maurier that he did not want to go; that he wanted to stay; that he would never leave her. She pointed out that in the first place she was married, in the second she was fourteen years older, and last, that he had a national duty to perform by returning to London and marrying the future Queen. Meekly, the sailor accepted his orders, put on his clothes, and left.

Whatever the veracity of this story, it caused the Windsors to experience not a little *schadenfreude* as once again they settled into an exhausting round of socialising. They were fed up with the smugness of Buckingham Palace, and its iron determination that the Duke should have no further place in public life. The best he had been offered as a follow-up to his tour in the Bahamas was something in Southern Rhodesia, an offer which he instantly dismissed as frivolous.

They spent a month cruising the Caribbean with Joe Davis, the former US Ambassador to Russia who was married to Jessie's kinswoman Marjorie Merriweather Post. Clearly this seal of royal approval had gone to Davis's head for when, the cruise over, he headed his yacht *Sea Cloud* towards Newport he found himself greeted with hoots of derision. As he stepped ashore and headed towards Jessie's rented home where Jimmy was also staying, the ambassadorial flag which normally adorned the nation's missions abroad was seen to be flapping from his mast. It was clear, said communophobe Newporters, that the man had had his mind bent while serving behind the Iron Curtain, and no longer knew whether he was in an embassy or a tub. What they meant was that Davies had caught what people around Buckingham Palace call 'red-carpet fever'. Not *everybody* adored the Windsors.

By mid-1949 another Paris house had been found for the

couple and they moved to 85 Rue de la Faisanderie. The wedding of Princess Elizabeth and Lieutenant Mountbatten came and went without the presence of the bride's uncle and aunt, a slight which the British press did not hesitate to exploit; and the momentous decade, which had started in conflict and ended in privation for all but a fortunate few, drew to its close.

CHAPTER 8

LOCKED IN A TRANCE

No particular attention was paid to the departure of the RMS *Queen Mary* on 24 May 1950 as it slipped its moorings at Pier 90 on New York's East Side and headed down the Hudson River, out past the Statue of Liberty towards the Atlantic Ocean. Of its 1,754 passengers there were few to excite the interest of the dockside reporters. They had seen the Duke and Duchess of Windsor too many times; there was no other celebrity of note aboard. Having scoured the first-class passenger list they had found nothing more than a smattering of well-heeled manufacturers and City men with addresses in Belgravia and the deeper reaches of the British Home Counties. Most travelled with their wives, some with their mistresses, a few with their valets. A J. P. Donahue appeared among the fourteen first-class passengers travelling with a valet, but his name raised no special interest.

For the Windsors, the *Queen Mary* was one link with a kingly past that no one could take away. Named after the

Duke's mother, the Cunarder made her maiden voyage in those fleeting few months when David was King. He had taken a childlike interest in the liner's construction and had been on a stem-to-stern inspection of the ship which had taken all day. To the Windsors it was 'their' ship, and the Cunard line were happy to concur with this particular fantasy. Each time they sailed in her, the large outboard suites assigned to the royal couple were repainted, re-hung with new curtains, re-laid with new carpet. At sea the Duchess favoured a shade of grey in which no other suite was allowed to be decorated; flowers specially chosen by the ship's gardener, Davis, were changed daily, the bed linen twice daily.

The Duke loved seaboard life: its bell-ringing luxury, the panoply of his surroundings, the pleasant mental torpor it induced and the sense of removal from everyday concerns. He made a particular friend of the *Queen Mary*'s captain, Commodore Harry Grattidge, and took pleasure in being lured onto the bridge and into the engine room. The Duchess cared for none of these boyish attractions, though as far as is possible the *Queen Mary* was the marine embodiment of her personality and spirit and appearance; an Art Deco masterpiece, a spectacular palace where dreams were born among the ebony, jacaranda, zebra wood and calamander-lined rooms, in the shadows of its bars, in the hidden corners of its decks, and on its dance-floors late at night.

It was here, on the high seas, that the Duchess of Windsor fell in love with Jimmy Donahue. He was thirty-four and she was fifty-four.

'Make no mistake, it was Wallis who made the running,' says one of the Windsors' intimates. 'Jimmy cannot have anticipated what was going to happen, much less manoeuvre himself into the position where he, a homosexual, was going to make a play for a woman. Heaven knows what drove the Duchess to

153

do it – anger, frustration, boredom with her lot in life? The onset of the menopause? No one has adequately explained it – but it happened on board ship, on the way from New York to Cherbourg. When they got on board they were friends. By the time they disembarked, they were lovers.'

The cars at Cherbourg took them in convoy, but separately, to Paris. The Windsors in their Rolls Royce to the Rue de la Faisanderie, Jimmy in his black Cadillac to the Ritz in the Place Vendôme. Within minutes the lovers were on the telephone to each other, whispering, conspiring. A couple of days later the Windsors and Donahues arrived together at the first big ball of the Paris season at the Hotel Lambert on the Ile St Louis. Barbara Hutton, wearing an enormous emerald necklace, was accompanied by Prince Igor Troubetzkoy and among the other guests were Henry Ford, Cecil Beaton, Lady Diana Cooper, the Duc and Duchesse de Brissac, Margaret Biddle and the Baron de Cabrol. 'The setting was absolutely beautiful,' recalls one guest. 'The main hall, where the orchestras were, was decked out in antique red velvet. On the higher surrounding floors were the boxes, occupied by the chosen few – the Windsors and Donahues among them. There was a beautiful garden, buffets with magnificent food, and champagne flowing like water, and on the top floor there was a night club which stayed open till 8 a.m.' The Duke left at midnight. Two of the last guests to leave, it was noted, were Jimmy and the Duchess.

A week later Barbara returned the compliment, hosting her own ball at the Cercle Interallié with 500 guests and the hostess appearing in a pink Indian sari and the famous Hutton ruby necklace, each stone the size of a large grape. Once again the Duke retired early, his wife and escort staying until dawn rose on the City of Light.

In the beginning, the Duke was almost as taken with Jimmy as Wallis was. Jimmy's jokes, his risqué anecdotes and his eagerness to pay a restaurant bill were new, fresh, deliciously acceptable to both Duke and Duchess. Her biographer Stephen Birmingham observed: 'With each successive rebuff from Downing Street and Buckingham Palace, the Duke had become gloomier and harder to divert, and trying to penetrate his sadnesses and dark moods had become increasingly difficult. With Jimmy Donahue it was just the opposite . . . he even helped her by sharing the burden of cheering up the Duke. Then there was the Duke's tightfistedness, which over the years became a considerable cross for his wife to bear. When the bill arrived at a restaurant when they were entertaining guests for dinner, it was often downright embarrassing to watch the Duke gazing balefully at it, fingering its corners suspiciously, then pushing it away from him just slightly, obviously in the hope that it would go away or someone else would pick it up. With Jimmy Donahue in tow, there was *no* such problem, it was *always* his treat.'

There was a madness about Jimmy and Wallis in the early stages of the relationship. The staff in Barbara Hutton's suite, observing with fascination the state of the bed linen, took note of what was described as 'activity' in Jimmy's room. At the Rue de la Faisanderie, Jimmy would leave evidence of his nocturnal play with the Duchess. He would dip his fingers in the icing of a cake and scrawl on the kitchen mirror: 'Dear Chef, we love you.' Soon they were to be seen *à deux* at all the fashionable night clubs.

Very quickly the press picked up on this new friendship, though with Jimmy's extravagant mannerisms it was quite clear he was gay, so little more was thought of it. Still, as one columnist observed: 'Jimmy escorts the D and D everywhere and stays up playing cards with the Duchess long after the Duke has retired.'

The writer Charles Murphy, engaged to ghost the Duke's memoirs, *A King's Story*, was in Paris at the time and noted later: 'They danced together. They sang duets of the sentimental song hits of the season: "La Vie en Rose" and "Autumn Leaves", "If I Were a Bell" and "C'Est Si Bon". If they did not happen to be seated side by side, they wrote notes to each other and passed them behind the intervening chairs, and each's languishing glance seldom left the other's face.'

Jimmy celebrated his thirty-fifth birthday on 11 June with a dinner at Maxim's; his guests of honour were the Windsors. Contrary to popular belief, Jimmy received no $15 million ($103.5m) inheritance on his thirty-fifth birthday with which to fund his costly adventure with the Windsors. Instead he received the small portion of Jim Donahue's estate, a negligible sum, which had been held in trust since his father's suicide in 1931. The next four years of wining and dining, sybaritism and seduction, were paid for, like everything else in her sons' lives, by the omnipresent Jessie. Many believed that Frank Woolworth had made individual provision for his grandchildren, but his estate passed in its entirety to the three daughters and, in Jessie's case, she never let go. Nonetheless, when it came to the Duke and Duchess, Jimmy rarely found himself short of cash: 'Jessie's purse is as wide open as her heart,' wrote Maury Paul.

When Jimmy's affair with the Duchess of Windsor became known among their circle – and, once it took hold, neither was in the mood to hide it – several people admitted to having introduced them; for to have triggered this most extraordinary of marital deceptions was to lay claim to a piece of history.

Among the most clamorous was the publicist Guido Orlando, who had previously done great work for the Windsors' profile during the war, and now insisted it was he who had finally put Jimmy and the Windsors together. But he went one stage further, for he claimed that behind the liaison between Jimmy and Duchess lay a darker secret – that it was actually Jimmy and the Duke who were having an affair. Orlando told the author Charles Higham that the Duke had fallen in love with Jimmy, that the Jimmy-Duchess connection was a smokescreen constructed by Orlando, and that Orlando – who certainly had the ear of the Windsors – was instrumental in the Duke's vocal detestation of all homosexuals.

This claim chimed with certain facts which were known to the cognoscenti: that while at Oxford the Duke, then Prince of Wales, was linked by gossip with his tutor, Henry Hansell; they had been commonly referred to as Hansel and Gretel. The brother to whom he was closest, the Duke of Kent, was a well-known bisexual who had a brief fling with Noel Coward. 'Even by the late 1920s the prince was what the French call a *demivierge*,' wrote Charles Higham. 'His homosexual leanings, deeply repressed, were revealed in what became an almost hysterical aversion to anyone homosexual.'

Orlando's claims, however, were wide of the mark and demonstrated his ignorance of the couple he claimed were his friends. Jimmy and the Windsors had already known each other for six years when Orlando came on the scene; and the Duke's sexual proclivities lay elsewhere. His official biographer Philip Ziegler quotes Ulick Alexander, a courtier who was perhaps more devoted to the Prince of Wales than any other, describing him as being possessed by 'the sexual perversion of self-abasement'. Jimmy later told his cousin Barbara that the Duchess had informed him that, when the Duke was a child in his mother's bedroom, he glimpsed some of the Queen's fantastic jewellery on the bed and put it on. Queen Mary discovered him wearing her jewels and gave him a sound thrashing on his bare bottom, 'about the only time she ever touched him'. Amateur psychiatrists might read into his relationship with Wallis, upon whom he showered jewels and who in return treated him with something approaching contempt, a squaring of this circle. On his deathbed, his last words to Wallis were 'Mother' – a reference, it is said, not to Queen Mary, but to Wallis herself.

By 1950 the couple had been married for thirteen years and had been intimate for sixteen, though the Duke always ferociously denied he had premarital relations with his wife. Whatever, for all this time, to all intents and purposes, it had been one-way traffic, with much gratification for the Duke but none for the Duchess.

Duff Cooper, the British Ambassador to Paris, observed: 'She is a nice woman and a sensible woman – but she is hard as nails and doesn't love him.' Higham quotes an unnamed source as saying: 'It is doubtful whether he and Wallis ever had sexual intercourse in the normal sense of the word. However, she did manage to give him relief. He had always been a repressed foot fetishist, and she discovered this and indulged the perversity completely. They also, at his request, became involved in elaborate erotic games. These included nanny-child scenes: he wore diapers, she was the master. She was dominant, he happily submissive. Thus, through satisfying his needs, needs which he probably did not even express to Mrs Dudley Ward and Thelma Furness, she earned his everlasting gratitude and knew that he would be dependent on her for a lifetime.'

Another intimate of Jimmy's at this time was Ethel Merman, the so-called Queen of Broadway. She recalled: 'Jimmy would give the Duchess beautiful jewels and the little Duke just closed his eyes to everything.'

They went out as a foursome to El Morocco. 'The Duchess was dancing with Jimmy and everyone else except the Duke. He and I danced, but the Duchess kept dancing with Jimmy until I got irked about the whole thing. I said to her, "Why don't you get off your ass and dance with your husband?" And she did.'

Those who were closest to the Windsors speculated constantly on their intimate life together. Even to the most inexperienced eye it was clear that the Duchess held the dominant, and the Duke the submissive, role in the relationship.

Jimmy told Ethel Merman that the relationship with the Duchess was a bumpy one. One night they had both been drinking and 'the little Duke' had gone to bed. 'Jimmy and the Duchess got into a big fight, yelling and screaming and trading insults. Finally she looked at him and said, "And to think I gave up a king for a queen."'

⁂

June 1950 was an exceptional time for fashionable Paris, with parties, dances, balls, dinners, receptions and salons. At the month's end, Jessie was in Biarritz, and the Windsors needed little persuasion to join her there. The royal couple stayed at the Hôtel de Paris, Jimmy at his mother's rented villa. They all met each day at the Casino, and again at night at a number of houses and restaurants. The Duke played golf, and cards; Jimmy and the Duchess did not. But at night a pattern had already established itself: by 10.30 or 11 o'clock the Duke would complain of tiredness and, summoning the Duchess, prepare to head for bed. But, in the company of Jimmy, the Duchess had discovered new reserves of energy. She would tell the Duke: 'You go. I'll be along soon', and be head-to-head in conversation again with Jimmy before her husband had even pushed back his chair.

They returned to Paris. By now their close friends were watching closely. It was the old Marquesa de Portago, according to Charles Murphy, who was the one to finally say what everybody else was thinking: 'Why, they're in *love*!'. Murphy added: 'Appalled, she looked around her. No one had heard, least of all Jimmy and Wallis, locked in their trance.'

Wallis's behaviour became extravagant, silly. Murphy recalled an evening at the Monsiegneur, where the Duke left early after buying a gardenia for his wife from the flower girl. 'Jimmy had bought her one too. As soon as the Duke had gone, the duchess snatched his flower from her corsage, flung it into the champagne bucket, and tamped it down in the ice with a bottle. Jimmy's flower she then tucked into its place . . . Jimmy took her hand and they wept.'

Murphy, a senior editor at *Life* magazine, observed much of this because his ghosting of *A King's Story* was far from over, even though the book was due in the shops that autumn. Clearly the deadline was going to be missed, and Murphy now tried to tie his subject to a schedule: 'The Duke, moved as much by the consideration of the handsome royalties at stake as by his contractual obligations, attempted to discipline himself and cut short his partying and nightclubbing,' he wrote later. 'A side effect of his self-reform was to throw Jimmy and the Duchess even more into each other's company.'

The Windsors' schedule called for them to return to New York on 16 November and to begin a two-month round of social engagements. The Duke suggested postponing the trip until his work with Murphy was complete, but the Duchess claimed this would be a discourtesy to their friends and dismissed the idea, leaving her husband in a dilemma: it meant either abandoning the book, or being abandoned by his wife while he worked on in Paris.

The time for their departure grew nearer but progress on the book was slow, and getting slower: relations with his ghost-writer sank daily, for Murphy was as punctilious as the Duke was negligent, and in the end when the *Queen Mary* sailed, it was without the Duke. He bade farewell to his wife at the Gare du Nord and next morning wrote: 'It was terrible watching the train take you away from me and I feel so desperately lonely without you. Please don't ever do this to me again . . . I miss you and love you more and more and more.'

For the Duchess, it must have been a relief to be removed, however briefly, from such claustrophobic pleadings. In any event there lay ahead the prospect of at least a fortnight's respite from her loving but abject husband; Jimmy was already in New York, having promised 'all sorts of delights' in their time alone together.

How much of this the Duke knew, and how much he surmised, is an open question but Bryan, by his co-author's side daily during the following weeks, recalled his increasingly frantic behaviour: 'The *Queen Mary* usually took five days to cross the Atlantic. On the sixth day the Duke telephoned their apartment in the Waldorf Towers. The Duchess was not in, so he left a request for her to call back. She failed to. The following afternoon, Paris time, he called again, expecting to catch her before she went out to lunch. Their private phone did not answer.'

It did not answer for four days. Now, said Bryan, the Duke began calling at five and six in the morning, Paris time, between her return from dinner and her bed-time; he was still unable to reach her. The maid who answered the phone was unable to say where her mistress was or when she would be home. When he finally caught up with her she said she had been with 'friends' and changed the subject.

What the Duke did not yet know, and what no one was ready to tell him, was that Jimmy and the Duchess were very publicly painting the town red. Their relationship was now six months old and, freed from the constraints of Parisian society, they began an unbridled romp around New York. While their public behaviour stopped short of the improper, more people were rapidly coming to the same conclusion that the Marquesa de Portago had reached in Biarritz – that the Duchess and her homosexual escort, young enough to be her son, were in love. Since neither was prepared to be found canoodling in some second-rate restaurant or bar, they continued attending the places they liked best – the Colony, 21, El Morocco – where the word spread fast.

It was only a matter of time before the gossip columnists started their insinuating pieces, written in such a coded form that only those who already knew the story could understand what they were trying to say. Meanwhile Murphy, desperate to get the Duke to finish the task in hand, took him off to Fontainebleau to stay at Margaret Biddle's country house. Relations between the two men had foundered, each believing that the other had neither the will nor the sense of urgency to see the job completed. On balance it would appear Murphy had right on his side.

'That evening the Duke was abstracted, lost in some private anxiety,' noted Murphy. 'He had more to drink than usual and retired to bed early, on the excuse that he wished to look over the draft chapters. Instead, he was up half the night, vainly trying to reach the Duchess.' No work was done the next day, and the evening was devoted in making fruitless calls to New York. The same pattern occurred on the next day, though on the following day he made some effort to get on with the book.

He broke off from reminiscing to Murphy and Murphy's secretary – his method of 'writing' the book – to say: 'The Duchess is very proud, you know. Very independent.' Then he went on to list several more of her attributes. Later, he steered the conversation round to the Korean war, which had recently started. It was, he said, jeopardising some of his investments. He was acting strangely, and declared, 'My friends in the British and American embassies have warned me that Russia is secretly preparing to enter the war, and may well strike in Europe. If this happens, I intend to be with the Duchess, as I was in the last war.' Murphy, an expert in military affairs, knew the threat did not exist, but the following day the Duke announced he would have to return to Paris: something had come up he had to attend to.

Nearly two weeks had elapsed since the Duchess's departure for New York and the Duke could no longer contain himself. One morning at seven o'clock he telephoned to say: 'I've been up all night. I've decided to sail for New York and join the Duchess. I'm taking the boat train for the *Queen Elizabeth* this afternoon . . . I'm sorry. I've got to give up the book. But with the risk of war what it is, I must in duty join her.' The writer got the impression that the call was curtailed because the Duke was about to burst into tears.

In the Duke's room was found a batch of press clippings which had been sent from New York. As he glanced through them he was startled to discover quite how often the Duchess and Jimmy's name had been coupled by the gossip columnists, reporting them in one night club after another. Walter Winchell, in the New York *Daily Mirror* snidely observed: 'The Duke and Duchess of Windsor are phfft!' As he set sail, the papers back in New York continued to warm to their theme: Jimmy and Wallis had been the last to leave Gogi's Larue nightclub, said the New York *Journal American*. The *Mirror* reported, while he was on the high seas: 'The Duke and Duchess thing is now a front.'

As much to protect his investment as anything else, Charles Murphy, set sail with the Duke in a last-ditch attempt to use the time aboard to catch up with the doomed autobiography. The Duke's secretary Anne Seagrim[1] observed: 'Murphy is just

---

1 Quoted in *The Secret File of the Duke of Windsor*.

like a sour grape, and being incredibly objectionable both to me and to HRH. He is the most horrible man to have around.' But Murphy was protecting his reputation, and the nearly two years of work he had put into *A King's Story*. In this he had not been helped by the Duchess who, according to Charles Higham, 'proved to be infuriatingly interruptive, constantly irritable, and resentful of the irregular absorption of her husband of the task in hand. She would burst into the various dens of the homes they occupied ... she would scream out: 'Stop talking about the past!' and she would insist that the Duke go, with or without Jimmy Donahue, to nightclubs and restaurants until late at night so that he would be too exhausted to tackle the writing in the morning.'

In his extensive writings about the Windsors, Murphy did not dwell on the Duke's behaviour aboard the *Queen Elizabeth*, but later he told one of the Duke's godchildren that he would not allow the Duke out on deck alone at night because he feared for his state of mind. The former king had been put on suicide-watch.

Given the pent-up emotions of the Duke – 'He was of course quite wild with excitement,' wrote Anne Seagrim – and the anticipation of the New York press, the reconciliation at Pier 90 was bound to be electric. The *New York Journal-American* reported: 'The Duke threw his arms around the Duchess, gave her a few affectionate, fervent smacks – seven times they kissed! – and kerflooie, there went flying all those juicy rumours that the famed lovebirds had finally drifted apart.' The *New York Times* was rather more circumspect, less ready to hope for the best: 'The couple denied published reports that they were estranged, and embraced for the benefit of camera men.'

But Walter Winchell in the *Mirror* would not leave it alone. 'The Duchess certainly put on a swell act at the dock. Tch-tch, hmph,' he wrote the following day. Later in the week he wrote:

'The Duke of Windsor explained his prolonged stay in France, where "I had to read the proofs of my memoirs." No more air mail, you know . . .' And Winchell's final word on the subject – for now: 'The Duchess of Windsor's friends are the ones who are embarrassed. The Duke is a very sad person these days.'

With this dramatic and highly public reconciliation Jimmy may have been put on ice, but not for long. The Duke still had a responsibility to turn out his memoirs and during the day tried his hardest to work on them; but by the cocktail hour his concentration had evaporated, and at night all three would troop off to El Morocco, the Duke apparently helpless in this spider's web. At midnight, when the Duke left for home, wrote one observer, 'Jimmy came into his own, wisecracking, cavorting, camping, telling naughty stories and gossiping about the other patrons – all for the Duchess's delight.' He would return her to the Waldorf Tower, sometimes via 834 Fifth Avenue if Jessie was not in residence, and when the Duke went to her room to check on her, he would find scrawled notices like 'Keep Out', 'Stay Out' or 'Don't Come in Here'.

Next day the Duke would go back to his memoirs while the Duchess and Jimmy lunched and shopped. Cartier, the jeweller where the Duke had squandered so much money on his wife, was a favourite stopping-off point – more, at this stage, as a resting-post than as an end in its own right, for Jimmy preferred to buy at Van Cleef and Arpels. Wallis went on to Mainbocher for fittings and consultations, and also to Hattie Carnegie's where, one afternoon, out of fifty Carnegie dresses paraded before her by mannequins, Jimmy encouraged Wallis to pick out thirteen in as many minutes. The dresses started at $450 ($3,105); Jimmy paid for them all. They moved on to Elizabeth Arden, where Wallis picked out fifteen suits designed by Mr Castillo, then on to Sophie Gimbel's Custom Shop.

Urged on by Jimmy, Wallis started to acquire a substantial

wardrobe of furs, collecting full-length sable, ermine, and mink coats as well as neckpieces, capes and short jackets in ermine and mink. She developed a passion for broadtail, the fur of young or premature Karakul lambs, and had a complete suit made by Maximilian which she wore under a mink coat. Jimmy and Wallis drove about town in Jimmy's Cadillac, chauffeured by his uncomplaining servant Twaddy, or in Wallis's special-bodied Cadillac, driven by her English chauffeur Dolan. Their favourite lunching-places were the Colony and Le Pavillon, and after they had dined they would continue their shopping, stopping off at the milliners Florelle and Mr John's. Though the Duchess's maxim was 'the less hat the better' this did not apply to the numbers they bought – she would order up to forty-five a time at Florelle and thirty-five at Mr John. None cost less than $100 ($700), but Jimmy was happy to pick up the tab.

In the days leading up to Christmas 1950, the pair devised a grotesque plan over lunch. Jimmy had maintained his close contacts with the Roman Catholic Church and Cardinal Spellman, and through Spellman had met Monsignor Fulton J. Sheen, a crusading prelate who had a reputation for converting high-profile Protestants to his Church. There can be no question of Jimmy's own faith, but the idea that he might encourage the Duchess of Windsor to join the Roman Catholic Church was promulgated, not by religion, but by mischief. He asked her whether she would attend Mass at St Patrick's Cathedral on Christmas Day. She said she would think about it, but did not know what to do with the Duke. 'Why, bring him too!' roared Jimmy.

Having cuckolded the Duke, Jimmy was following up his coup by an even greater act of treachery. The Duke, as King, had taken on the ancient, hereditary mantle of Defender of the Faith – the Protestant faith. The rules of his kingship forbade him to have a Catholic wife. Though no longer king, his pledge and vow to the senior religion of his country was unrescinded: for his wife to bow to the Church of Rome would be a shattering, fundamental, blow. Was this, as some thought, Jimmy's plan – that if his adultery would not break the marriage, then might his religion?

On Christmas morning, the ill-starred trio attended Mass at St Patrick's Cathedral. Sophisticated, emancipated New York couldn't care less about an ex-king breaking his 'house rules', even though the Duke may have been the first British monarch, or ex-monarch, to take the sacrament from a disciple of Rome since the reign of Charles I three hundred years before. The moment passed almost without comment in society or in the newspapers. Disappointed, Jimmy followed up this damp squib by urging the Duke and Duchess to give luncheon for Cardinal Spellman, and on 3 January the archbishop was received with due ceremony at the Waldorf Towers. However, as a private visit, it went unrecorded in the press, thus saving the Duke and his extended family much embarrassment and serving further to frustrate Jimmy.

During the ensuing months a series of half-hearted meetings took place between the Duchess and Monsignor Sheen but, despite encouragement from Jimmy, her heart was not in it. Sheen later allowed that although he had tried to persuade her to a more profound religious view, he could not get her to convert. Nonetheless, Charles Murphy claims in his book *The Windsor Story* that the Duke himself had attended some of these preparatory talks. If so, it demonstrated how completely he felt he had burned his boats with Britain and its royal family. And how much he loved his wife.

At the end of January all three members of this curious, but by now well-established, *ménage à trois* travelled south to the Horse Shoe Plantation at Tallahassee, Florida, the home of the banking heir George Baker, but by St Valentine's Day they were back in New York as the guests of Jessie at the Venetian Ball at the Sherry Netherland Hotel. At this time Jessie's grip could not have been tighter on the Windsors, giving rise to speculation among friends that she had 'bought' one or other of them, much in the way that she had 'bought' the writer and socialite Elsa Maxwell with substantial cheques at Christmas and birthday, and the columnist Maury Paul. Certainly she was funding Jimmy's reckless spending on the Duchess, which now extended to their joint passion for antique gold snuffboxes. In decking out one of her houses years before, Jessie had found one which allegedly belonged to George III and later presented it to the Windsors. Now Jimmy and the Duchess sought out more examples of the genre, shopping with a passion, and giving them to each other as unincriminating love-tokens.

Despite all the whispering which went on behind their backs, the Windsors were still a social catch – but were they now, weighted down with Jimmy, quite top-drawer any more? Strong arguments still range over the nature of the Windsors' social status at the time. Nancy Mitford encountered them and observed: 'They both look ravaged with misery', before adding cattily, 'I do hate that Duchess'. It is argued by some that by late 1950 they had become *déclassé*, and the rise of Jessie Woolworth Donahue to be their close friend and confidante was directly related to their own social fall. The Duke's brother King George VI had minuted, on his sister-in-law: 'Recent reports show that no woman in Paris wishes to meet her', and in a curious twist, Britain's wartime ambassador to London, Joe Kennedy, himself only very lately arrived and still not a fully accepted part of Palm Beach society, ordered his wife not to call on the Windsors. But Jessie's money enthralled both the Duke and Duchess and, just as she had caught her son Jimmy in her web by the skilful use of it, now too did she do so with the Windsors: she gave them a free ticket to the world.

It could not buy their health, however, and in February 1951 the Duchess became ill: cancer of the womb was diagnosed and a hysterectomy required. On 19 February, less than a week after the Venetian Ball, the Duke's diary noted: 'To hospital with Her RH' – an underscore of the vain hope that the family which had pushed him away would, one day, officially recognise his wife as their equal. Wallis was operated on for the removal of a fibroid tumour, and the operation was judged a success. Both Jimmy and the Duke visited Wallis at the Harkness Pavilion of the Columbia Presbyterian Medical Center, though at different times; the Duke's secretary fielded the inevitable press calls, but expressed amazement that, in asking after the Duchess's health, one reporter had the temerity to also ask after the state of her marriage. It really should have come as no surprise.

During Wallis's incarceration, the Duke went into limbo, refusing to see people and aimlessly pottering about the Waldorf Towers. Lord Beaverbrook, his old ally from Abdication days, came for morning coffee but did not stay to luncheon. Finally, after a week, he was forced out to lunch with Mrs Vanderbilt before scuttling off to hospital to visit his wife. Wallis stayed in hospital for just under three weeks, the Duke noting in his diary for March 9: 'Her Royal Highness returns from H.'

Two days after she left hospital, she and the Duke hosted a small dinner party at which Jessie and Jimmy were both guests. A few days later the Duke left alone for Palm Beach for a fortnight's sunshine. Wallis remained behind in New York for radium therapy.

In a rare, possibly unique, gesture towards the Duchess, Queen Mary wrote to her son: 'I feel so sorry for your great anxiety about your wife, and am thankful that so far you are able to send a fair account so we must hope the improvement will continue.' But in real terms, it meant nothing. In his official biography of the Duke, Philip Ziegler indicates that by this point the Duke had given up hope of his wife ever being officially recognised as HRH.

⁂

Elsa Maxwell, despite a daunting and unlovely exterior, occupied a curiously powerful position in New York society at the time, writing articles for tabloid newspapers and hosting increasingly extravagant parties, always at someone else's expense. Though of spectacularly unaristocratic origin, she had become society's ringmaster: 'She created, for bored and exhausted members of high society, a range of stimuli in the form of soirees that featured a mixture of movie stars, playwrights, authors, politicians, composers and artists,' wrote one observer. 'She brought them all together and moved among her guests, with a somewhat toadlike but persistent waddle, fixing everyone in sight with her charming, always fascinated stare, snapping out deliciously squalid gossip, and making sure that all the guests were happy with their company and that their champagne or cocktail glasses were never empty.'

For some years, Miss Maxwell had given the Duchess a bad press. She despised the Abdication, questioned the Windsors' marriage, raised her eyebrows at Wallis's Baltimore origins. Some of her closer friends wondered whether or not she was in love with Wallis and disappointed that it could not be reciprocated; Charles Higham recalls their meeting in Vienna in 1935 when Elsa was riveted by the Duchess's strong, forceful stride across the lobby of the Hotel Bristol. All in all, her present attitude was creating difficulties, the Duchess told Jimmy one day. Jimmy spoke to his mother, and during the first months of 1951 a rapprochement, reluctant on both sides, was arranged by Jessie, to whom both women owed considerable favours. On 11 April Elsa joined Jimmy and Jessie when they entertained the Windsors to dinner and the circus; a week later Jessie met the Windsors to discuss Maxwell's warming to them; then on 24 April the Windsors were Elsa's guests to dinner and the theatre. The problem had been finessed; for the time being at least.

By now Jimmy and Wallis had been lovers for almost a year 'though not as often as he would have wished', according to one friend. In Paris, Biarritz, Monte Carlo and on the succession of sea cruises the Windsors were fond of taking – away from their native America – Jimmy and Wallis became increasingly open, holding hands and laughing. In front of the Duke and the Duke's friends, they initially maintained a distance but, as with all relationships, the disguise started to wear thin as time went on. The Duke, bleakly, tenaciously, clung on to his wife, perplexed by her closeness to this patently homosexual figure.

On 24 May all three sailed for Cherbourg, just as they had the year before, when Jimmy and the Duchess had consummated their love for the first time. Jimmy returned to his cousin's suite at the Ritz while the Windsors made their way to the Rue de la Faisanderie. Jessie, ever eager, had been waiting for them when they arrived.

Early in June, Jessie, Jimmy and the Windsors spent the evening at the Pre Catalan, a fashionable restaurant in the Bois de Boulogne. Jessie hosted a dinner for eight and one of the party later recalled: 'That was the season that haute couture sponsored the *jeune fille* look, perhaps its cruellest infliction on ageing beauties. Dior's interpretation was a strapless gown, ballerina-length, in palest pastel shades, worn with low-heeled slippers. Unfortunately, both the hostess and her guest of honour had chosen this model that evening: the Duchess, very dark, very thin, in pale blue; and Mrs Donahue, golden blonde, rosy-cheeked, and plumpish, in pale pink. The orchestra struck up, and Jimmy whirled the Duchess on to the floor, while the Duke led out Mrs Donahue. Again unfortunately, she had added to her costume a pink tulle scarf, yards and yards of it, and almost at once the diminutive Duke found himself swaddled and almost smothering. He stopped dancing and fought for his breath, only to swaddle himself worse. The whole room watched his exertions – everyone, that is, but Jimmy and the Duchess. They glided on, unnoticing, lost in the dance and in each other.'

Not long after, the Windsors gave a dinner for twelve at home. The Duke's back was troubling him, and after dinner he tried to switch on a lamp near his chair, but he could not quite manage it. 'The Duchess, whispering with Jimmy at the other end of the room, came over to help him,' recorded their biographer Murphy. 'As she reached across him to reach the lamp, he patted her, affectionately. She stiffened, threw him a freezing look, and marched back to Jimmy, to resume their whispering.'

It was at this point that the Duke left for England, alone, to visit his mother at Marlborough House, and the afternoons in the Quai Branly resumed their usual routine. The affair increased in its physical intensity, the Duchess almost mad with the pleasure Jimmy gave her. The Duke stayed away for a week, during which time the lovers painted the town red. Mournfully, in between visits to his ailing mother, the Duke spent his under-utilised time wandering round the Grosvenor House Antiques Fair, showing a particular interest in the gold snuffboxes which had become a binding interest between the Donahues and Windsors. On his return to Paris, no one dared to mention his wife's extraordinary behaviour, but if he hoped there might be some respite from Jimmy's company, there, in his diary, was the entry: 'Dinner. Mr Donahue.'

Worse was to come. At least in Paris this curious threesome did not share a roof. Now, with the onset of the summer-holiday month of July, the Windsors prepared to travel south to St Tropez where they would board the *Sister Anne* for a month-long Mediterranean cruise. Jimmy came too – but then, why not? Jessie had paid for the charter . . .

A map exists of the three-week journey which took in Antibes, Monte Carlo, Genoa, Viareggio and Elba (the real Elba). At Portofino, the party were guests of the British actor Rex Harrison and his German-born wife Lilli Palmer, who recalled in detail in her memoirs that receiving the royal party was an honour, but not an unmixed blessing: she detested the protocol which went with such visits.

One evening, while Jimmy and the Duke and Duchess were dining with the Harrisons, there was a telephone call from Greta Garbo and her companion George Schlee: could they come and visit? 'It was a historic moment,' Lilli Palmer wrote.[1] 'The two women sat face to face and sized each other up from head to toe. Both knew they were legends of the twentieth century. Looking at them, I thought that life casts people in roles that a good script would never assign them. The woman for whom a man would be willing to give up his throne should obviously have been Greta Garbo, forever the world's most beautiful woman, unique and unattainable.' To Miss Palmer, the Duchess in her jewels and 'something white and exquisite' was no match for the actress in her old blue slacks and a faded blouse. As for the Duke, his blond hair, she observed with her trained actress's eye, was touched up.

---

1 In her autobiography *Change Lobsters – and Dance.*

Next day, the Harrisons, Garbo and Schlee turned up at the *Sister Anne* only to discover a furious Duchess: 'It's Jimmy. He went ashore this afternoon and he's not back yet. He knows perfectly well that the Duke insists on punctuality. It's simply a question of manners, that's all.' Before long Jimmy climbed aboard, tossing exuberant greetings in all directions and depositing in the Duchess's lap a large bouquet of gardenias by way of a peace offering. She swept them to the floor and barked: 'Do you know what time it is?' Jimmy brought his wristwatch to within an inch of his eyes. 'Well, well, what do you know!' he said. 'I'll be damned!'

Included in the guests was a retired American senator who, by the time dinner was served, was quite clearly drunk and in the mood to castigate the British for their apparent desire to sacrifice the flower of American youth in pursuit of empire interests. All were embarrassed, but still the senator droned on. Lilli Palmer pleaded with Jimmy to change the subject. A first attempt failed to stop the senator's flow so Jimmy stood up, strolled to the rail, and casually vaulted over it into the water.

The *Sister Anne* was tied up in dock, and the dinner party was taking place on the quarter-deck in full view of a large crowd of impoverished natives which had gathered to watch the proceedings. Jimmy's noisy entry into the water, still clad in midnight blue velvet dinner jacket, patent leather pumps and diamond cufflinks, produced a ragged cheer from the unwashed onlookers. 'The boy has no manners,' said the Duchess to her fellow guests. 'I'll ask you not to speak to him when he comes back. We'll act as if nothing has happened.'

Lilli Palmer recalls that even this departure from protocol failed to still the senator's monologue about the awfulness of the British: 'The Duchess signalled to the steward,' she wrote, 'who distractedly handed the dishes round again, although our plates were still full. Suddenly Wallis said, loudly and rudely, right into the Senator's lecture, 'Of course, it's all his mother's fault. It's all Jessie Donahue's fault. On the one hand she pampers him, and on the other she keeps him so short of money that he doesn't care what he . . .'"

Jimmy reappeared, his hair wet but otherwise immaculate. He had changed into another set of evening clothes, this time a green velvet dinner jacket. The Senator continued on his meandering conversational path. 'Oh for God's sake,' cried Jimmy, 'we'll just have to try again!'

Lilli Palmer continues the story:

> He stood up and made for the rail once more. This time, however, he didn't bring off his vault quite so elegantly, because Greta had jumped up and was hanging on to his trouser leg. 'Don't, don't!' she pleaded. 'Not again! You'll get sick! Stop! Ouch!'
>
> He had given her a vigorous push, knocking her backwards onto the deck. Then he jumped over the rail, laughing, and disappeared into the black night.
>
> Splash! The people on the dock broke into frenzied cheering, 'Bravo! Hurrah!' or simply aboriginal screams of delight.

Once more Jimmy returned looking immaculate, but the dinner party was over. Palmer, her husband, Greta Garbo and George Schlee, together with the drunken Senator and his wife tiptoed away as Jimmy, the Duke and the Duchess retreated into the library where they were involved in what Miss Palmer described as a 'passionate conversation'.

Whatever their differences, they continued the cruise, arriving back at Antibes on 28 July. Jessie was given a full account of her son's misdemeanours a week later when she and the

Windsors dined together.[1] Jimmy was not invited, and had decided in any case to stay on in the South. During the whole of August Jessie became the royal couple's closest companion, following them as the entourage moved on to Biarritz. There they met daily for lunch or dinner, at the Café de Paris and the Hôtel du Palais as well as the casino, with Jessie arranging an exhibition of Spanish dancing as a precursor to them all travelling across the border to watch a bullfight.

Jimmy joined them at the end of the month and, recalls Aline, Countess of Romanones, took up where he had left off in the Duchess's affections. 'My husband and I would be there with them at the Wunderbar in the Casino and after playing, we'd be sitting with them for a long time. The Duke would go to bed earlier, maybe one o'clock, and we'd be there till five in the morning. She and Jimmy would be laughing and joking with each other, they'd be upstaging each other making clever quips about things.

'The Duke was out of it, I don't think he liked Jimmy at all. They'd be polite to each other but then the Duke was always polite, determined not to let anything show, certainly not in front of other people. When he'd gone back to the Hotel du Palais the Duchess would ask me to stay on – she would never stay alone with Jimmy, she had to have someone else there. Jimmy made a big thing out of being gay, laughing and joking about it, and I think that helped confuse people about the

---

1 When she wrote to her aunt Bessie Merryman on 4 November the Duchess described the voyage as 'delightful', which may say something about how much she filtered the news being passed back to her relations in Baltimore. 'Don't pay any attention to those vile US newspapers. There never has been a cross word between the Duke and myself and we laugh at all their nonsense.'

New love – Jimmy brings the Duchess home to 834 Fifth Avenue, 1950.

A new twist to the phrase 'royal patronage' – Jessie Donahue helped bankroll the Windsors' expensive life for four years. Here she entertains the Duke at 834 Fifth Avenue, 1950.

A night in Jimmy's, Paris, where Jimmy and the Duchess made public their love for each other on the dance floor.

A token of love: the fantastic sapphire ring Jimmy ordered from Cartier and which the Duchess wore on their night of abandonment in Paris, 5 June 1951.

Reunion: the Duke finally catches up with his runaway wife after rumours surface in the New York newspapers of a rift. The Duchess had spent three weeks in the company of Jimmy Donahue while the Duke became suicidal at the thought of losing her.

Jimmy and the Duchess at a fancy-dress party in the Champs Elysées, summer 1952. His apparent homosexuality convinced the world's press that there was no affair, despite the couple's obvious closeness.

At your service – the Duke and Jimmy with Mrs Lytle Hull at the Duchess of Windsor's Ball, New York 1953.

Yet another evening of wearisome celebration – Jimmy, a family friend, Jessie, the Duke and Duchess.

Love rules the waves
. . . Jimmy and the
Duchess aboard the
Sister Anne in the
Mediterranean, 1951.
Looking on is Elsa
Maxwell's lover, Dickie
Fellowes-Gordon.

No longer a king,
barely a husband – the
Duke poses alone while
Jimmy and the Duchess
seek amusement
elsewhere. Austria,
1954.

Rather the devil you know – Jimmy and the Duke, 1954.

There are two men in my life: the Duke holds on tight while the Duchess whispers to her lover. Austria, 1954.

The cruellest cut – the Windsors at El Morocco, New Years Eve 1953. Jimmy had found the paper crowns and presided over the couple's public 'coronation'.

Quintessential Jimmy: partying at 21, 1954.

Broadhollow, Long Island.

Last love – British-born dancer Don Walker, whom Jimmy plucked out of the chorus-line of the Folies Bergère.

The other side of the coin: Jimmy (centre) carries the American flag behind the Archbishop of New York in an outdoor ceremony, circa 1960.

A final Christmas together –Woolworth, Jessie and Jimmy at 834 Fifth Avenue, 25 December 1965.

Where are the cufflinks? The Woolworth mausoleum at Forest Lawn, New York, Jimmy Donahue's resting place.

nature of their relationship. But those of us who saw a lot of the Windsors were very surprised at the Duchess and Jimmy's closeness. People were forever speculating on what sort of a romance it was.'

Nevertheless the sometimes difficult *ménage à trois* staggered on, the Duke's diary noting 'Dinner. Mr Donahue' on 7 September. A few days later the caravan headed back to Paris after two months in the sun, and celebrated with dinner at Le Cremaillère, presided over by Jessie. The afternoon visits to Count Jean de Baglion's apartment resumed, while in the evening Wallis, Jimmy and the Duke dined at the Tour d'Argent.

On 18 September the Duchess gave a dinner party at the Rue de la Faisanderie. The seating plan exists to this day:

Mr de Courcy	Mrs Lytle Hull
Baron de Cabrol	Mrs Donahue
Mr Donahue	Mrs Nelson Slater
Mr LaCaze	Mrs Biddle
Mr Aldau	Hon Mrs Fellowes
Mr Slater	Mrs Austen Gray
Mr Richman	Mrs Hearst
Mr Lytle Hull	Mrs de Courcy

These people represented, at that time, the Windsors' inner circle. There were other friends, and advisors who became friends, but these were the people closest to the Duke and Duchess. Jimmy and Jessie had become indispensable to both.

September drifted into October, and at last a chance came, with a General Election, to see the re-election of the Duke's friend, Winston Churchill, who had been pushed out of office so ignominiously in 1945 and kept out again in 1950. But Churchill's new administration had no more wish to see a return to Britain of the errant Duke, and his continued representations for some kind of official job fell on deaf ears. With post-war reconstruction and a sagging economy to face, the Duke was one political hot potato the premier could well do without.

Two days before the Election, the Duke and Duchess took the ferry for England, putting up at a house in Upper Brook Street in Mayfair. On 28 October the Duke made a private visit to Frogmore, the royal mausoleum at Windsor where, it had finally been decided, he would be interred at his death. For a time, feeling acutely the rejection by his brother, his family, and his former subjects, he had toyed with the idea of being buried alongside Wallis in Baltimore, an idea originally suggested by Jimmy to the Duchess ('rest in peace in your own back yard') but he had come to the realisation that if he was to have a place in history, he must be buried in the country where once he reigned.

The next day he went to see the new Prime Minister, Churchill, and for the fourth time of asking sought some official position. Though by now he had grown lazy through inaction, and in any event was still preoccupied with the promotion of his autobiography, he reasoned that via an official position he might once again raise the issue of recognition for his wife. But that afternoon he returned to Upper Brook Street and the Duchess knew from his drawn, pinched face that he had failed again. 'Was it no?' she asked. His raised his hand and turned his thumb down. 'I hate this place,' she said bitterly. 'I shall hate it to my grave.'

The writer Adela Rogers St Johns, who had been to visit Wallis in Nassau, wrote: 'Her bitterness, dark and real and terrible, against the waste of this man's gifts, was partly for herself. They had sat out St Helena [the Bahamas] as good soldiers – that wasn't her idea of a *life*. Now with years and years ahead of them, growing older years, what would they do with their lives, with the days?'

Maybe it was then, on that cold, foggy day in London, or maybe it had been earlier, looking out over the River Seine in Jean de Baglion's black-draped apartment, that Wallis began to fantasise about leaving yet another husband. She said, bitterly, to a friend: 'You have no idea how hard it is to live out a great romance.'

CHAPTER 9

LOVE OR WHAT YOU WILL

There is still a debate among those who knew Jimmy and the Windsors intimately as to when the question of marriage came up. The writer Philip van Rensselaer believes it was discussed early on in the affair; others suggest it was later, when the heat had gone out of the relationship and Jimmy was seeking to keep the mischief alive. All are agreed that Wallis quite seriously considered the eventuality because a friend, probably Sylvia de Castellane, mentioned it to Jessie. All are agreed that the notion was extinguished by Mrs Donahue, who threatened to cut her son off without a penny if he tried to push through such a horrifying idea.

And yet there can be no question of her complicity in the romance, given Jimmy's continued demands on her purse to support his extremely expensive habit, of his depth of commitment to the Duchess.

'Wallis was infatuated, ready to do almost anything,' says one of the Duke's circle. 'Jimmy had got carried away by his

own self-importance – he really did have control of her, probably the only person who ever did. Whether he himself believed
this crazy idea would go anywhere, who knows? He wanted
something, though it's hard to know what; maybe he wanted
the mother he never had, maybe it truly was love, maybe that
crazy egotism – the belief that he could do anything he wanted
– had got the better of him. But he definitely proposed marriage,
and she definitely thought about it.

‘But Jessie, who took a curious delight out of her son's intimacy with the Duchess – though she never knew the details –
was devoted to the Duke, and when she thought the relationship was getting out of hand, she told Jimmy that if he did anything to damage the marriage he wouldn't have a penny. He only
existed on her allowance – she really did control the show.'

Quite what Jessie harvested from this *liaison dangereux*
beyond a social vindication, a quasi-ownership of the royal
couple, is unclear; but her determination to stick close to the
Windsors at all costs was beyond doubt. She and the Duchess
were of an age; yet when the Donahues and Windsors dined
together, observed Elsa Maxwell, it was as if Jessie and the
Duke were one generation, and Jimmy and the Duchess
another. Some argued that Jessie, who had spurned all suitors
since the death of her husband twenty years earlier, was
sexually attracted to the Duke. But if that is so, it was not
reciprocated. What made Jessie appealing to the Duke was her
easy conversation, that with all her millions she deferred to
him and called him Sir, and the fact that, if a bill needed paying,
she paid it.

There had been many crises in the lives of the Windsors but
this, a betrayal at the most fundamental level, was the worst.
‘Few were aware,' concurred Charles Murphy, an eyewitness to
Wallis's abandoned pursuit of Jimmy, ‘how close the Duchess's
folly had carried her to irretrievable disaster.'

The Duchess, still beautiful in her unique way, glimpsed in the mirror a woman in her prime. Weighing in the balance the two men in her life, she saw, on the one hand, someone still young, handsome, zestful, indescribably wealthy, adventurous, stimulating and sexually appealing. On the other, her husband was now starting to collect ailments, some psychosomatic. His forcefulness had faded; he constantly worried about money; he was feeble both with and without her; his ambition had gone, and his life had adopted a highly predictable annual cycle. Whatever intimate life they had once shared – never, ever, satisfactory from the Duchess's point of view – was now over. The plus sides of the Duke were that he had kept his name and looks intact, and was a universal object of fascination.

It was quite evident to many who saw the Windsors regularly at this time that the Duchess found herself at a crossroads, with no idea which way to turn. To choose Jimmy – if she dare – would mean even greater notoriety, and almost certain annihilation at the hands of the world's press. The idea that a king could give up his empire for the woman he loved and that, mere years later, she could give up the king for a spoilt, mother-reliant homosexual misfit, simply beggared belief. Yet that was not the whole story: the stolen afternoons in the Quai Branly, the illicit sex heightened by the very perversity they shared, was a drug to which she had become wholly addicted. In addition, Jimmy could not turn off the money-tap: he paid for everything from cars to Cartier. At one stage, according to Philip van Rensselaer, he even encouraged his cousin Barbara to support this most expensive of habits, the Duchess: 'Barbara loved it, she loved the whole clandestine thing,' he recalled. 'She used to give Jimmy money for the Duchess's presents. She paid out anything up to half a million dollars – the Duchess was really greedy.' Jimmy's way of saying thank you was to pile bouquets of roses from floor to ceiling outside the door of his cousin's Ritz suite so that when she opened it she was literally bowled over.

The lunches at the Méditerranée and the dinners at the Relais des Porquerolles continued – 'I married David for better or for worse, but not for lunch,' Wallis mocked. On one occasion an English aristocrat, lunching with Jimmy at Le Pavillon, noticed the Duchess sitting at a table on the other side of the room. 'Towards the end of luncheon she was making her face up, with a particularly ugly way of putting lipstick on her lips, moving her mouth round the whole time,' he recalled. 'Jimmy turned to look at her, then turned back and in a stage-whisper said, "Look at her, she's doing her exercises. I'm seeing her after lunch."'

Temporarily in two minds, the Duchess had by no means abandoned her life with the Duke. She was having her cake, and eating it. On Tuesday 30 October she and the Duke drove out of Paris to Gif-sur-Yvette to view a seventeenth-century millhouse, the Moulin de la Tuilerie. The Duke became so excited by its possibilities as a country residence that they returned the next day at 3 p.m. and offered to rent it from its owner, Etienne Drian, the fashion artist and stage designer, with a view to purchase. Participating in such a forward-looking venture is not the act of a woman about to leave her husband, though some might construe in her actions a plot to find him something to do while she turned her attentions elsewhere. For this was to be the Duke's plaything, a re-creation of his pre-abdication home Fort Belvedere, on French soil. Such was Wallis's indifference to the place that it was sold immediately after the Duke's death.

The seasons of the year moved on, and it was time to head back to America. In December the couple set sail and, upon arrival, sat down to dinner with Jessie and Jimmy. Ten days later, Christmas Day, all the hard work that Jessie had put into these last fourteen years cultivating the former king-emperor paid off. He and his wife came to her house for Christmas luncheon. It was the high water mark of Jessie Donahue's social life. If the moment was a trifle spoilt by the knowledge that the Windsors were going on to dinner that night with her arch-rival, the higher-born Margaret Biddle, she could at least reassure herself that the royal couple would be back in her lair in two nights' time. If the frequency of home visits was the only yardstick in her battle with Mrs Biddle, then Jessie was winning.

About this time the Windsors were invited to a party in Long Island by Nelson Slater and his wife Martha. One guest recalls: 'It was a tremendous affair with an orchestra and many people. Towards the end of the evening the orchestra packed their things up and just the pianist stayed behind. The Duke had, as usual, gone off to bed and there was just Jimmy and the Duchess and one other couple dancing. Everyone else had gone.

'Suddenly the Duke reappeared, standing on the stairs in a robe and muffler. He looked down at Jimmy and the Duchess for a moment, then addressing the Duchess, he said, "Yankee, Go Home." But it had no effect, the Duchess kept on dancing with Jimmy, and finally she went upstairs at about 3 a.m. Bear in mind this was someone else's house, and no protocol about sleeping arrangements was about to be broken here.

'The men were left drinking. Next morning the hostess went downstairs to hear the staff putting out glasses for cocktails where various locals were to be invited before luncheon. She went into a coalhouse where she found Jimmy lying, fast asleep, hands crossed on his chest, still looking immaculate in his dinner jacket. It was nearly midday. Sidney, the Windsor's butler, and the hostess's own butler carried him out to the car and sent him away somewhere where he got changed and arrived back, half an hour late for cocktails but otherwise not missing a beat.'

⚬

Back in England the man who inherited the throne because of his brother's obsession was making his final curtain-call. King George VI, a well-meaning but lacklustre monarch with a furious temper and an obsession with uniforms, succumbed slowly to the effects of a lifetime's tobacco addiction. In September he had undergone surgery for the removal of his left lung, together with certain nerves of the larynx, but the royal radiologist Sir Harold Graham Hodgson opined, 'The operation was six months too late', and so it proved. The King went to sleep and was discovered dead in bed by his valet on the morning of 6 February 1952.

No biographer of the Duke and Duchess of Windsor has attempted to analyse the couple's feelings at this point. But by now, with their life a meandering path leading nowhere, it is unlikely that they would have seen in their actions sixteen years before the cause of this monarch's premature death. The king's widow, Queen Elizabeth, had no such vagueness about the events of 1936. The Duchess, she declared, was 'the woman who killed my husband'. One can only speculate as to her feelings had she known that, the night the Duke set sail from New York to attend his brother's funeral, the woman who killed the king was about to take advantage of her own husband's absence to engage in a night of complicated sexual games with a homosexual playboy twenty years her junior.

The Duke had a clearer picture in his mind of what would transpire while he was away. It was barely a year since he had had to chase across the Atlantic, suicidal with despair, to

185

recapture the woman he so famously loved. His behaviour aboard the *Queen Mary* on this occasion was hardly less distracted. The ship's captain, his old friend Commodore Grattidge, reported that throughout the voyage he paced the decks day and night like a lost soul, yearning for her. He monopolised the radiotelephone and cable facilities for hours on end, bombarding her with affectionate talk. But he could do nothing about how she spent her evenings.

Such was the Duke's anxiety that, although he and his wife were to sail to France the following month, once the royal funeral was over and he had made his obeisance to the new sovereign, Queen Elizabeth II, he headed straight back to New York rather than travel the shorter journey to the French mainland and await Wallis's arrival in Paris. 'Quite simply he could not live without her, he was a hundred per cent dependent,' recalls one who was part of their intimate circle. 'At this stage, he was forced to accept life on her terms – whatever she wanted, he would put up with. And that included Jimmy.

'The relationship between Wallis and the Duke was much stronger than any mere physical relationship, because it was a form of complete control, the kind of control I have never witnessed anywhere else, ever. It was hard to understand, while the Jimmy thing was going on, just how the Duke could put up with it. The small group of people who saw them all the time were just staggered.'

This intimate makes it clear that conjugal relations between the Duke, now 57, and Duchess, now 56, had long since ceased. 'You can be absolutely sure that for a long period there was little or no contact of that kind between them – it's impossible to imagine the Duke and Duchess doing anything. She was *so* involved with Jimmy.

'It was, by any standards, unbelievably humiliating for the Duke, but he never showed it. This man must, everybody

186

thought, be going through hell because of his wife's behaviour; but in public he behaved with complete serenity and dignity. His manners, always, were exquisite. But seeing the three of them together ... it wasn't a comfortable threesome. Being around Jimmy wasn't a comfort zone.'

Wallis's control exerted itself across the water. Her letters to the Duke during his London sojourn are full of instructions: wear a uniform, be careful with Mountbatten,[1] make sure your statement is graceful. As for their last-ditch attempt for some official role from the new regime she warned: 'Do not mention or ask for anything regarding recognition of me'; but she may as well have been barking at the moon. Her obsession was with squaring the King's widow, now titled the Queen Mother: 'I hope you can make some headway with Cookie and Mrs Temple Jr.'[2] The Duke made virtually no progress, but was allowed to meet President Auriol of France, a privilege which had evaded him in Paris despite Auriol having been in office for five years. Gleefully, pathetically, he wrote to his wife, 'We have a foot in the door of the Elysée!'[3]

During his time with the Duchess, Jimmy had not abandoned that other part of his life. While the Duke returned to New York ('If the boat gets in at dawn shall I come down? Because

---

1 Mountbatten switched allegiance from the Duke to his brother King George VI in the aftermath of the Abdication.
2 The Queen Mother, and Queen Elizabeth II, sometimes referred to as Shirley Temple.
3 Elysée Palace, the president's official residence. The Duke was wrong in his assumption.

of the press I think I should, don't you?' wrote the ever-alert Duchess), Jimmy was back in France. He cruised the boulevards of Paris in his black Cadillac, seeking adventure where he could find it. A favourite haunt was the Club Sept, a highly fashionable homosexual restaurant and dance bar near the Place de l'Opéra. Indeed the Duchess, whom he once took there, later confided to her friend Cappy Badrut: 'All the best-looking men in Paris are at the Club Sept.' All the men at the Club Sept were bi- or homosexual.

In the spring of 1952 Jimmy encountered the composer Ned Rorem, then a young protégé of the Vicomtesse de Noailles. Rorem later recorded in his Paris diary: 'The dirtiest words I know are J———— D————. With shame, I admit that while drunk recently I allowed this person to drive me all over Paris, he must have spent 200,000 francs on champagne, tips, private entertainment and such ostentation, not a sou of which he would have disposed on me as a composer. He told me his personal detectives had informed him that I was a pale-pink Communist, which is the most idiotic accusation I have ever received.'

There were no personal detectives, of course, but according to Jimmy Douglas, Jimmy Donahue enjoyed the power his Woolworth money brought him and would use it lustfully, manipulatively and vengefully on those whom it could influence – and few were immune to its power. Ned Rorem recalls: 'We met at the Boeuf sûr le Toit, which was an expensive gay nightclub on the Right Bank. I don't think he knew I was a musician with a certain reputation already, nor did he care. His main interest in me was physical. He was pretty drunk and I remember he drove me home. I lived in a fairly humble place, but he didn't want to come up. We did something in his car, I don't remember quite what. But he spoke ill of Marie-Laure de Noailles and that was it.'

If the international press knew about the Jimmy-Duchess affair, they were still not writing about it. Among the press corps based in Paris, Jimmy's homosexuality, his great cloak in this huge subterfuge, was an amusing talking-point; nobody bothered to look beyond it. In a piece heavily larded with sarcasm, the writer Audrey Whiting got nearest to saying something substantial when she reported for the London *Daily Mirror* on 11 June: 'Top American party-hostess and socialite Elsa Maxwell took an unhappy Duchess of Windsor under her wing last night. At the last moment the Duke of Windsor felt too tired to join in the merry-making at the fancy-dress ball Elsa held at a chic Champs Elysées restaurant. The Duchess was persuaded to go, reluctantly, without him.

'In the red-carpeted ballroom, she met an old American friend, Mr Jimmy Donahue. The Duchess, who arrived an hour after Mr Donahue, was seen earnestly talking to him.

'Soon, holding an orchid-bedecked mask to her face, she was chatting with other guests – the cream of French, British and American society. But the Duchess did not stay long, however. She was escorted home by Mr Donahue.' Whose home, Miss Whiting could not – or would not – say; but then perhaps she had never heard of Count Jean de Baglion.

The summer months of 1952 were devoted to the remodelling of the Moulin de la Tuilerie. The Duke concentrated on creating an informal English landscape with a rock and water garden, spending many days moving rocks and planting fruit trees and shrubs, while the Duchess went to work on the main building which, when complete, was a little too theatrical for some tastes. Cecil Beaton complained: 'Overdone and *chichi*. Medallions on the walls, gimmicky poufs, bamboo chairs. Simply not good enough!' Wallis had in effect created a living Windsor Museum at the Mill, one where her husband's history could be seen and digested.

Though Jimmy had had a hand, both artistic and financial, in furnishing the house in the Rue de la Faisanderie, his involvement in the creation of this ducal home-from-home was minimal. However, Jessie managed to leave her mark, paying for the redecoration of Wallis's bedroom which was all white, with the beams waxed to a dull gold, and dominated by a vast four-poster bed, 'mountainous with pillows and canopied with lawn' as one visitor described it. The Duke slept elsewhere, in a modest little room with a barracks cot.

Nonetheless when the work was completed Jimmy's was the first name to appear in the Mill's handsome calf-bound guest book. The Duchess was proud of her work and wanted to show it off to the one person whose opinion she valued. Viewed today the book, bearing the royal coat of arms, is an interesting indicator as to whom the Windsors favoured at that time: apart from Jimmy's childlike scrawl, signatures include those of the Princesse de Polignac, Christopher Dunphy, Charles Blackwell, Carroll Portago, Gray Phillips, the Earl of Dudley, Lady Alexandra Metcalfe, Alastair Mackintosh, Martha Slater, Edith Baker and Charles Cushing.

Though another sea-cruise was planned for July, there was to be no repeat of the ill-fated voyage of the *Sister Anne* the previous year. Even the Duchess had to concede that, in the relatively cramped conditions of a private yacht, Jimmy was *de trop*. So when the Windsor caravan headed south for the Mediterranean, Jimmy sailed for America. The Duke and Duchess's charter, a vessel called the *Amazon,* headed off on the familiar route, taking in Genoa and Portofino before heading south for Rome. Even here, however, Jimmy's influence could not go unnoticed, for the audience the Windsors had with Pope Pius XII, had been arranged through Jimmy's New York friend, Cardinal Spellman. At this time, the Duke and Duchess were still thirsty to meet world leaders, who were growing ever less eager to meet them. Jimmy's intercession earned him grudging thanks.

If there was no embarrassment this year about Jimmy tossing himself overboard before an adulatory crowd, the Duke still managed to draw attention to himself by succumbing to an acute case of food poisoning. He and the Duchess were put ashore at Montecatini and made their way back to Paris by train. Their subsequent trip to Biarritz, where Jessie awaited them, laden with cash, revived their spirits. 'Jessie used to take $300,000 ($2.07m) gambling money with her every year when she went to France,' says someone who knew her then. 'She would gamble until it had all gone, and then she would gamble no more.'

Another intimate adds: 'She was like a lady-in-waiting to the Windsors. She took some of the burden off the Duchess. He said to me: "Do you know, I live with a woman who gets by on four hours' sleep a night?" Jessie just loved to be alongside them.'

While the Duchess was absorbed with her ailing husband, Jimmy went to stay with Barbara Hutton in a rented house at Hillsborough (near San Francisco). Freed from the courtly constraints of escorting the Windsors around, he and Barbara took themselves off to the Beige Room, a gay club which featured female impersonators. According to David Heymann, Barbara had been told that one of the transvestite acts was a send-up of herself and the 'other' richest woman in the world, the tobacco heiress Doris Duke. The women were portrayed travelling across America in the back of a limousine when they stop at a service station to visit the bathroom. Barbara goes first but on her return warns there is no toilet paper. Doris, desperate, rummages through her bag but finds no substitute. 'You should have said something earlier, Dee-Dee,' remarks Barbara. 'If I'd known I would have saved you a traveller's cheque. I just used my last one.' The real Barbara, and her cousin, broke up laughing.

⁂

Jimmy opened 1953 with a New Year's Day party for Wallis and the Duke at El Morocco. A few days later the Duke welcomed Randolph Churchill, who came to tea at the Waldorf Towers. An ardent monarchist, an incurable romantic and a faithful friend, Randolph had continued to publicly support the cause of the Duke of Windsor long after it had become unfashionable. But the truth was that Randolph had become an insufferable bore, given to endless monologues, and it was only with difficulty that the royal couple could escape after cocktails, using Elsa Maxwell and a visit to the theatre as their excuse.

On 5 January the Windsors returned the favour by giving a cocktail party in their rooms at the Waldorf Towers. They then descended in the elevator to the hotel below where were gathered 1,200 of New York's most glittering members of the Social Register. They walked into the vast ballroom to thunderous applause. In their diary the event was described as 'Veterans' Ball', but to their social group it was being billed by the foghorn-voiced Elsa Maxwell as The Duchess of Windsor's Ball.

Sitting at Jessie Donahue's table, set against a backdrop designed by Cecil Beaton, the Windsors entered into the spirit of the affair rather more than usual. After dinner, the drums rolled, the curtains parted and out stepped Wallis wearing a white taffeta and coral dress. She followed this revelation with a quick-change routine, emerging in two more dresses before leading a parade of mannequins on to the dance-floor to the strains of the specially-composed 'Windsor Waltz'. This found

192

immense favour, and was calculated so to do. But later that night, according to an eyewitness, Geoffrey Bocca, Jimmy and the Duchess 'had their heads together, and were buried deep in conversation that made now one then the other gurgle with laughter. The Duke across the table . . . listened in desultory fashion to the gales of laughter, and seemed preoccupied.' This was nothing new. But it was new that the word was starting to leak out about this curious threesome.

Until now that Jimmy and the Windsors were an 'item' was known only to an intimate group of people. Often hostesses would receive instructions that when an invitation was being issued to the Duke and Duchess, Jimmy should be included as well. 'Can my naughty boy come too?' the Duchess playfully wrote, more than once.

As usual in late January they took off for the annual duck-shooting party hosted by their friends George Baker and his mother Edith on the Horse Shoe Plantation at Tallahassee, one of the Duke's great treats. On their return, they found that during their absence, Barbara Hutton had nearly died from an overdose of Seconal.

Since Jimmy's visit to San Francisco the previous autumn, Barbara had gone into decline, convincing herself she had only a year to live and that she was dying of some unspecified ailment. Her Hollywood physician impotently reported that she was on 'Seconal, Codeine, Demerol and anything else she could get her hands on.' She was admitted to hospital, then released, then rushed back in after it was discovered she had swallowed two dozen Seconal tablets. Not for the first time she had come within a whisker of death. Boredom, loneliness and too much money constantly drove her to seek her own dance with the devil. She travelled to Paris in March but almost immediately tried again to commit suicide, this time by slashing her throat and her left wrist with a razor blade. Her doctor was of the opinion that this attempt was simply a cry for help. Like her cousin Jimmy all she wanted was attention, love, and admiration.

Back in America the Windsors moved south to Florida, where the Duke spent every day, as he now did wherever he went outside New York, fruitlessly trying to improve his golf technique. He was at Clearwater when he heard that his mother, the eighty-five-year-old Queen Mary, was nearing the end of her life. He had visited her at Marlborough House the year before when he attended the king's funeral. Now, he prepared to return to Britain once more, via New York. After a hasty meeting with his tax consultants on 5 March he went to collect his sister, the Princess Royal, from Idlewild airport. She had flown there from Trinidad, where she was spending the winter. The Duchess went too, meeting her sister-in-law for the first time in sixteen years. Next day brother and sister – but not the Duchess, who was still unwelcome in Britain – set sail on the *Queen Elizabeth*, taking with them a maid and valet. In the first-class passenger list for that voyage the Duke describes himself as 'Edward Windsor', and his proposed address in the UK as 'Buckingham Palace'. Quite whether he thought, as former monarch, that this would be a suitable place for him to rest his head is unclear, but there was no bed for him in his former official residence. In the end he stayed with his brother the Duke of Gloucester in the less glamorous surroundings of York House, St James's.

The *Queen Elizabeth* sailed from New York on 6 March and the Duke did not return until the beginning of April, the longest period the Windsors had ever been apart. His days were filled with the lingering passing of his mother, and with meetings with various members of his family. On Thursday 12 March he went to visit Queen Mary at Marlborough House, then on to Buckingham Palace to pay his respects to the new

sovereign, his niece. Next day he consulted his doctors before
going to spend the weekend in the country with his friend the
Earl of Dudley.

Though Queen Mary was dying she seemed in no hurry –
'hanging around someone who has been so mean and vile to
you, my sweetheart, is getting me down,' the Duke wrote to
the Duchess – and, frustrated at having exhausted his small
social circle in London, he decided to spend a few days in
France. He took the cross-channel ferry and drove down to the
Mill to inspect the progress being made on its garden, forbore
to spend the night alone there and returned to Paris, then
repeated the same process the following morning. Without a
guiding hand, he was lost as to how to fill his days. He returned
to London and met Sir Harold Nicolson who agreed to help
him with an article he was writing on the Coronation, then
retreated to Lord Dudley's house for another golf-filled weekend. On 23 March he had a meeting with the Prime Minister,
Winston Churchill, before returning to Marlborough House
the next day to be witness at his mother's deathbed.

So completely unwanted was the Duke during the flurry of
activity which followed Queen Mary's passing that, after
attending family prayers, he took the ferry back to France and,
while the British nation mourned, spent the next three days
playing golf and pottering around in his garden at the Mill.
These actions put paid to the sentimental gloss put on the death
of his mother by successive biographers. Nor, given her own
history, does it seem in the slightest likely that the Duchess,
on hearing the news of Queen Mary's death, sat and wept as
was implied by her private secretary. The old Queen had been
her implacable foe, the instrument of her husband's exile and
the cause of their nomadic downward spiral. To describe the
Duke as 'grief-stricken', as some have done, is far wide of the
mark. He wrote to Wallis: 'I somehow feel that the fluids in

her veins must always have been as icy-cold as they now are in death.' He played no part in the organisation of the funeral service, and only a vestigial role in the ceremony itself. He was viewed with barely-concealed hatred by the Queen Mother, and with suspicion by the powers-that-be at Buckingham Palace. The Queen, influenced by her mother and the private secretary, Sir Alan Lascelles, who had played such a large part in marginalising the Duke under the previous sovereignty, kept her distance.

As soon as he decently could, the Duke drove to Southampton and headed back to New York. 'What a smug, stinking lot my relations are and you've never seen such a seedy worn-out bunch of old hags most of them have become,' he scribbled furiously in his last letter to Wallis. 'I've been boiling mad the whole time that you haven't been here in your rightful place as a daughter-in-law at my side. But let us skip this rude interlude and enjoy our lovely full life together, far removed from the boredom, the restrictions and the intrigues of the Royal Family and the Court. You don't know how much I love you, my Sweetheart, and . . . I'll not relax until I can hold you tight again.' These were sorry words, written, as so much of the Windsor correspondence appears at this distance, with half an eye on posterity.

During that long month's separation, the Duchess and Jimmy had had free reign. Conscious that she must keep a low profile during her husband's period of mourning, she donned black and at first stayed away from public places. But Jessie Donahue was away in Palm Beach for the season, and according to the reports of staff at 834, Wallis spent many evenings at Jimmy's apartment in Jessie's absence.

'There was a little restaurant just off Park Avenue and 59th,' recalled the interior designer Billy Baldwin. 'I heard an absolute roar of laughter from the entrance of the restaurant, and into

the room, like two children, rushed the Duchess and Jimmy
... to the furthest corner at the back-back-back of the room
where there was practically no light ... After, they would
quietly go to Jimmy's apartment.'

There they planned the apartment's re-decoration and talked
about the future. But this was an uncomfortable time for
Jimmy. Not a man given to introspection and, until now,
allowed only stolen moments with the Duchess, he found her
undiluted company difficult to handle. Even though he had
mentioned marriage, he had never quite envisaged having this
woman, twenty years his senior, occupying every waking
moment of his life. Apart from anything else, their lifestyles
were entirely different: and though when night fell they became
as one, the Duchess would rise early the next morning, steely
and disciplined, to set about a programme of activities. With
no quasi-public role to play, and with no job to go to, Jimmy
preferred to linger in bed and contemplate a more languid levée.
Though sexually compatible, they remained in many other
respects poles apart.

None the less, on the night of Queen Mary's funeral, while
Britain came to a standstill and flags were lowered to half-mast
across the nation, they went out 'to celebrate', in Jimmy's
words. They went to dinner at the Colony, then on to El
Morocco where they danced and drank a great deal. As they
left, Jimmy gave the *maître d'* a one hundred dollar bill and
declared loudly, 'I am now going to have the best blowjob in
all America', before wafting out into the night.

It is not difficult to imagine the Duke's state of mind on his
return to the Waldorf Towers. Some who knew the Windsors
then take the view that Wallis used Jimmy as just another stick
with which to beat her subservient husband; and to this extent
he was prepared to put up with his rival's continued presence.
Certainly Wallis was in no mood to hide Jimmy from the Duke

after their month alone together; the Duke's diary despairingly notes for 13 April: 'Dinner. Mr Donahue.'

During April, immediately after his return from his mother's funeral, the Duke dined with Jessie sometimes twice a week, but she did not have the couple all to herself. Her rival, Margaret Biddle, still had the ability to score a victory or two: the famous photograph of the Duke and Duchess, watching with solemn regret the televised coronation of his niece Queen Elizabeth II on 2 June 1953, was taken at Margaret Biddle's Paris home. Jimmy watched the ceremony at the Ritz in his cousin Barbara's suite: she herself had sufficiently recovered from her *douleur de vie* to head for London in order to witness the Coronation at first-hand.

To celebrate the Coronation, and the Queen's official birthday which followed within a few days, the British Embassy in Paris staged a ballet, followed by dinner. Oliver Harvey, the ambassador, who had a particular dislike of the Windsors, was under instructions to 'do something' with them, so invited them to the ballet but not to dinner. After the ballet, the Duke and his wife slunk home where they dined alone. Fortunately their friends, high-born and not so high-born, rallied round at this time: the Earl of Dudley came to pay a visit, and drove out to the Mill to witness its progress towards becoming a mini-Fort Belvedere; and Jessie arrived from New York, her annual $300,000 gambling money stowed about her person, ready for an amusing few summer months in France. Her first act was to cheer the doleful pair with a dinner at Maxim's and indeed, there was at last something to celebrate: on 22 June the Windsors signed the lease on a house in the Route du Champ d'Entrainement, on the edge of the Bois du Boulogne, fifteen minutes from the centre of Paris, which was to be their principal residence for the rest of their lives.

Next, there was a jostle to help the Duke celebrate his 59th birthday; once again Margaret Biddle won the day and was his hostess that night. Jessie's own celebrations would have to wait till the following evening. Jimmy chipped in with his own small birthday celebration for the Duke at the Tour d'Argent two days after that.

Some friends found it curious that the Duke should accept from Jimmy an expensive birthday present of gold cufflinks inlaid with sapphires; indeed that he had accepted other such gifts in the past. His supporters put this down to the Duke's preternatural good manners, that he would shrink from refusing for fear of giving offence. Others took a less charitable view, arguing that there was a word for men who accepted presents from their wife's lover. Whatever, there were occasions when a spontaneous gesture such as the donation of a pair of cufflinks could improve the shining hour – as the retiring former Captain of the *Queen Mary*, Sir James Bisset, discovered when he was called to the Windsor stateroom on one transatlantic voyage and was unexpectedly handed a pair of gold links. Whether they were a pair Jimmy had given the Duke, no one knows. It was curious that when Sotheby's came to sell the Windsor jewels at auction many of the Duke's cufflinks were missing from the collection.

⚘

Given the fury Jimmy's presence generated on board the *Sister Anne* two summers before, it seems extraordinary that the Duke and Duchess should wish to cruise the Mediterranean with him ever again. Yet when he offered to charter a yacht to repeat their disastrous voyage of 1951, they accepted with alacrity, for the organisation and cost of such delights was beyond the Windsors. First, July was spent in Biarritz with Jessie Donahue and Eric Dudley as their mainstay companions,

199

dining repeatedly at the Pélican and the Villa Carlotta. Then as August approached the party headed east, Jessie going on to her rented villa in Monte Carlo and the Windsors arriving at Cannes to join Jimmy aboard the *Narcissus*. The schedule was not dissimilar to that of the *Sister Anne* cruise – patrolling the Gulf of Genoa, the yacht would take in Monte Carlo, Rapallo, San Remo and Portofino on a lazy four-week cruise.

According to Truman Capote, a week after the trio's departure from Portofino, Noel Coward arrived and had an outspoken discussion with Capote on the Windsor-Donahue-Windsor triangle. 'I like Jimmy,' Coward told him. 'He's an insane camp, but fun. And I like the Duchess; she's the fag-hag to end all – but that's what makes her likeable. The Duke, however, well, he pretends not to hate me. He does, though. Because I'm queer and he's queer but, unlike him, I don't pretend not to be. Anyway, the fag-hag must be enjoying it. Here she's got a royal queen to sleep with and a rich one to hump.'

For Capote, it was not sufficient that Jimmy and the Duchess were sleeping together, somehow the Duke had to be involved as well. In fairness he (or Coward, if Coward actually spoke the words ascribed to him) was not the first to try to turn it into a true *ménage à trois*. But whatever the Duke's own sexual complexities there is nothing to suggest that he was attracted to Jimmy, or Jimmy to him. The author Michael Bloch suggests that there may have been a repressed homosexual streak within the Duke, but if there was, Jimmy never caught a whiff of it. In later years, Jimmy was never averse to repeating details of his sex-life with the Duchess. But when one person raised the possibility of the Duke being queer, Jimmy snapped back a very sharp denial. If anyone were to know, it would have been Jimmy – Jimmy, or a woman the Duke had slept with. And in Caroline Blackwood's idiosyncratic memoir *The Last of the Duchess* she recalls a conversation with the Marquesa de Casa

Maury, the former Freda Dudley Ward who had been the Duke's mistress when he was Prince of Wales. 'The Duke was never homosexual. If the Duke had been homosexual, I would have known. I think he may have been a masochist.'

The trio ended their holiday with a short visit to Baden-Baden before returning to Paris on 8 September. Two nights later they were dining with Jessie. Jimmy had arranged the Mediterranean cruise, but it was Jessie's money that paid for it. Her payback was to hear from the Duke and Duchess how it had gone, and during the dinner conversation there was time for Jessie to recount how, once again, she had lost the $300,000 gambling money she had taken with her that summer.

As summer turned to autumn, work continued on the Mill, and finally the Windsors moved into the house at 4 Route du Champ d'Entrainement. By now they had forsaken all hope of returning to a permanent home in England – indeed, had come to dislike the idea of returning there with the inevitable discourtesies and snobberies they knew would await them. Now, a house they could turn into a palace-in-exile was envisaged, offered to them by the city of Paris at a modest rent. Grand, imposing, and formerly the residence of President de Gaulle, it could not have been more fitting. Faced with a beauteous stone façade, balconied, porticoed, having a rose-and-green marble entrance hall two stories high and a dignified iron gate with a high spiked iron fence redolent of Buckingham Palace, it was a truly fitting backdrop for these two historic figures.

With the new sovereign embarking on a six-month tour of the Commonwealth, the Duke felt it safe to creep with his wife into Britain for a week in late November. Jimmy was not invited; his presence could be tolerated in New York, Paris, Biarritz and the Mediterranean, but in ultra-critical London, where the Windsors had to step on eggshells, where their behaviour had to be superlatively *comme il faut*, Jimmy was too much of a risk. With his mother, he returned to New York; his own particular destination was the gay bars where he could behave as he liked, without constraint.

⚜

Maybe it was out of pique for being excluded from the London trip, maybe it was Jimmy just being Jimmy. Either way, as the coronation year of 1953 drew to a close, Jessie Donahue's favourite son perpetrated on his lover and her husband the most awful practical joke of his career.

On 31 December he and the Duke and Duchess arrived at El Morocco to see in the New Year. Somehow, somewhere during the evening he found two paper party-hats in the form of crowns and, as the El Morocco crowd looked on with roars of approval, Jimmy performed a coronation of his own – first on the Duke, then the Duchess. People laughed, but it was a tragic, awful moment.

Later, as the royal couple donned their coats and waited in the lobby for their car to take them back to the Waldorf Towers, Jimmy encouraged a photographer forward to record the couple's departure. Captured for posterity is an unhappy portrait of the former King Edward VIII and his consort at their lowest ebb, crowned not with hushed reverence before his peers at Westminster Abbey, but in a drunken, noisy New York nightclub.

Some time later, when the affair was over, the society photographer Jerome Zerbe had lunch with the Duchess at La Côte Basque in New York. He told his old friend: 'The only thing you've ever done that I disapproved of was running around with Jimmy Donahue.' The Duchess made some vague comment about Jimmy being a pleasant escort. Zerbe said: 'He

202

was a man who destroyed everything he touched. He destroyed your reputation.'

The Duchess said she had never thought of it like that.

CHAPTER 10

A Bloody Shin

Jimmy's cousin Barbara Hutton, having cast off her princeling husband Igor Troubetzkoy, was fast approaching another marital dalliance. This time, though, her attitude towards the solemnised state was more like a rich woman walking into a shop, buying a fur, then casting it in the gutter because she changed her mind on the way out.

For her fifth husband, Barbara chose the playboy and Dominican diplomat Porfirio Rubirosa, who at the time was engaged in a passionate liaison with the actress Zsa Zsa Gabor. The manner in which they came to marry was similar to her discussion with Oleg Cassini some years before: You seem suitable, I will pay you a lot of money, drop everything and marry me.

Jimmy was appalled. He became the go-between in a complex financial deal which was, effectively, a pre-nuptial contract to buy Rubirosa's services as a husband, and to limit his claim against Barbara when the inevitable occurred. Rubi, as he was known, initially refused to settle for less than $3m ($20.7m); eventually he was beaten down to $2.5m. Everyone, including the two participants, knew the marriage was doomed even before it started, and though the ceremony took place in New York, the journey from 834 Fifth Avenue to the Dominican Ambassador's residence – a five-minute car ride – proved too much for Jessie and for Jimmy: 'They asked me if I wanted to come and I said no,' he told reporters stiffly. Barbara headed south to Palm Beach where, discovering her new husband was not welcome at Cielito Lindo, she set up a marital home at the Maharajah of Baroda's villa just down the road. Within six weeks she had moved out into the Everglades Club, and the rift between her and her aunt Jessie was patched up: 'Barbara is definitely through with that disgusting man,' was the matriarch's haughty comment.

Officially the marriage had lasted fifty-three days and, apart from his marriage settlement, Rubi had picked up around $1m ($6.9m) in gifts. It was all Palm Beach could talk about when the Windsors arrived to stay with Jessie at Cielito Lindo. Delighted to be able once again to show off her house-guests to island society, Jessie put her niece's problems to one side and organised a dinner-party for sixty guests in the beach-house – 'more like a film set than a mere house by the beach', as the columnist Suzy remarked.

This was no ordinary dinner-party, for Jessie had ambitions. She wanted the evening's entertainment provided by her guests, and ringmastered by her best friend the Duchess. It would be an evening the like of which Palm Beach had never before seen, an evening which would conclusively prove that Jessie was queen of the island and settle once and for all the question: who, of all the Palm Beachers who had opened their doors to the Windsors, was most fitting to be their hostess? The idea for the party's entertainment came from Jimmy but, after the debacle of the New Year's Eve picture of the Duke and Duchess at El Morocco, it was filtered through his mother. Responding slowly at first, the Windsors said finally that yes, it would be good to have an informal cabaret and yes, they would agree to participate. Jimmy, determined to make Wallis dance, spent hours with her in the library of Cielito Lindo showing her how to make the most of leading a conga-line. The Duke went away and prepared his own contribution.

Come the night, the Duchess stood up behind a microphone and announced herself to be the MC for the evening. The first act was her husband, as part of a barber-shop quartet including Lord Dudley, Charles Cushing and Palm Beach luminary Milton 'Doc' Holden. Rumba, hulas and a paso doble followed a competition where couples had to dance with an orange held between their foreheads (winners: the Windsors) before Jessie got up and demonstrated to her unsuspecting neighbours that the gossip columnists had been right all along. As a result of her singing lessons she *could* sing. Jessie executed an aria from *Rigoletto*, before the Duchess ended the evening by leading the whole party in an energetic conga. The effervescent Jimmy for once confined himself to a side-of-stage role, occasionally helping out by conducting the Meyer Davis orchestra. Barbara, too drunk these days to entertain anyone much, stayed in the shadows.

Given that within a few short months she was to be cast into darkness, despite all her billets-doux and her presents and her jewellery and her chartered yachts, the evening was a merciful climax to Jessie Donahue's social rise. After three or four days the Duke moved on to stay at other houses in the resort, but Jessie had triumphed.

Jimmy returned to New York alone, then went on to Long Island to stay at his brother Wooly's estate at Riverhead. Wallis followed. The Duke stayed behind in Florida to acquire a driver's licence,[1] and for four days Jimmy and Wallis re-enacted the month of cohabitation they had enjoyed while the Duke had been mourning his mother in England. The Duke snatched back his prize on 13 March, noting with anticipation in his diary 'W arrives', and the next week the couple made their first return to Nassau, the little kingdom they had ruled a decade before. On their return to New York they dined with Jessie before setting sail on the *Queen Elizabeth* for France.

During this period the Windsors learned – not from Buckingham Palace, but from their friends in New York – that it was the Queen Mother's intention to visit America in the Fall. This news was greeted with horror by the Windsors, who considered America 'their' territory, but with hilarity by Jimmy, who promised all sorts of pranks to discomfit the royal progress. As time had gone by, the bitterness had increased rather than diminished, and the Windsors would now discuss quite openly their feelings for their sister-in-law who, in Britain, had achieved an extraordinary status, almost unprecedented in royal history, of universal love and approbation. There, not a word was heard in criticism against her, but, *chez* Windsor, the Duke referred to her as 'that fat Scotch cook' and 'the Loch Ness monster'. When she appeared on television, the Duke yodelled, 'Here comes the Blimp', while the Duchess now called her 'that fourteen-carat beauty' and 'the monster of Glamis'.

Back in Palm Beach a friend who had a beauty shop on Worth Avenue sent Wallis a box of new powder called 'Duchess of York'. 'Thank you,' she responded crisply. 'And you know where I'll put it.'

---

1 When asked to enter his occupation he wrote 'None.' His friend Eric Dudley jokingly advised him: 'make that "Peer of the Realm"'.

Backed by the likes of Jessie Donahue, Elsa Maxwell was now the doyenne of party-givers, both in America and Paris, and wielded further power through her newspaper columns and books. Though grateful to Jessie for the cheques which arrived, regular as clockwork, four times a year, she loathed Jimmy, who loved to mimic her. He once turned up at 21 in a dress stuffed with pillows, wearing odd shoes and a five o'clock shadow, claiming to be Miss Maxwell, and noisily demanding her usual table. She disliked the fact that he publicly paraded his homosexuality without apology and got away with it, while she had to contain her lesbianism ('she is the oaken bucket in the *Well of Loneliness*,' quipped Wallis). And she hated the fact that he was having an affair with the Duchess.

It seemed all wrong to her, and when she spoke sharply to the Duchess about 'discretion' in her personal life it was the same voice that had condoned a hundred other high-society affairs. Jimmy and the Duchess perplexed her, and she took it out on Wallis. Later she wrote: 'I no longer see the Duchess of Windsor. She has become so completely engrossed in herself and in her pursuit of pleasure that she neither knows nor cares what others are thinking or feeling. Had she been more conscientious about her position in history, she would not have to search so constantly for excitement and amusement. It's my considered opinion that many of the things she has done in this search, largely because of the high-handed, selfish way in which she has done them, have contributed to her final frustration – the fact that the Windsors' prestige is not what it was, not what it used to be.'

Maybe, indeed, they were now *déclassé*, as the British Ambassador had suggested a decade before, but the Duke and Duchess still carried about them a glamour which Miss Maxwell could never possess, and a sort of plangent appeal which she could never conceive of. And yet her words struck home.

By now, after a month of commuting daily between Paris and Gif-sur-Yvette, the Windsors were ready to receive weekend guests at the Mill, even though the refurbishment was not yet complete. Jimmy, along with Princess Ghislaine de Polignac, was the first to stay. 'The Duchess used to call me her guinea-pig,' recalls the Princess. 'I was supposed to try every room every weekend and tell her what was missing, what was wrong. She listened to me because I could offer criticism with a joke and a laugh – she had a great sense of humour. That first weekend, it was hardly finished but she wanted to start slowly, see how everything went. She was a dedicated hostess.'

Virtually derelict when they had taken it over, the Mill now positively glowed with the Windsor style. The millhouse was the main residence, while an old one-and-a-half storey barn had been opened up to provide a summer dining room. Outbuildings became guest rooms, with walls of yellow felt, or black-and-white quilt. The rooms were fitted with every article the traveller might require, from cluttered drinks trays to razor, soap, brushes, pen, ink, cigarettes, radio and a telephone to connect to eighteen other extensions in the house. It was, by rural French standards, a revelation; for the general rule was to live in a château, big or small, not convert a building created for the *paysannerie*. Soon, however, emboldened by the Windsors' lead, others followed suit.

This first weekend, with Jimmy and the Princess, was deemed a success. Wallis moved on to invite others to whom she owed much, both in terms of hospitality and favours done. The great supporters – Eric Dudley, Gray Phillips, Alastair Mackintosh, Martha Slater, 'Fruity' Metcalfe, the Marquesa de Portago, Charles Blackwell – all came, entered their name in the visitors' book, stayed two nights, and signed themselves out again. Jimmy stayed often, usefully making up uneven dinner-party numbers. While the Duke showed his guests around the garden he had created, Jimmy stayed indoors and gossiped with the Duchess. One guest, the Guinness heiress Mrs Aileen Plunket, recalled that at dinner he loved to embarrass the footmen by making loud remarks about their genitals: 'The unfortunate footmen would go scarlet in the face and their hands would shake so much that they nearly dropped the plates.'

Jimmy thanked his hosts with more dinners in Paris, and helped draw up the list of next guests – Count Czernin, the Baron de Cabrol, the Maharajah of Baroda and Madame Embiricos. For two months, until they headed south-west for their usual stay in Biarritz, the Windsors entertained at the Mill at an increasing pace, the Duke enamoured with their new creation. Jimmy took particular delight in teasing Wallis with the amount of Woolworth money which had gone into the Mill's makeover, but she was unmoved: if people wanted to give, she was more than happy to receive.

In Biarritz, the Windsors met up again with Jessie, her purses once more loaded down with her $300,000 gambling money and, with Jimmy once more in attendance, they entertained on a grander scale than hitherto. Maybe it was the financial underpinning of the $1 million ($6.8m) the Duke was supposed to have received from *A King's Story*; maybe Jessie was bankrolling them; or maybe the couple had suddenly developed a taste for providing their own entertainment rather than relying on what they sometimes considered the inferior offerings of their friends. Whichever, they hosted entertainments almost every other night during their fortnight's stay, dining out only once with the Marquis and Marquesa de Portago.

Towards the end of July, the Woolworths and Windsors headed east for the second part of their holiday, Jessie travelling by chauffeur-driven Rolls Royce, taking the same route she had used to escape the Second World War fourteen years before, and the Windsors and Jimmy breaking with tradition and flying to Cannes. There awaiting them once again was the *Narcissus*, crewed with a complement of fifteen, chartered by Jimmy and paid for by Jessie.

This, the third lengthy summer holiday taken by all three was to be more ambitious than its predecessors. First the *Narcissus* docked at Monte Carlo where Jessie, based at the Hôtel de Paris, was already hard at work pursuing her life's passion. She and her equally enthusiastic gambling friend Dorothy Strelsin were labelled 'the two white birds' because their dedication to the game kept them from the plentiful sunshine outside. The British columnist William Hickey, observing Jessie at play one night, opined to his readers in the *Daily Express*:

> If reports from this gilded playground fill you with envy, may I offer you this small piece of consolation. The wealthy and the famous who spend their lives on the giddy international merry-go-round don't appear to get very much fun out of it. I have seen the same faces here as I have in Miami, Havana, Jamaica, Paris and New York. Bored. Empty. Discontented. The sad masks of poor little rich folk going round in circles and getting nowhere.
>
> Take the Duchess of Windsor's friends, the Donahues, for instance. They have more money than they could spend – or even count! – in a lifetime. And they are nice people I am sure. But oh, how abysmally bored they always look.
>
> Each night, beautifully gowned and wearing a fortune in furs and jewels, Mrs Donahue plays chemin-de-fer in the Casino. She sits in solemn silence for hours, monotonously staking £200 (£3,160) on each turn of the cards. And, win or lose, the sad expression on her chalk-white face never alters.

If this seemed a dreary way to pass the month of August, then Jimmy, Wallis and the Duke were to have no part of it. Tied up alongside Aristotle Onassis, the King of Monte Carlo – Rainier was merely the prince – and his yacht, the *Christina*, encouraged them to think big. From their familiar landfall at Rapallo they would sail on to Capri, Naples, Ischia, Ponsa, Livorno – then Venice. The holiday would end with a few days in Austria, with a trip over the border to Munich.

After four years of each other's company, this tight-knit threesome were beginning to weary of each other: Jimmy, because of the Duchess's need to possess outrightly anything she deemed was hers; because of his boredom at having to address the Duke constantly in a courtly fashion in order to please both; and because of their capacity to endlessly sop up Woolworth money without ever asking whether the spigot might run dry. There was little chance of that, but even in this mega-million world there were times when you stopped to count the cost. Jessie had sold tranches of Woolworth stock to fund her lifestyle, which included the expensive Windsors; Jimmy had had to borrow from Barbara as well as his mother to keep the thing afloat. The Windsors gave little in return, save for themselves. Other friends like Margaret Biddle asked for little more, but then she was not bankrolling the Windsors in the way the Donahues were; consequently her expectations of the royal couple were, realistically, lower.

If Jimmy was tiring of this *ménage* – later he complained to his sister-in-law: 'I hate playing cards and I got stuck *every afternoon* with the Duke, playing gin rummy' – so too were its other members. The Duchess, now fifty-nine, had with Jimmy sated the banked-up passions of her arid love-life and begun to dwell on the other aspects of his personality.

'Jimmy was not an all-rounder,' says someone who knew him at that time. 'The world which Wallis had entered by a process of osmosis was still largely a closed door to Jimmy. He knew nothing of affairs of state, was uninterested in meeting politicians and statesmen, and many of the people the Windsors dwelt on in later life – the Moncktons and the Metcalfes – were people he had never met and who meant nothing to him. He was worldly, but politics bored him, which they did not the Windsors. He was sophisticated but did not know a Fragonard from a frog. He was a brilliant gossip, prankster and joker – but there was never a *quiet* moment when he was around.'

Maybe the Duchess had finally begun to regret her too-public dalliance; that finally the imprecations of Elsa Maxwell and her social superiors had begun to take root. As a woman approaching sixty she may possibly have sensed the truth of what Jimmy was saying behind her back – that her face, on the pillow, looked like that of an old sailor.

The last member of this trio had played a long game, but then there was nowhere else for the Duke to go. He had given up his throne and empire for the woman he loved; a martyr he could be for the history books, and gladly, but a cuckolded martyr does not have quite the same ring to it. He simply had to ride out the storm, for history's sake. One of his godchildren told this writer: 'He never seemed to have a moment's regret about what he did, quitting the throne. But if he *did* have any regrets, it would have been during the Jimmy period. It had been, by anyone's standards, unbelievably humiliating for him, but he never showed it. He considered the Duchess the perfect woman.'

Certainly the atmosphere aboard the *Narcissus* was different from the previous years. 'Jimmy had got so carried away with his own self-importance,' says one of the Duke's old circle. 'He really did have control of her, he was probably the only person that ever did. She was *so* involved with him.' Having wrested control of Wallis from the Duke, having considered and dismissed marriage, what more was there to do? Though part of Jimmy remained besotted by her, the other part of his life, his homosexuality, was now a resurgent and energising force.

The *Narcissus* stopped at Capri. The Duke and Duchess stepped ashore and went shopping. They dined in a small restaurant and continued their walkabout, happily acknowledging the applause of the crowds. Jimmy, meanwhile, whisked away and made for a sailor's bar. Some time later, when everyone had returned on board and the yacht slipped anchor and headed towards Naples, there was a commotion. On returning to his cabin Jimmy discovered that six sports jackets, a golden rosary, his passport and a wallet containing $2,000 ($31,750) had been stolen.

The Duke was furious. He called the police, as once before he had called the police when his friend and benefactor Sir Harry Oakes had been murdered in Nassau, ten years before. He did not like dealing with them, but felt that as the senior figure on board he should appear to be in charge. To the Duchess he implied that the culprit must have been a sailor Jimmy had picked up on Capri, or else a member of the fifteen-strong crew whom no doubt he had been seeing below-decks.

The Duke hated the publicity, which he found demeaning. Jimmy was no happier. There was something about the robbery which was a tainted reminder of the great jewel heist perpetrated by his father all those years ago. Knowing that, most likely, he had only himself to blame he felt acute embarrassment and no little loss of prestige. Unlike Jessie's priceless jewels, however, the money, the coats, the rosary and passport were not recovered despite a minute search of the *Narcissus*. In a sour mood, the yacht-party continued its cruise.

Finally the party found landfall at Venice, where they decamped and parked their bags at the Gritti Palace, the palatial home-from-home on the Grand Canal. The next few days were spent in blissful calm and comfort, paid for by Jessie, though the irritations caused by too long an exposure to sun, sea and each other – three is such a difficult number – remained in the background.

From Venice the party continued its journey by road to Austria. A motorcade of five cars – the Windsors' Rolls Royce, Jimmy's Cadillac, a staff car and two others containing luggage, wound its way to Lake Worthersee and the baroque charm of the Schloss Velden, a hotel situated at the edge of the warmest alpine lake in Europe. This was the Duke's section of the holiday: the yacht cruise, in the end, was endured on sufferance, and now he was able to return to a part of the world he loved and whose language he spoke fluently. Here he was able to pick up his golf clubs after six weeks' abstinence and tackle the hotel's eighteen-hole course. Though the surroundings were magnificent, there was little for Wallis and Jimmy to do since neither was inclined to take walks in the woods or in the beautiful surrounding parkland. Wallis and Jimmy, trapped in a place they did not want to be, and after so long in each other's daily company, began to grate even further on each other's nerves.

In the evening of 28 August, the party set out for the summer residence of the Duke's kinsman, Prince Maximilian Windisch-Graetz, at Sekirn, seventeen kilometres away on the other side of Lake Worthersee. The Duchess had ordered a hire-car so that the chauffeurs in the royal motorcade could go to bed early before setting out the next day for Munich. Instead they spent the night drinking in the Wieser Hotel until nearly four in the morning.

The driver hired to take the Windsors to their party recalls: 'The road was totally cleared of all traffic for them, and the Duke talked to me in excellent German throughout the whole journey, about how things were in the country now the war was over, about the kind of car I was driving. But his wife often interrupted him, quite inconsiderately. Time and again she broke into his conversation, finally she stopped it completely by insisting that we were not on the correct route.'

Increasingly frustrated at being left out of the conversation in a language she could not speak, Wallis became hysterical, accusing the driver of not knowing the way. The Duke was forced to ask him to stop and ask at a house whether they were on the right route. The man came back and assured them they were and, five minutes later, they arrived at the Windisch-Graetz lake house, Karinderhutte. But the evening had already been ruined by the Duchess's shrewish behaviour. They had had too much leisure; it was high time they all went home.

Next morning the entourage of twelve – the Windsors with their valet and maid, Jimmy with his valet, plus a bodyguard and five drivers – set off in a disagreeable mood for Munich. It had been seventeen years since the Duke had set foot in the city during his ill-starred tour of Nazi Germany in October 1937. Some would argue that in the intervening seventeen years, the Duke had learned nothing. Munich was anxious to accord him visiting-monarch status, he equally anxious to accept. If the official red carpet was no longer rolled out in the capital cities of Europe, then why not remind oneself of how it used to be, here in this friendly and accommodating place?

The Windsors' first call was to tea with the German Ambassador to Madrid, Prince Adalbert of Bavaria. It little mattered that the prince was a kinsman of the Duke; the whole episode of the German attempt to suborn the Windsors in Spain at the outset of the war was too recent for comfort, and British officials who hovered in the background winced at this very public reminder of his close ties with the Nazi regime. But the red carpet had been laid at their feet and the Duke and Duchess were determined to walk down it. Next was a visit to Prince and Princess Constantine of Bavaria at Nymphenburg Castle, coupled with a tour of a local porcelain factory, and a walk round the Schonheiten Gallery and the Marstall Museum. The royal progress concluded with a meeting with the German culture minister Dr Keim, and a visit to the ballet at the Gartnertheater and a meeting with the director of the State Opera, Bruno Neissen.

It had all the hallmarks of a state visit and wherever the Windsors went, Jimmy went too, still bronzed and handsome from the *Narcissus* cruise; a beautifully-dressed young man who, to the adoring crowds, was clearly the aide-de-camp to the royal couple. He played up to the role magnificently and the two-day stopover was considered a triumph for all concerned: a fantasy tour for the protocol-starved Windsors and an amusing diversion for him. The Windsors rode out of Munich in their motorcade, surrounded by police outriders, happy in the knowledge they could still turn it on when asked.

⚜

The end of the affair was shocking, brutal, abrupt.

The final stop on the tour was Baden-Baden, the ancient spa town where the Duke's grandfather, King Edward VII, had demonstrated his skill at international diplomacy with consummate ease half a century before. Their destination was the Brenner's Park Hotel, a sumptuous nineteenth-century establishment where in 1860 Napoleon III attended a summit with the Crown Prince of Germany in which a fruitless non-aggression pact was agreed (the Franco-Prussian War followed soon after). The hotel had remained a favourite of European monarchs, both reigning and deposed.

The Windsors were greeted by the mayor of Baden-Baden, Dr Schlapper, and the hotel's owner, Kurt Brenner. Photographs were taken, and the honoured guests retired to adjoining suites. The plan was to spend five 'off-duty' days and nights at the hotel where the Duke would play golf and cards while Jimmy and the Duchess sunbathed and synchronised their schedules for the autumn in Paris and New York. On the first night, dining together as they had so often dined over the past weeks, there was no inkling of what was to come.

On the second day, the Duchess went sightseeing with Jimmy, wandering around the ancient spa town in the early autumn sunshine. All three met up again for dinner. But by the third day Jimmy was getting restless. Baden-Baden's atmosphere was too soporific, too jaw-achingly dull for him. After breakfast he headed off alone, in search of mischief. The Duchess remained behind at the hotel while the Duke continued his hopeless pursuit of the golf ball. The arrangement was that they should meet again for dinner at eight.

As they sat down, the Duchess remarked that Jimmy's breath smelt of garlic, and that it was selfish and crude to share his consumption of such a repellent commodity with others. Jimmy, no more so than his two companions, had drunk cocktails in anticipation of supper; he saw red. In a burst of temper he kicked the Duchess on the shin, under the table. 'She yelped with pain and jumped up. Her stocking was torn and her shin bled,' went Charles Murphy's account. 'The Duke called for the maid to fetch towels and Mercurochrome and helped the Duchess to a sofa, where he wiped away the blood and dressed the scrape. Only then did he turn to Donahue.

'All he said was, "We've had enough of you, Jimmy. Get out!"'

After four years and three months of being cuckolded, the worm had finally turned.

CHAPTER 11

ABDICATION

The end, when it came, was unforgiving and all-embracing. The name Donahue was not to be mentioned again in the presence of the Duke and Duchess. The hapless Jessie, who had lavished her Woolworth millions on them – feeding them, watering them, paying for their holidays, buying their jewels – was cast into the same dark abyss as her son.

Jimmy was determined to take it lightly. Asked by a newspaper columnist about the rumours that there had been a split between him and the Windsors, he quipped: 'I've abdicated.' He then explained that he now sought a quieter, less social life. No one was taken in for a minute. Later he was to be found sauntering down Fifth Avenue with a young male companion. 'Let me introduce you,' he whooped, 'to the boy who took the boy who took the girl who took the boy off the throne of Merry Old England.'

The Duke's diary, which for four years had weekly featured the name Donahue, was no longer thus adorned. The Duchess's

219

memoirs, published soon after the rift and entitled *The Heart Has Its Reasons*, make no mention of Jessie, nor of the colossal debt both the Duke and Duchess owed her. Perhaps more understandable, given the Duchess's determination to promulgate the belief that hers was the marriage of the century, was that there should be no mention in her pages of Jimmy. History had been swiftly re-written, the Donahues effectively airbrushed out, but the Duchess 'never forgave him', according to Barbara Hutton's secretary Mona Eldridge.

It was nothing new. The Windsors had a habit of cutting out of their lives those they needed most. 'Fruity' Metcalfe, the Duke's defender and supporter, equerry and best man, was dropped after the Duke ran out on him in the early stages of the war, abandoning not only Metcalfe but his military post, and chasing after Wallis to Biarritz. Later he wrote to another benefactor, Robert Young, describing Metcalfe as a 'four-flusher', that is to say, a cheat; a terrible and utterly unworthy assessment of his friend. Walter Monckton, another of the great heroes who gave much in their support of the wilful Duke, was upbraided by the Duchess after he was created Viscount Monckton of Brenchley: 'You got yourself a title, but you didn't get *me* one!' Monckton fumed to his wife: 'This from *her*, after all I've done for the Windsors! – selling Sandringham and Balmoral,[1] and getting the money out of England for them, and persuading the French Government to let them live here without paying taxes!'

Quite as much as Jimmy, it had been Jessie's habit over the past four years to shadow the movements of the Windsors – the annual tour would lead them from Palm Beach to New

---

1 Owned privately by the Duke and sold to his brother George VI on his abdication.

York, Paris, Biarritz, Côte d'Azur, Paris, and New York again, with Mrs Donahue patiently trailing behind. Now, with the awful prospect of being seen to be ostracised by her former best friends, she hastily retreated to New York where she began a furious and ostentatious round of socialising.

So too did Jimmy. Paris was now a busted flush and he rarely travelled there. Princess Ghislaine de Polignac recalls: 'He never made any true friends in Paris, he never tried. He was often invited where the Windsors went, but when the relationship ended he never came back to Paris. He had got bored with the Duke and Duchess, and bored with too much high society. Really what he wanted was to get back to his totally wild life in New York.'

The Duchess took out her friend, the Marquesa de Portago, to luncheon and announced, 'I have decided not to see Jimmy any more.' The Marquesa recalls it being said without any emotion, as if it was nothing more than a page had been turned.

Back in New York, and mindful that their paths were likely to cross once the Windsors returned to the Waldorf Towers, Jimmy set about finding a project to keep him, and his money, occupied. Inspired by what he had seen at close quarters of the Duchess's home-making skills, he now decided to create a backdrop of his own, a mirror-image of the Route du Champ d'Entrainement and the Moulin de la Tuilerie all rolled into one.

For the first home of his own – he was now nearly forty – Jimmy selected a neo-Georgian forty-room pile in the rich country of Long Island: Broadhollow, on Cedar Swamp Road at Old Brookville which carried with it a 108-acre spread. The previous owner, railways and Bromo-Seltzer heir Alfred Gwynne Vanderbilt who, valued at $25 million ($170 million) was rather richer than Jimmy and owned Belmont and Pimlico race tracks, had lived at Broadhollow for four years, using the house as a retreat where he and his wife, Lourdes, could entertain with lavish parties and soirees. The marriage foundered and Vanderbilt sold the estate to Jimmy for $400,000 (£2.7 million). 'Here,' proclaimed Jimmy, 'I shall only entertain the beautiful people.'

The layout of Broadhollow was certainly grand enough for that. From a vaulted Gothic hallway, doors led to a card room, library, drawing room and dining room. The windows, from floor to ceiling, shed bright light into the rooms; a courtyard gave on to sloping lawns and formal gardens. Though the house had only been built in 1928 it had acquired a patina of age and exuded a sort of grandeur, like many of the mansions on the north shore of Long Island, known as the Gold Coast, which had sprung up after the First World War. It was no architectural gem, but it served its purpose well.

Jimmy set to work to remodel the house, opening up vistas and using light and space in much the same way he had seen the Duchess alter perspectives at the Moulin de la Tuilerie. He spent a further $400,000 filling it with furniture and topping it off with a display of gold snuffboxes, some of which the Duchess had given him, many of which he had bought alone; somehow, though, visitors were left with the impression that *all* these boxes were the spoils of love. Certainly many visitors would have sworn that the Duchess had come to the house and ordered its redecoration herself. In this they were mistaken, perhaps deliberately misled by Jimmy, who liked to dine on stories of the Duke and Duchess and the ancient set that surrounded them in Paris. It took his particular brand of *joie de vivre* to stop it from sounding like a bitter remonstrance against the old couple who had taken him up, and dropped him. Ethel Merman, a regular guest at Broadhollow, claimed that all the staff who waited on table had to be partially deaf: 'The trusted head butler who did the hiring saw to that. That was to prevent their overhearing what was said, and telling other servants.' She enjoyed the camp atmosphere which prevailed in this most staid-looking of houses: 'I was very close to Jimmy. He adored me. When he was on the wagon, I never met a more refined, cultured man in my whole life.'

Another reason Jimmy sought to establish his own home was that, without warning and without referring to either of her sons, Jessie sold Cielito Lindo, that massive monument to social ambition, and had taken instead an enormous suite at the Everglades Club. Unlike 834 Fifth Avenue, there was no provision here for Jimmy to stay. If he wanted an out-of-town residence he was going to have to find one for himself, as his brother Wooly had already done, buying a large hunting estate in upstate New York, and another mansion in Palm Beach at 300 South Ocean Boulevard.

During that autumn Jimmy took some amusement in witnessing the triumphant arrival of the Queen Mother in New York. The woman the Duke and Duchess called Cookie and 'the fat Scotch cook' was beating them at their own game. When, according to the author Michael Thornton, she went to see the hit Broadway musical *The Pajama Game*, the audience rose as she entered the theatre and remained standing and applauding for so long that she was forced to rise from her seat and tearfully wave her hand in acknowledgement. That had never happened to Wallis.

If he felt resentful of being cast into the outer darkness beyond the Windsors' gilded circle, Jimmy certainly did not show it. Whatever feelings of rejection he may have harboured would have been lightened when on 8 November, a British Government document was issued which contained allegations by Count Julius von Zech-Burkersroda, the former German minister to the Hague, suggesting the Duke's indiscretions, while a serving officer in France at the beginning of the Second

World War, had alerted the Nazi high command to the Allies' 1940 strategy regarding the invasion of Belgium.

The Duke's name appeared in two letters from the count, the first of which suggested that in 1940 he was dissatisfied with his purely nominal job in the military, sought something more active, and was disgruntled when his request was turned down. A second report was more specific: the Duke had referred to a German invasion plan found in a crashed airplane, and had talked about the Allied War Council's strategic policy on the possible invasion of Belgium and the Netherlands.

The Duke's biographer, Philip Ziegler, quoting Michael Bloch, says that the Duke's knowledge at the time would appear to have been the exact opposite of what Count Zech reported to his masters. However, on the day of the report's publication, Windsor hastened to London to meet with Sir Walter Monckton, his old friend and now a government minister. Later that day he issued a statement through his former solicitor, Sir George Allen, which denied his ever having met or had any communication with Count Zech.

This was fine insofar as it went, but occluded the fact that the Count had never claimed to have met the Duke, merely that he had heard what was said at his table. Allen's statement went on: 'In particular, it is absolutely untrue that the Duke discussed the alleged Allied war plans, as stated in the second of his letters' – yet the Duke was notorious for his indiscretion, and was sidelined in his military role in 1940 specifically because of fears of him learning too much, and repeating it. Count Zech never revealed the source of his information, but any waiter at any restaurant or private house in Paris during the 'phoney war' could have overheard the Duke and his injudicious comments.

Despite the Duke's denials, questions were asked in the House of Commons and Sir Winston Churchill rose to defend his old friend. The allegations, he said, could be treated with contempt. In this way three friends, all knights of the realm – Monckton, Allen and Churchill – preserved the Duke's reputation; but in the minds of clear-thinking people, the doubt remained. Soon after, the Windsors left for America. For the first time since the quarrel in Baden-Baden, Jimmy and the Windsors were in the same town.

The final breach left some embarrassment all round with both Jimmy and the Duchess hastening to tell their friends the affair was over, each wanting to get their version in before the other had a chance to tell it as they saw it. Carroll Petrie, then the Marquesa de Portago, remembers hurrying to the theatre one night with her husband when a car pulled up and Jimmy bounded out: '"I guess you've heard, we're not seeing each other any more,"' he started. 'He had to tell us, *on Broadway* of all places,' recalls Mrs Petrie with amusement. 'We had to say we already knew.'

Throughout the whole affair Jimmy had maintained his links with Cardinal Spellman and the Catholic Church. Given the godless nature of his existence this struck some who knew him as strange, but to Jimmy there was always hope of salvation while he prayed. He became an enthusiastic supporter of the Children's Foundling Hospital in New York and, though no one could claim he was pious – he called Spellman Fanny Spellbound – re-forged his links with the church. 'He was a pretty good Catholic, strange as it may seem,' recalls Billy Livingston. 'One day he went with the Cardinal "to get some new dresses made", as he put it. I suppose he meant going to the tailor. Sitting outside the fitting room he could hear the Cardinal instructing the tailor "More lace! More lace!"'

Through the Cardinal, Jimmy now arranged to go to Rome for an audience with the pontiff, Pius XII. When word of this somewhat laughable pilgrimage reached his brother Wooly in

Palm Beach, he snorted: 'Now he hasn't got the Duchess any more, I suppose he's gone to Rome to fuck the Pope.'

Relations between the brothers had not mellowed over the years. A former girlfriend of Wooly recalls: 'He was ashamed of Jimmy. Jimmy was his mother's favourite, but in Wooly's eyes his behaviour was beyond the pale. He was a sophisticated man and not easy to shock, but Jimmy did shock and embarrass him. Jimmy would go to nightclubs and behave appallingly, playing jokes on people, pouring drink all over the place, showering people with $100 bills, making passes at heterosexual males who didn't know how to cope with it. He'd wreck the joint and then pay for it. The devil was in him, all right – he just didn't care. If a reporter turned up, or a photographer, he would always claim to be Wooly – and these guys didn't know any better and would write in the paper that Wooly had been out on the town behaving badly. Any scrapes he got into, he'd always use Wooly's name.'

His brother believed he was bereft of any moral standards: 'He is a wild man, an absolutely wild man,' he would say. Nonetheless, he was a man who had abruptly been denied the luxury of his first lengthy relationship and, at thirty-nine, began to feel the need of a long-term liaison. He found it in the shape of Joey Mitchell, a part American Indian, whom he met in a New York bar. Joey was to stay with Jimmy for the rest of his life, 'though you'd scarcely call it a love affair,' recalls one friend. 'Joey was there for Jimmy, and devoted his life to him. He wasn't wonderful-looking and wasn't a great conversationalist. He may or may not have been a great lover, but in any event Jimmy was not monogamous. Joey could be relied on to go round picking up the pieces after Jimmy's latest *faux pas*, and that made him indispensable.'

Someone else who met him around that time recalls: 'Joey was of medium height with a fat, bloated face and a pudgy nose, bloated by the booze. In the looks department, Jimmy lasted the course but Joey did not. He looked a debauched character. I always found him rather crude, but you couldn't show it. If Joey didn't like you, you weren't invited again.'

Someone else who knew him recalls: 'I thought he was rather unpleasant and a taker. Jimmy bought him an apartment and stocks and bonds and so forth – he showered him with largesse. Jimmy and Barbara had the same approach – they paid for everything, so as not to be beholden to anyone.'

An early visitor to Broadhollow was Princess Ghislaine de Polignac. Though one of the Duchess's closest friends she, unlike many others, maintained contact with Jimmy after the breach. In recognition of this, he invited her to dinner at his newly refurbished home. 'He told me, "There will be twenty of us and I will send a car." When I arrived I discovered I was the only woman, the rest were all men. It all seemed rather pompous, these people looked like directors of museums, that sort of thing, all dressed very severely.

'After dinner we went into another room and suddenly there was very loud music and Jimmy burst in, dressed as a woman. He was wearing a corset and ostrich-feathers and he sang "Hello Dolly", and danced. It was a total *numero*. He was dressed exactly like his mother.

'There was a very good-looking young man who came and made a lot of fuss of me and after some time this young man started to make a pass at me. I was very surprised, this was clearly a man's party. I went over to Jimmy and told him I was embarrassed by the young man's attentions. "Oh *chou-chou*," he said. "I'm sorry. I told him you were a transvestite."' The princess left soon after, a chauffeur-driven limousine returning her to the relative safety of Manhattan.

Later, Mary Donahue remembers a similar evening: 'My husband told me: "You haven't met a lot of Jimmy's friends, please don't be upset." We drove out to Brookville in a horrible snow-storm and when we walked in there were a lot of people but I saw I was the only girl. Woolworth said to me, "*Told* you!"'

'We had dinner then Jimmy said he had a surprise. We were taken next door into the drawing room and, after a delay, some music started up – "Hello Dolly" – and all these people who'd been at dinner fluttered through the door, all dressed in costume, they did this huge routine.'

Soon after, Jimmy headed south to Palm Beach for Jessie's birthday, parking *en route* his entourage of boys at Wooly's house. 'We left the boys behind and went to the Everglades Club for dinner. Jessie showed some of her old movies but Jimmy was trying to get away because of all his boys waiting for him. Finally when we got back to the house to discover they had got in my wardrobe and were wearing my hats and things.'

There was a manic determination that life should be no less glamorous and amusing than in the Windsor days, but it was never quite the same for Jimmy, or the Windsors. They had returned to New York on 10 December but now their diaries, once so full, were virtually empty. At last the Duke seemed to have got his way and insisted on staying at home. Certainly the Duchess was no longer to be seen in El Morocco, on the arm of the Duke or anyone else. A curt little entry on 23 December – 'Donahue' – denotes the brief return of their benefactress, but whatever the conversation that transpired that day, whether dwelling on Jimmy or not, Jessie did not hook her erstwhile friends for Christmas Day. Instead they went to Long Island to stay with people they barely knew. Her name does not appear again in their diary for eighteen months, and, says her daughter-in-law, she never ever referred again to Jimmy and the Windsors in the same breath.

There was, to a certain extent, some deft footwork on the

part of Jimmy and the Windsors to avoid each other in New York and, earlier than was their habit, the royal couple returned to France to escape any possible embarrassments. The affair had changed them: strengthening their public and outward *contra mundum* alliance, but weakening the fabric of their relationship. One of the Duke's godchildren commented: 'There was this fascination, during the Jimmy period, that this man must be going through absolute hell because of the behaviour of the Duchess with Jimmy. It was by any standards unbelievably humiliating for him, but he never showed it. But the relationship could *not* have done more damage.'

Another person, closely connected with the Windsors, added: 'He was a splendid, tragic, man who gave up *everything*: there was nothing left but a rather poor golf game. I think it gave Jimmy a salacious pleasure to mentally whip this poor man by taking away the Duchess.' Jimmy headed south to Florida, but now with no home to go to in Palm Beach, he preferred to take the sunshine with Joey in Miami.

※

Here, where the atmosphere was rather more emancipated than in strait-laced Palm Beach, Jimmy made a home-from-home for himself at the Fontainebleau Hotel. One (heterosexual) friend who saw him there recalls: 'We had gone down to see Ingmar Johannsen fight and we met up with Jimmy. Porfirio Rubirosa was there with his wife, Jimmy had three or four boys in tow. We went back to Jimmy's place at the Fontainebleau to discover he had taken a whole floor, for three months. There were bars on the lift doors to stop strangers inadvertently getting out at the wrong stop. Jimmy took us up and there were boys all over the place. We sat down and had a drink, the women were pretty much at a loose end, and all these boys were cruising past Rubi because they knew what he had, it was a legend.[1] As a result Rubi, who got stuck into the drink, insisted on being chaperoned when he went to the loo – "Not you, Jimmy," he shouted. Meanwhile Jimmy drifted in and out of the bedroom, and we could see as the door swung open that there were six or eight men indulging in an orgy on the bed; he didn't mention it, and carried on as though nothing unusual was taking place. He was always so courteous and polite, the perfect host – but did he think we couldn't see?'

Another friend caught up with him at the Fontainebleau: 'We had a double date with these Siamese twins. They were famous in showbiz and the curious thing was that one drank and the other didn't. Jimmy kept plying his date with champagne and she got drunker and drunker as the evening progressed while mine stayed sober, but they both had to go off to the bathroom together. Jimmy thought that was hilarious.'

Back in Palm Beach, no longer the centre of attention, Jessie decided to remind her inferiors that while she may no longer entertain in such glittering style now that Cielito Lindo had gone, she still had the most dazzling collection of jewellery in the whole resort. A curious paragraph emerged in one newspaper, stating she had been tipped off by Palm Beach police that she was on the top of a list marked for robbery by a Miami gang. Two bodyguards were hired to shadow her day and night and, according to the story, her jewels were sent back to New York for safekeeping. It was a pathetic cry for attention.

She gave a flamenco party at the Everglades: 'I not only hated the stamping and clapping that went on during those terrible flamencos, but I had a nice supper prepared for my guests who

---

1 Rubirosa was considered to be the most prodigiously-endowed man in society.

came in after dinner, and the ten members of the troupe fell upon my food as if they'd never had a good meal in their lives,' she complained. 'I believe what they didn't eat they put in their pockets – there was nothing left for my guests at all.'

Though Paris had absolutely lost its charm, Jimmy still returned to see Barbara from time to time. On one occasion she gave a party for King Farouk, the libidinous and despotic former ruler of Egypt who had abdicated three years before and washed up in Paris. In the 1950s this exiled monarch exercised a fascination for many people in international society in much the same way the Duke of Windsor had done, only more so. He had retreated from his country carrying great riches and with an insouciant smile about his fleshy features, determined to enjoy life to the full. Unlike Windsor, the fussy, prim, anal-retentive, Farouk was a glutton, a sensualist, and a man with a huge sense of humour – when it suited him.

Jimmy put it to the test. As the king grandly held court at Barbara's party, Jimmy released a small pig which ran squealing straight towards the Islamic potentate. Pandemonium ensued and bejewelled women screamed, dropped their drinks, and fled. King Farouk bellowed wildly at his hostess, then followed the women. Jimmy collapsed, hysterical with laughter.

Farouk's biographer William Stadiem tells the sequel to this chaotic event. Returning to New York, Barbara went in search of a suitable present by way of apology for her cousin's outrage. She finally found what she wanted in a store on East 59th Street where she spent $50,000 ($335,000) on a jewel-encrusted antique tureen, which she ordered to be packaged up and sent off to Farouk. A month later, back in Paris, a package arrived at her apartment on the Rue Octave Feuillet which turned out, upon opening, to be the tureen – returned without a note. 'She opened it and was horrified,' wrote Stadiem. 'The tureen was packed with dried excrement. It is a

231

commentary on Hutton's own perversity that she became fascinated by what kind of excrement it was. At first she assumed it was camel dung, but then she realised there were no camels in Rome [where the king was based]. She sent a sample to the laboratory. It was human dung.'

⁂

The spectre of drink and drugs was never very far away. Jimmy took Seconal, Barbara took Seconal, so too did Jimmy's friend Libby Holman. With her Broadway career as a singer of torch songs now over, Holman indulged in an on-off affair with the bisexual actor Montgomery Clift, but despite immense wealth she could not find happiness and attempted to kill herself with a massive Seconal overdose. The attempt failed, but later she committed suicide in her garage by switching on the engine of her Rolls Royce and lying down on the passenger seat to await death's embrace.

Barbara married again but Jimmy, wearied by now of befriending each new spouse, stayed away from the ceremony at Versailles. His cousin was now the Baroness Gottfried von Cramm, wife of a former German tennis champion, homosexual, and alleged Nazi sympathiser. Unlike her previous marital encounters, she had known von Cramm for eighteen years but, like all the rest, the union was doomed from the start. Baron Jean de Baglion explained: 'The truth of the matter is they never consummated the marriage.' By the summer of 1957 it was all over.

During this period Barbara acquired a palace in Tangier, Sidi Hosni, and created an awesome Japanese-style house set in thirty acres in Mexico which she named Sumiya, the 'house on the corner'. Jimmy visited both, but though Tangier was a destination for many high-born homosexuals, where they could live or visit without fear of harassment, neither venue was particularly to his taste. Ruth Hopwood recalls his arrival in the city of Paul Bowles and David Herbert: 'He wasn't quite himself. In fact he was so unwell when he arrived at the airport that he had to be put in a chair and carried up to Sidi Hosni. He'd come for a big party which Barbara had organised, but nobody ever saw him. He stayed two or three days then moved on.'

In Mexico, Jimmy arrived at his cousin's house accompanied by three men. 'These three fellows were dressed completely in black,' recalls one of the house-party. 'Black suits, black shirts, big black hats. They had been instructed not to speak, just to follow Jimmy round. At dinner they stood, all three of them, behind his chair, never saying a word, just helping their master to whatever he needed. We said to him, "What is this, Jimmy?" "My three black crows," he replied. He never explained, it was just his joke for the night. Heaven knows where he found them or what he did with them after.'

On another occasion, travelling with Joey Mitchell in Mexico, he became bored by the typically leisurely service in a restaurant. In a very weary voice he bellowed at the pro-prietor: 'Just tell me the name of your country and I'll instruct the State Department to stop your foreign aid!' In Acapulco, with Barbara, he excused himself from a waterside dinner-party, plunged fully-clad in evening dress into the sea, swam to a pontoon from where water-skiers were making a circuit of the bay and, never having skied before on land or water, managed to complete a circuit of his own, pulled by a motor-launch. 'He was still fully dressed in dinner-jacket, complete with bow-tie,' recalls another guest.

The memory of his romance with the Duchess did not dull. 'He used to say how ugly she was and how he had to put a bandage over his eyes when he slept with her,' recalls Mona

Eldridge, Barbara's secretary at that time. 'He continued to take the mickey when it was all over, saying how awful she was, how old and ugly she was, and what an effort it was to have a screw with her. But he was obviously not happy.'

The jokes started to wear thin: at a formal dinner given by Barbara, and during a lull in the conversation, he looked across the table at Clark Gable and said: 'Oh, Clark, you were fantastic last night. It was ... *unbelievable*!' 'There was a dead silence,' recalls a fellow guest. 'The poor chap looked down into his plate, he was a married man, there was nothing he could say. People tried to cover the gap in the conversation but it was terribly embarrassing. Not *every* joke Jimmy attempted necessarily came off. He'd go to the bathroom in the middle of a dinner party and come back stark naked. Another time he announced to the Press that he was Queen of the Fairies and, with Joey Mitchell, would shortly be making a tour of the whole of the United States to visit his subjects. Barbara said to him, "You can't *do* that, giving that stuff to the newspapers", but he did. Given the climate of opinion at that time the press let him off very lightly indeed.'

The cousins met up in Venice where Elsa Maxwell, once again the Duchess's implacable foe, invited them to her Headdress Ball on the roof of the Danieli Hotel. This event, in August 1957, triggered a drawing-together of European society in Venice unprecedented in the twentieth century. Only those fond of irony would dwell on how impotent European society had become, now that it danced to the tune of an unlovely septuagenarian *arriviste* from Keokuk, Iowa. But Elsa's Headdress Ball was followed by a series of other equally lavish entertainments thrown by a succession of blue-bloods, along with a number of parties given by Aristotle Onassis – celebrating his new affair with Maria Callas – aboard his yacht the *Christina*, anchored in the Grand Canal.

Slowly the entourage made its way back to Paris, then New York, on the SS *United States*. En route Barbara had acquired as a companion the writer Philip van Rensselaer who was young, charming, handsome – and jealously regarded by Jimmy. Marianne Strong, then a columnist for the New York *World Telegram*, recalls boarding the liner at dawn as it prepared to dock and trying to evade Jimmy as she made her way to interview Barbara. 'I saw him running up the gangplank with a furious expression, like he was going to kill someone. He always had an aggressive stance and this time it was exacerbated by Philip. He was jealous, especially because Philip was one of the most devastatingly handsome men.'

The confrontation was avoided, but Mrs Strong detected a change in this once happy-go-lucky figure: 'Jimmy had become an incorrigible, furious kind of person. He would think nothing of slapping you in the face if he got too excitable. He was very rapacious – if anyone got in his way he would just push them aside. He had huge personal charm and of course a lot of people liked him, loved him; but you couldn't trifle with him and people were afraid of him.'

Not all, perhaps. But there had been a significant mood-change in Jimmy, as if he had become another person. One friend from that time says: 'The relationship between Jimmy and his mother changed, soured. She came to visit his house in Old Brookville and, you know, Jimmy loved flowers. He adored them. He had developed some lovely beds around the house but when he enthused to his mother about his handiwork she merely said, "We had gardeners to do all that." She ruined both her sons. Wooly had expressed, years before, a desire to go to medical school, she said no. Jimmy, she never let go of.'

Another acquaintance described Jimmy as 'A Manhattan Caligula', with Broadhollow becoming the backdrop for weekly gatherings of like-minded males whose activities sought

235

to emulate those of the Roman emperor. One woman, grand-daughter of one of Britain's foremost public figures, recalled being taken out to the house: 'I was very young. Jimmy liked to shock, but with ladies he wouldn't push things too far. He liked to repeat that line about the Duchess: "She married a King but screwed a queen." He showed me round the house, with black sheets on the beds, my eyes were on stalks. Then just as we were getting into the car to leave, he went up and kissed a man full on the lips. Nobody was looking at him, they were all looking at me, laughing. I had never seen anything like that before, my face dropped a mile. The chap he kissed worked in one of the trade showrooms in New York.'

Another friend from that time says: 'Once he settled at Broad-hollow, I didn't see too much of him any more. The people he invited were, generally, his social and intellectual inferiors. He felt better that way I guess, but it made for unattractive company.'

The riff-raff were cleared away for the visit of Barbara Hut-ton, who brought with her a new companion, Jimmy Douglas. A quiet, handsome, accomplished man, Douglas brought a measure of stability to her life and succeeded in weaning her off drugs. All that changed upon her arrival at Broadhollow: 'Jimmy Douglas was out of sight for a moment and the next moment she had a handful of Seconal,' recalls someone who was there. 'She hadn't had any for a long time, a year or so, and all of a sudden here she was a completely changed person, she went off her head. Jimmy Douglas was furious with Jimmy Donahue but it made no difference. Barbara ordered a car, and she and Douglas were whisked into New York.'

Fuelled by drugs and alcohol, Barbara's primeval urge to spend once again reared up and she ordered the chauffeur to drive to East 59th Street to her favourite shop, A La Vieille Russie, where she had bought King Farouk's tureen. 'There she was in this dreadful condition, she just started buying things left and right. Jimmy Douglas was trying to stop her but she wouldn't. She bought him a Fabergé snake bracelet made of emeralds and with ruby eyes. She carried on buying, madly, but it was such a huge amount of money that when the bill was presented to Graham Mattison, her lawyer, he refused to pay it and all the stuff had to go back. Douglas had already returned the bracelet. The best thing she could do was get away from the influence of her cousin, and after a few days she headed off towards Mexico.'

Some who knew Jimmy well declare that after the Duchess, his life was over. She had set an agenda for him, filled his days with thoughts and experiences, and with her restless energy invigorated his daily life. Now, though he did not lack energy, he lacked motivation. He had put his energies into creating a Long Island Moulin de la Tuilerie, and developing a garden the Duke would have envied. Soon, though, the job was done; he had no one to show it to.

Out of boredom and frustration, he started to drive about with Joey, looking for things to do. One day he decided to drive down to Atlantic City where there lived a link with his past. Louise Mack, now in her seventies, had been a dancer with Ziegfeld's Follies and had retired to the New Jersey resort to start a bar, Louise's, in Snake Alley. There he met a seventeen-year-old, Arthur Pavlow, who became his companion over the next month or two. Pavlow recalls being taken to a mansion near Pleasantville which Jimmy claimed was actually Barbara Hutton's, though there is no record of her ever having owned or rented such a place. 'Jimmy was a party person,' recalls Pavlow. 'There was cocaine, marijuana, and plenty of booze.

Whether he was an addict, I can't say. One weekend he took us up to New York and we went to see this famous madam, Lucille Mallon: he hired some guy to defecate on a glass-topped table while someone else was underneath. I didn't watch. That aside, he was a witty, funny man. He was pear-shaped and his blonde hair was thinning, and he wore glasses some of the time. He was flighty and feminine, and he didn't dress well, he was wearing Hawaiian shirts hanging out, the look didn't gel. But he was a very nice man. He was happy, you might say proud, to let you know he was Barbara Hutton's cousin but when I met him I had no idea who he was.'

It took care of a summer. Back in New York, and under the influence of Cardinal Spellman, he tried to turn his attention to good works, visiting the New York Foundling Hospital and agreeing to interest himself in its operation. The hospital had been founded nearly a hundred years before in the aftermath of the Civil War, when hundreds if not thousands of infants and children had been abandoned in the city streets. A new building was being prepared for occupation at 1175 Third Avenue, and Jimmy became an enthusiastic fundraiser before accepting the posts of secretary of the advisory board, then president of the appeal fund. He gave $100,000 ($660,000) to the Metropolitan Opera House being built at the Lincoln Center in New York, and he appeared on early televised telethon appeals for the Cerebral Palsy Fund, matching donations from the public with his own money. He also gave lavishly to the Jerry Lewis Muscular Dystrophy Foundation as well as a number of other leading charities. Ethel Merman recalled: 'He never paid much in taxes because he gave his money away. Every year, for instance, when Jane Pickens[1] would raise money

---

1 An actress

for children with muscular dystrophy or multiple sclerosis, Jimmy would double the amount she raised.'

Merman, the so-called Queen of Broadway, now played a significant part in his life. Paying engagements were becoming fewer with the passage of time but Dorothy Strelsin recalls, 'Sometimes they would go to a club on 53rd Street and she would get up and sing. Jimmy would applaud, even if there was nobody else in the club he'd make enough noise for fifty.'

Another friend, Al Koenig, drove her around New Jersey looking for antiques and occasionally Jimmy would go along too. They would return to her Manhattan apartment and Jimmy would trawl through the exhaustive collection of acetate discs the singer kept of all her performances. They talked of a revival of *Annie Get Your Gun*, the Irving Berlin show which, starting in 1946, ran for a thousand performances and gave her an undisputed theme song: 'There's No Business Like Show Business'. The show had been hijacked by Hollywood and the inferior Betty Hutton given her lead role; she wanted to prise it back and Jimmy talked about backing the show. The theatre world he had so loved, so desperately wanted to become part of, continued to remain a mirage, always just beyond his grasp. 'It was not too late,' recalled a Palm Beach friend. 'The problem was that Jessie had robbed both her boys of ambition.' These days the best he could do was to be a stage-door Johnnie for the likes of Ethel Merman and Martha Raye.

His nocturnal activities became more extreme. He staged an elaborate psychosexual prank involving him lying shrouded in a coffin in a candle-lit room while a female prostitute hurled abuse at him before finally closing the lid and claiming her five hundred bucks. It was a solitary, and very sad, plateau he had reached.

CHAPTER 12

LUCKY

Lucky is a dangerous name to go by. No one knew quite how David Morra came by it, but in many ways it suited him. Tall, slim, almost beautiful, he made his living as a fashion model in the early 1960s and dabbled in the restaurant trade. His companion was Tommy Dowling, who had a place on East 43rd Street. When it burned down, they started again with a sumptuously upmarket establishment called Regent's Row on East 58th.

In this post-El Morocco, post-Windsor period, it became a regular haunt for Jimmy: less public, less stuffy, more openly gay, while retaining an exclusive atmosphere. It was there that Jimmy met and fell in love with Lucky. As is the custom, Morra moved from Dowling's protection to Jimmy's and was bought an apartment on the upper East Side.

At the time they became partners Jimmy was forty-six, Lucky twenty years his junior. 'This affair cured Jimmy of the depression he had suffered since his break-up with the Windsors,' says someone who saw them together. 'You can't say Lucky was a substitute for the Duchess, but it gave him something to chase after.' For Lucky was capricious, elusive and bisexual. He had, according to Jimmy's sister-in-law Mary Donahue, fathered the child of a well-known socialite. Jimmy told this story against himself, but with less than his usual glee.

Soon Lucky moved into Broadhollow and made his home there. Joey Mitchell, Jimmy's partner for all these years, continued to be part of the *ménage*. As a sop, he had been bought an apartment in Manhattan but soon he came to tolerate the presence of the new member of the household. Life continued much as before, but instead of travelling to Europe, Jimmy now preferred to break up his year by flying down to Hawaii and taking up residence there, sometimes for months at a time.

His life had changed, and he no longer felt the need to rationalise his complex bisexuality. Prudently he kept his boyfriends away when he visited Jessie in Palm Beach, sending them on to Miami and the Fontainebleau while he went to pay his respects during the season. But the world was beginning to change. The 1950s had seen the publication of *The Homosexual in America* by Edward Sagarin, a book which, according to Charles Kaiser, was 'a call to arms, an attack on every anti-homosexual prejudice', and at last the unseeing eye of the heterosexual American majority slowly opened to the inescapable fact that a significant part of the population was not as they were. Though homosexuality was still illegal, the gay political debate had begun.

Change was in the air everywhere. In New York the rock'n'roll age ushered in new styles, new manners, a new elite. No longer was it fashionable to cross the Atlantic by sea, wear white tie, sport a gardenia in one's buttonhole, make physical contact with your partner on the dance floor. The generation that had weathered the war carried a set of values which no longer seemed relevant, it seemed constantly to be looking back, rejecting both the present and the future.

While others were feeling the stirrings of gay liberation, Jimmy was too old, too set in his ways, to take part in a movement which was finding a voice to claim its civil rights. He was too circumscribed by his social position to do anything other than carry on as before, keeping his homosexuality contained, private. Sagarin wrote, 'The inherent tragedy – not the saving grace – of homosexuality is found in the ease of concealment.' And Jimmy concealed – from his mother, from his mother's friends, from the boards of the various charities on which he sat.

All this may have been a struggle, but it was not a tremendous struggle. The real changes between the 1950s and 1960s which affected Jimmy were simply the passage of time. He had grown older, drink and drugs had fattened the once-perfect figure and coarsened the once-beautiful face. His brother Woolworth, though more conventional than Jimmy, had become an alcoholic. Though the world was liberating itself, it was too late for Jimmy, as he regretted in an aside to Mary Donahue on his fiftieth birthday: 'It's terrible when you have to pay for what you used to get free.'

In a sense Jimmy had always paid, had always been ready to pay. He had bought friendship, often with cash, only occasionally with goodwill, almost never with love. Now, at last, he *was* in love, with the aptly-named Lucky. In the winter of 1962 the couple travelled south to Mexico to meet Barbara Hutton. For nearly thirty years now, his cousin had been introducing her latest loves: the count, to date, was six husbands. The latest beau was Lloyd Franklin, a twenty-five-year-old former trumpeter in the Coldstream Guards. Jimmy wanted to return the favour and introduce Lucky to Barbara in much the way that Barbara had introduced her Franklin: 'There, take a look. Isn't he *gorgeous?*'

The visit coincided with the arrival of Lance Reventlow, Barbara's son, now twenty-seven. Jimmy had attended Lance's wedding to the actress Jill St John in San Francisco a couple of years before, but already the marriage was foundering. Dudley Walker, once valet to Cary Grant and now fulfilling the same role for Lance, recalled: 'Lance was saying all sorts of things he shouldn't have said. It had to do with all the publicity [his mother] was getting because of her affair with Lloyd Franklin. Lloyd was a nice enough chap but he was younger than Lance and Lance found it demoralising. Anyway, one day Lance says to Donahue, "Where's that drunken cunt of a mother of mine?"'

Jimmy, in effect Lance's uncle, went to Barbara and angrily repeated what her son had said. Walker continued: 'That was the end of Lance. She cut him off without a cent, including his trust funds. He had to sell his house and buy a smaller one.'

Eventually Barbara would repent and reinstate Lance, helping him to fix up his new home. But that was later. In Cuernavaca, in late 1962, the atmosphere was not conducive to a long stay, and Jimmy and Lucky hastened away. Next summer the couple, their relationship barely a year old, decided to take a longer trip, down to Hawaii for an extended holiday. They should never have gone. Before long, people were saying that Jimmy had murdered his boyfriend.

꧁꧂

Jimmy took a suite at the SurfRider Hotel on Waikiki Beach at the beginning of July 1963. The pair stayed there amicably enough for several weeks, meeting up with John Gomez, who managed the Black Point estate of Hutton's rival in wealth,

Doris Duke. Jimmy and Gomez were old friends and Jimmy had been Doris's guest at her house, Shangri-La. But by the beginning of September, the holiday had run its course; there had been too much booze, too many pills, too much sun. Though they were due to stay until the end of the month, both men had grown irritable of the other's company. Finally, after one particularly drink-sodden day, there was a row. Lucky stormed out, saying he was going back to New York. Jimmy, Gomez and another man, Jack Sheppard, the manager of the Gourmet Bazaar in the International Market, tried to calm Lucky but he was determined to go home, so they drove him to Honolulu airport.

But Morra's condition was such that he was turned away by airline officials and not allowed on the flight. The trio were forced to take him back into town. He was dumped, still arguing vociferously, at Jack Sheppard's apartment on Seaside Avenue, and the others returned to the SurfRider where they spent the rest of the evening in a convivial mood. The following morning, Sheppard walked past Morra, asleep on his couch, and went to join Jimmy and Gomez for breakfast at the Royal Hawaiian Hotel. After breakfast, as Sheppard set off for work, Jimmy and Gomez drove back to Sheppard's flat to collect Lucky.

He was dead.

A first autopsy by the local medical examiner, Dr Richard Wong, proved inconclusive. After further tests the doctor stated that Lucky's death was due to 'an accumulation of fluids on his lungs', though the tests failed to reveal the cause of the fluids, or any disease which could have caused them. The inconclusive nature of his findings was most unusual, to say the least.

Lucky's parents were grief-stricken at the loss of their son. Bill Morra, Lucky's brother, recalls: 'I spoke to Jimmy a few times because he wanted to organise David's funeral in Hawaii.

But I didn't want that, I wanted the body to be flown back to New York, and we buried him here. There was a great deal of confusion over his death, and no death certificate was ever produced by Donahue. The whole thing seemed very strange.

'I arranged for David's body to be examined when he was brought home, and it was confirmed he had had a heart attack. He was only twenty-nine, but foul play was ruled out. He never had a heart problem that we knew about. He was a fit and healthy young man who lived life in the fast lane – David was attracted to Donahue because he wanted a fast life.

'I made Donahue send back all his belongings to my house. I didn't want him to have anything to do with the burial, so I had him send the body back and we buried him in our family plot in New Jersey. He was so young and so beautiful. My folks never really recovered, and of course we felt Donahue was to blame in some way, although there was never any proof.'

Various stories have circulated since Lucky's death about Jimmy's actions that night and subsequently. The popular legend is that Jimmy murdered Lucky.

In part this theory is underpinned by the not-so-subtle attempts at a cover-up. First, several telephone calls were made to New York in the immediate hours after the discovery of the body, and a representative of Jessie's law firm flew out to Honolulu on the next plane. Second, and some say as a result of the first action, the Hawaiian police authorities pursued no thorough investigation against Jimmy or the others involved. Third, no action, and hardly any investigation, took place on Jimmy's return to New York, even though both he and Lucky were residents of the state. To this day, the events surrounding the death of David 'Lucky' Morra are indistinct. Despite an investigation by the Hawaii police, another inquiry by the New York Police Department and two autopsies, no one can actually be sure of what took place.

It would not be the first time Woolworth money had bought silence – from Jim senior's bungled attempt to steal his wife's pearls, to the ravished salesman left to freeze on an icy street-corner. In addition, the New York press, the same press that had been so keen to trail Jimmy down the street as he reluctantly joined the army, the same press that had hinted so furiously and yet so impotently at his affair with the Duchess of Windsor, remained uncharacteristically silent on the matter of Lucky Morra. Everybody, it seemed, except Morra's family, wanted the episode forgotten.

One person who knew Jimmy's family intimately told the author: 'The barbiturate addiction of both Jimmy and Barbara Hutton was an absolute catastrophe and had ramifications in their lives that very few people realise. Morphine and heroin do not change the basic personality of an individual, whereas barbiturates do. Jimmy and Barbara – especially Jimmy – had the capacity to take Seconal in large doses and while it was supposed to be a depressant, in huge quantities it had the opposite effect. Just because Jimmy could take it didn't mean that others could.'

The theory promulgated among the drug cognoscenti, those who were closest to Jimmy's lifestyle, was that he killed Lucky with too large a dose of Seconal. With an undiagnosed heart weakness, with too great an ingestion of alcohol, Lucky had been given – maybe clandestinely, maybe force-fed – some pills to quiet his still-angry mood. They had been too much for him. It may not have been murder, but it was no accident either.

Jimmy went home to Broadhollow and to Joey Mitchell. Within a few weeks, the country was plunged into darkness by the assassination of Jimmy's contemporary Jack Kennedy. It was the blackest period of Jimmy's life. He did not emerge from it for two months, until the arrival of Barbara with her latest fiancé, 'Prince' Raymond Doan Vinh Na Champassak, a

Vietnamese chemist for a French oil company based in Marrakesh, who had peremptorily parted with a wife and children in order to prepare himself for marriage to the world's richest woman. That woman had, by way of gratitude, driven round to the Laotian embassy in Rabat and bought him an Indo-Chinese princedom for $50,000 ($310,000). The title had no validity anywhere in the world, but at least it meant she could call herself Princess again.

By now the cousins were completely isolated from the society which was once theirs to conquer with money and charm if not with breeding. Frank Woolworth's millions had bought them an expensive entrée to American society and opened doors to the finest salons in the Western world. But, in the end, the rudderless existence each of them lived led them back to each other; for who else could understand why they behaved the way they did?

Having sailed from Casablanca to New York, Barbara and her fiancé made straight for Broadhollow to escape the attentions of a press ready to sneer contemptuously at her latest hook-up. It was Christmas, the chilliest time of the year for all descendants of Frank Woolworth in that loveless family. Barbara's biographer David Heymann records: 'Jimmy's French chef had prepared a sumptuous Christmas Day repast that was marred by an altercation between Barbara and her intended.'

He quotes Jean Mendiboure, part of the Hutton entourage: 'In the middle of the meal Barbara started raving, "I'm going to kill him! I'm going to kill him!" She bolted out of her seat and ran into the kitchen where she grabbed a butcher's knife and came out swinging at 'Prince' Doan. The chef managed to wrestle the knife away from her. She then went to her room to sulk for a few hours and when she returned she said, "It's these pills and drinks that are making me crazy."'

She decided to leave for New York for treatment but Mendiboure, who was ready to accompany her, slipped in the snow which lay a foot deep outside the house, and broke his wrist. The pair checked in to the Lenox Hill Hospital in Manhattan, but checked out again soon after and repaired to the Pierre Hotel where at least there was a decent room-service and the drinks were cold. Three months later Barbara married her prince in a brace of ceremonies at her Mexican home, Sumiaya; Doan was to be her seventh, and last, husband.

About this time, someone new came into Jimmy's life, an English dancer called Don Walker. A friend of Walker's, Gerry Atkins, recalls: 'In 1964 the Folies Bergère was taken from Paris to Broadway for a season in the New York World's Fair. It was the type of show that appealed to Jimmy and he came to see it several times – but mainly because he was attracted to Don. I think they met in a bar or restaurant. Eventually Jimmy got Don released from his contract with the Folies and he went to live with Jimmy out on Long Island.'

The dancers were invited, on their day off, to visit their erstwhile colleague at Broadhollow. A chauffeur-driven car arrived to collect them: 'We would usually spend all day round the pool. I don't think Jimmy ever appeared before the cocktail hour but Joey, who still lived with him, used to make an appearance. I never really liked him, I always found him rather crude.

'Sometimes we would play croquet. Then dinner would be served in the dining room by one or two uniformed waiters complete with white gloves. There was never any bread on the table – Jimmy didn't allow it, he thought it was only for the poor.'

The evenings would round off with Jimmy doing his well-worn version of 'Hello Dolly', with the boy dancers lifting him onto their shoulders for the final chorus.

Don Walker's friends little realised it but Jimmy had, once

again, fallen deeply in love. He started to fantasise about a better life, a cleaner life, an existence where the detritus which had piled around him – Lucky's death, his mother's still-pervasive presence, his continued purposeless existence – could be resolved. He told his sister-in-law he wanted to get married.

'Jimmy wanted to marry this fellow in Honolulu,' recalls Mary Donahue. 'He said to me that he was trying to make arrangements with the church. He talked to someone who was trying to get the litigation through and he felt he *could* get married in Honolulu. He was so sincere about it. I tried to make a joke about it but he was deadly serious. We were down by the swimming pool, walking around and talking about it. He had talked to priests about it, and when I asked about the legality of it he assured me it was legal.'[1]

Mary and Wooly went to stay with Jimmy at Broadhollow prior to their marriage at Christmas 1965, and spent a bibulous dinner with their host before moving on by chauffeur-driven limousine to their own estate at Riverhead. The previous evening the two brothers, reconciled after years of enmity, had been to pay their respects to the materfamilias in her apartment at 834. Now Wooly and Mary asked Jimmy to be their best man at the service which was to take place the following day.

In the morning they had a call: 'Jimmy, you're up so early!' said Mary.

'I haven't been to bed. I've got a terrible hangover, and there's so much snow, I'm never going to make it.'

So Winston Guest, socialite godson of Winston Churchill and pillar of Palm Beach, was best man, with Stanley the game-keeper as witness, while Jimmy packed his bags and headed south to catch some Miami sun. A couple of days later Mary

---

1 It was not.

had a call from her new mother-in-law: 'Dear, what *can* you two be thinking about? It's in all the papers!'

'What's in the papers?'

'It says that Wooly was in this Miami nightclub and he was making paper airplanes out of $100 ($620) bills.'

It was Jimmy again. 'My husband got on the phone to him and told him it was undignified, but Jimmy just thought it was hysterical. He'd given his name as Woolworth Donahue again, he always did.'

Jimmy continued to see his mother daily in New York, and in Palm Beach on the few occasions he visited. Ethel Merman recalled: 'He was a wonderful son to her. Jessie had a vertigo condition that made it impossible to get about, but every night when he was in the city Jimmy would sit with her until after she had had her dinner, then he'd be on his merry way.'

Chagrined by the breach caused by her son's affair with Wallis, Jessie tried her hardest to re-establish a close friendship with the Windsors. But the diaries which had borne her name on a weekly basis for so many years now had no mention of it. On one occasion she managed to catch them for lunch in Palm Beach; but fearful of the gossip and the laughter which was sure to follow her ruthless attempts to rekindle the relationship, she arranged for the party to be held at 300 South Ocean Boulevard, Wooly's house. Nonetheless, the lunch over, she could not wait for the world to know the Donahues and Windsors were back on speaking terms; and the ever-faithful Cholly Knickerbocker dutifully recorded the Windsors' tepid social embrace. Jessie marked the occasion by commissioning a gold bracelet for the Duchess from Van Cleef and Arpels: regal, understated, just the right mood.

The restitution of relations had progressed sufficiently for Jimmy to hazard issuing an invitation to the Windsors to Broadhollow. They came, the Duchess remarking coolly as she gazed at the way it had been furnished, 'This seems familiar', and then they were gone. No longer did Jimmy's money, or his charm, or his naughtiness, work for them. The world had moved on and left him behind.

In their twilight years, the Windsors managed to regain some of their lost stature. To them, of course, it had never gone. At their Paris house the footmen wore royal livery, visitors entered under the Duke's personal Garter banner and moved, as if in a real palace, through the long blue and silver drawing room with its fine eighteenth-century furniture and full-length royal portraits. This elaborate backdrop allowed them to become, as memory faded, the grandest of royal outcasts, exemplars of exiled dignity and *comme il faut*. The Duchess occasionally broke loose – she would be photographed in a nightclub dancing The Twist, for example – but there were no more love affairs. Accepting her fate as the years advanced, she realised there was nothing for her beyond the Duke. The wild moments when she discussed leaving him to marry Jimmy were forgotten. Jimmy was her single indiscretion.

⁂

On 21 September 1966, Jimmy attended the opening night of Ethel Merman's revival of *Annie Get Your Gun* at the Broadway Theatre. He had been instrumental in encouraging Merman to reprise her most famous Broadway role and had backed it with his own money. On this occasion, rather than an epic 1,000-performance run as she had achieved in 1946, the show was for a limited eight-week engagement only. During the next few weeks he drifted into the theatre, wafted backstage, took the star out to dinner afterwards. To celebrate the successful conclusion of the run he threw a black-tie dinner and dance at Goldie's restaurant on 42nd Street. So delighted was Merman with the success of her come-back and Jimmy's generosity that she ordered some gold cufflinks to be made up by her jeweller in Jimmy's initials. Next morning Jimmy went to the offices of Meyer Handelsman, the family lawyer, to order the rewriting of his will. He promised Handelsman he would look in later in the week to sign it.

Two days later Mary Donahue, at home on Long Island, was woken by a telephone call from Joey Mitchell who was in the apartment at 834 Fifth Avenue. He didn't know who to call, he said. He was sorry to wake her, but Jimmy was dead.

Mary, still half-asleep, took a moment to take in the news. The voice became more insistent. Nobody knew how to tell Jessie the news, nobody knew what to do, could she and Woolworth come into town and take charge?

At about the same time as an appalled Mary and Wooly Donahue stepped from their chauffeur-driven limousine outside 834, there was a knock on the door of Jessie Donahue's friend and near-neighbour Dorothy Strelsin. A young man of her acquaintance stepped in and agitatedly told her the news that Jimmy was dead. He had just run up Fifth Avenue from 834. He then mentioned that he had some Van Cleef and Arpels cufflinks, and would she like to buy them. 'I told him I wasn't interested. He clearly needed money.' The young man let himself out of the apartment and disappeared, the stolen jewellery still in his hand.

Meanwhile, confusion reigned at 834. Jessie, sensing something was happening, came to the entrance of her apartment as the elevator doors opened to reveal Wooly and Mary Donahue. She expressed surprise at seeing them there and asked why. Some excuse was made, and the couple plunged on into Jimmy's apartment. Wooly, unequal to the task that lay ahead, delegated responsibility to Mary, who ordered the family physician Dr Faulkner to be called – no one had so far thought of this simple requisite. The police arrived and Handelsman the attorney; a large group including members of staff and Joey Mitchell now crowded the drawing-room. No one seemed willing to go into the bedroom to identify the body, so Mary started forward.

'Would you like a drink?' inquired Joey, solicitously.

'This isn't 21!' she snapped back.

Then she stepped in to the darkened room to discover Jimmy in dark blue silk pyjamas in bed, his face a livid purple, his body already stiffened by rigor mortis. Having been formally identified, someone had to tell Jessie that her favourite son was dead; he had died, choking on his own vomit, after yet another night of too much alcohol and too much Seconal. The doctor, the attorney, Joey and Wooly all demurred. It was left to Mary to step down the hallway and confront her mother-in-law.

She said, 'Jessie, something terrible has happened. Jimmy is dead.'

Jessie's face was a mask. 'Oh,' she replied. 'This is the worst thing that can happen to me.'

***

Twenty-seven limousines followed Jimmy's coffin from the funeral mass at the Mater Dei chapel of the New York Foundling Hospital to Woodlawn Cemetery, where the Woolworth family mausoleum stood. Up at the front of the cortège, solemn, dark-faced, were leading members of New York society – Astors, Vanderbilts. Down the back end was a collection of cars filled with tearful, excitable young men dressed a little too garishly for such an occasion, chirruping noisily. It was all going reasonably smoothly, though in the midst of all the arrangements Mary Donahue had received a call from Ethel

Merman: 'You know, Mary, I can't believe it! We were together last Tuesday! He gave the most divine party for me and I've had these cufflinks made for him, they're beautiful, they're gold and sapphire. *You've got to get them put on Jimmy!*'

The cars arrived at Woodlawn and circled the massive mausoleum built by Frank Woolworth for himself and his sorry dynasty, with heraldic sphinxes brought all the way from Egypt to stand guard at the entrance. The massive bronze doors were thrown wide, revealing the resting place of America's five-and-dime czar, his wife, his daughter Edna Hutton and her husband, and his son-in-law Jim Donahue. Now it was Jimmy's turn to pass, for the last time, through a pillared portico into a marbled palace. For once, there was no chilled champagne to greet his arrival.

The casket, still open, was rested in its bier. While other backs were turned, Mary and Wooly Donahue hastily stepped forward and Mary, whispering, 'God bless you, Jimmy, with love from Ethel', flung Merman's cufflinks into the void. The priest stepped forward and the marble slab slid into place. There had been no time to put them on his wrists, but Mary was determined to fulfil her promise that Jimmy should be buried with them. They laughed, as they drove away, knowing how he would have loved the black comedy of it all.

When Mary Donahue stepped into Jimmy's bedroom on the morning of 8 December 1966 the only adornment it contained was thirteen framed photographs of the Duchess of Windsor.

The same week he died, the Windsors sold yet another milk-and-water account of their lives to the New York newspapers. Needless to say, though the royal couple's account was exhaustive, it never once mentioned Jimmy Donahue. And nobody much seemed to notice the few short paragraphs on another page noting Jimmy's passing.

Afterword

Jimmy Donahue never did inherit the Woolworth millions. His will went unpublished but he left the bulk of his fortune, estimated to be around $1million ($5.1 million) to the New York Foundling Hospital which does not disclose details of personal bequests. Reports which suggest that he left the Duchess of Windsor $50,000 are inaccurate. He left her nothing but may, at the time of his last unproven will, have been ready to change its contents at least partially in her favour. The *rapprochement* at Broadhollow, however fragile, gave him cause to hope that, twelve years after the breach, the friendship could be re-established. It meant something to him; but it meant nothing to the woman who once considered becoming his wife.

Jessie Woolworth Donahue, the architect of her son's demise, died in 1971 at the age of eighty-five. Her mansion, Cielito Lindo, was long gone – torn down by developers to make way for an estate of smaller houses. Just two wings of Cielito Lindo still exist to this day, as two separate houses. A road drives through the middle precisely where, in 1941, Jessie first entertained the Windsors and gained her social validation.

Jessie wanted to make sure that her jewellery would be sold on her death and that it should not fall into the hands of the beneficiaries of her estate. Among the pieces that went on the auctioneer's block were a pair of ear-clips containing eight marquise diamonds weighing 39-carats, a large round yellow diamond ring weighing 57-carats and an emerald ring weighing 22-carats. To her daughter-in-law Mary, the only other woman of the family, she bequeathed a small diamond ballet-dancer pin. Three-quarters of her vast but undisclosed fortune, estimated to be $27 million ($115.56m), went to the American Cancer Society. The Duke and Duchess of Windsor, upon whom she had showered millions but who, in the end, turned their backs on Jessie and her largesse, went unremembered in the testament.

Wooly died six months after his mother, a victim of cancer, though he actually died of a heart attack. He was fifty-nine. Had he lived – come to that, if Jimmy had lived – the sons still would not have got their hands on the elusive Woolworth millions. In death as in life, Jessie was determined they should not have it, and Wooly received for the short remainder of his life a bequest of $100,000 and $1million ($4.28 million) in trust of which he was allowed to draw no more than $100,000 in any one year. It was a derisory, almost contemptuous, sum.

A friend wrote at the time: 'It was well known that Jimmy was Jessie's favourite son. She closed her eyes to his scandalous escapades and frequently bailed him out of serious trouble. In her will she stipulated that, should there not be sufficient funds to honour any bequest Jimmy made in his will, she, Jessie, would honour them in hers.' It was a grand, but as it turned out, utterly futile gesture.

Within a couple of years of Jimmy's death, life closed in on Barbara Hutton. Her biographer David Heymann records that by 1968 her daily intake was twenty bottles of Coca-Cola a day; alcohol, vitamin pills, intravenous megavitamin shots (often mixed with amphetamines), a soybean compound, Metrecal, cigarettes, and a mixture of drugs which included Empirin compound, Codeine, Valium and Morphine. When, in 1972, her only child Lance Reventlow was killed in a plane crash, she was too ill to attend the funeral. Life became a downward spiral, lived out in Tangier, Paris and the Beverly Wilshire Hotel in Los Angeles. It was in that city that she died, aged sixty-six, on 11 May 1979.

The Duke of Windsor had gone seven years earlier, in May 1972. The Queen had visited Paris a few days before, to pay a last call on her uncle, dying of cancer of the throat. His biographer Philip Ziegler wrote: 'As they had been for nearly forty years, his thoughts were all with his wife who had so filled his life and who would now have to face the future alone.' Sixty thousand mourners filed past his coffin as he lay in state at St George's Chapel, Windsor. It was a touchingly grand finale for one whose life had gone so wrong.

The Duchess of Windsor, who had for four years and three months given herself to Jimmy Donahue, was the last to die, finally succumbing aged eighty-nine in April 1986 after a woefully long illness. In her last days, wrote her biographer Michael Thornton: 'Her chair would be placed by the tall French windows of her bedroom, and there she would sit each day, staring out unseeingly at the trees and the flowers in her garden. Sometimes, for a fleeting moment, the still beautiful blue eyes would come alive with the gleam of memory. Sometimes they would fill with tears.'

Whether she shed a tear for Jimmy Donahue in those long, last days – the laughing, joking, dancing Jimmy, the naughty, camping, outrageous Jimmy, the spoiled, abandoned, devilish Jimmy – no one will ever know.

Acknowledgements

The principal research for this book took place in New York, Paris, London and Palm Beach. I am indebted to many people in each of these places, not only for the generous way in which they gave their time, but in many cases for their kind hospitality as well. Sadly I am unable to thank everyone who helped this enterprise, since some significant figures I spoke to asked that their anonymity should be preserved. To them, first of all, I issue my thanks for their kindness and for the information and material they made available.

In New York I owe a special debt to Mrs Nancy Holmes, whose zeal in uncovering new leads was often in danger of outstripping the author's, and in Paris to James Douglas, who provided many leads and gave great moral support. I thank Mrs Marianne Strong, whose comprehensive knowledge and kind help were generosity itself, and I am also deeply grateful to Mrs Mary Woolworth Donahue, both for her memories and insights, and also for the photographs from her personal album which play an important part in the telling of this story.

May I also thank E. Haring Chandor, Countess Vivian Crespi, Philip van Rensselaer, Oleg Cassini, Igor Cassini ('Cholly Knickerbocker'), Ned Rorem, Mrs Ariel Eweson, Ms Liz Smith, Mrs C. Z. Guest, Mrs Dorothy Strelsin, Mrs Anne Slater, Mrs Aileen Mehle, Mrs Carroll Petrie, Ms Kate Duffy, Ms Geraldine Hugo, Billy Livingston, Cliff Robertson, Charles

Kaiser, Ned Moss, St Clair Pugh, T. Roderick McCubbin, Al Koenig Jr, Kenneth Jay Lane, Arthur Pavlow, Richard Mineards, and David Heymann.

I am most grateful for the assistance and guidance of Sister Marguerita Smith, archivist, Archdiocese of New York; Elizabeth Oravetz, New York Foundling Hospital; Patsy Kirschner, the Hun School, Princeton; Charlotte Murphy, Choate, Wallingford; Robert MacKay and the Society for the Preservation of Long Island Antiquities; Colonel Leonard Blascovich, Civil Air Patrol; the Federal Bureau of Investigation; the External Affairs Office, NYC; Roger Seybel, Northrop Grumman History Center, Bethpage, NY; and the staffs of the John Fitzgerald Kennedy Library, Columbia Point, Boston; The Connecticut Historical Society, Hartford; the Greenwich Historical Society; the Oyster Bay Historical Society; New York Historical Society; NYC Department of Health Records; New York Police Department records office; and Friends for Long Island History.

I am most thankful to the Director and staff of the New York Public Library, and to the House Committee and staff of the Union League Club.

In Palm Beach I thank Mrs Alyne Massey, Mrs Walter van Durand, Mrs Linda Mortimer, Charles Amory, the late Charles van Rensselaer, Princess Martha Kropotkin, Mrs Celia Lipton Farris, the Hon. Robert Spencer, Frank Quigley, Jock Sullivan, Miss Ann Hall, Bob Jackson, Kae Sanderson. Extra thanks to Molly Charland of the Four Arts Library, Clemmer Mayhew and the staff of the Palm Beach Historical Society, Shannon Donnelly of the *Palm Beach Daily News*, Michael Macdonald of the Everglades Club, Donald Trump and the staff of Mar-A-Lago, the staff of the Flagler Museum, and the Palm Beach Chamber of Commerce.

Elsewhere in the United States I would like to thank my old friend Christopher Hitchens, Zsa Zsa Gabor, Bill Robertson,

Dante Stephenson, Noonie Fortin, Floyd Conner, Mr and Mrs Richies, Litchfield, Illinois, and a special vote of thanks goes to Dick Bielen of the US Locator Service, and to Bill Pugsley of the Texas Information Network for his tireless, patient and intuitive work. Also to the staff of the City and County Medical Examiner's office, Honolulu, and the Hearst Corporation.

In Paris I would like to thank Princess Ghislaine de Polignac, the Hon. Lady Mosley, Roderick Coupe, Suzanne Lowry, Charlotte Mosley and Major Walter Lees.

In Tangier: the late Paul Bowles, Mrs Ruth Hopwood, Thor Guniholm, Joe McPhillips. In Spain: the Countess of Romanones. In Portugal: Gerry Atkins. In Italy: Francesca Forni, Gritti Palace, Venice, Alexander Moncada, Milan. In Austria: Maria Mattle and Alexandra Fortunat of the Veldener Tourismusgesellschaft. In Germany: Martina Gott, Brenners Park, Baden-Baden. In London: The Duchess of Devonshire, Hon. Artemis Cooper, Hon. Lady Murray, Lady Aberconway, David Metcalfe, Count Paolo Filo della Torre, Kenneth Rose, Michael Bloch, Peter Townend, Mrs Caroline Pocock, Anne Seagrim, Mona Eldridge, Christiane Sherwin, Christine Carter, Jane Mays, Dale Lawrence and Lufthansa Airlines; Georgina Sullivan and the management and staff of the Ritz Hotel; Barney Perkins and staff of the library, Victoria & Albert Museum; Alexandra Rhodes, Sothebys, and Emily Barber; Jo Wallis, Victoria & Albert picture library.

Of those who helped me most closely I would first like to thank Rik Carmichael, Mike Carmichael, Bill Whalley, Michael Wilson, Edward Seymour Taylor and Clive York for their unique contribution. Jeremy Dore provided me with books I thought were untraceable, Laurence Malden once again provided a suitable backdrop; and I am indebted to the translation expertise of Uli Zupnickl (German), and Avril Bardoni (Italian). Laurel Wilson helped put the finishing touches to the manuscript, and I applaud the patience and determination of Elaine Kitt and Dee Adcock whose research I gratefully acknowledge.

I am indeed fortunate in finding myself once again published by the inspirational figure of Val Hudson, Publishing Director of HarperCollins, and edited by the sublime hand of Andrea Henry. I would especially like to thank my editors at St. Martin's, Charles Spicer and Dorsey Mills, for their support and enthusiasm in bringing this book to U.S. publication. Lastly, as always, a profound thanks to my wife Carolyne Cullum.

Bibliography

Polly Adler, *A House is Not a Home* (Rinehart & Co., 1953)

Charles Amory, *Who Killed Society?* (Harper, New York, 1960)

Anthony Beevor & Artemis Cooper *Paris After the Liberation* (Penguin, 1994)

Stephen Birmingham, *Duchess* (Macmillan, 1981)

Caroline Blackwood, *The Last of the Duchess* (Macmillan, 1995)

Michael Bloch, *The Duchess of Windsor* (Weidenfeld & Nicolson, 1996)

–, *Secret File of the Duke of Windsor* (Bantam, 1988)

Jon Bradshaw, *Dreams That Money Can Buy* (Jonathan Cape, 1985)

Iles Brody, *Gone with the Windsors* (John C. Winston, 1953)

James Brough, *The Woolworths* (McGraw Hill, 1982)

J. Bryan III and Charles J. V. Murphy, *The Windsor Story* (Granada, 1979)

Art Buchwald, *I'll Always Have Paris* (Fawcett, 1996)

George Chauncey, *Gay New York* (Basic Books, 1994)

Floyd Conner, *Lupe Velez and Her Lovers* (Barricade Books, 1993)

Diana Cooper, *The Rainbow Comes and Goes* (Hart-Davis, 1958)

Duff Cooper, *Old Men Forget* (Hart-Davis, 1953)

L. J. Davis, *Onassis and Christina* (Gollancz, 1987)

Frances Donaldson, *Edward VIII* (Weidenfeld & Nicolson, 1974)

The Duchess of Windsor, *The Heart Has Its Reasons* (Michael Joseph, 1956)

Mona Eldridge, *In Search of a Prince* (Sidgwick & Jackson, 1988)

Neal Gabler, *Walter Winchell* (Picador, 1994)

C. David Heymann, *Poor Little Rich Girl* (Hutchinson, 1985)

Charles Higham, *The Duchess of Windsor, The Secret Life* (McGraw Hill, 1988)

Dean Jennings, *Barbara Hutton* (W. H. Allen, 1968)

Charles Kaiser, *The Gay Metropolis* (Harcourt Brace, 1997)

Stanley Karnow, *Paris in the 1950s* (Times Books, 1997)

Ralph G. Martin, *The Woman He Loved* (W. H. Allen, 1974)

John Maxtone-Graham, *Cunard, 150 Years* (David & Charles, 1989)

Elsa Maxwell, *I Married the World* (Heinemann, 1955)

Suzy Menkes, *The Windsor Style* (Grafton, 1987)

Ed. Charlotte Mosley, *The Letters of Nancy Mitford* (Hodder & Stoughton, 1993)

Malcolm Muggeridge, *The Thirties* (Hamish Hamilton, 1940)

Regine, *Call Me By My First Name* (Andre Deutsch, 1988)

Philip van Rensselaer, *Million Dollar Baby* (Hodder & Stoughton, 1979)

William Stadiem, *Too Rich* (Robson Books, 1992)

C. L. Sulzberger, *A Row of Candles* (Macdonald, 1969)

Michael Thornton, *Royal Feud* (Simon & Schuster, 1985)

John K. Winkler, *Five and Ten* (Robert Hale, 1941)

Philip Ziegler, *King Edward VIII* (Collins, 1990)

-, *Mountbatten* (Collins, 1985)

Index